TOWARDS A
SURVEILLANT
SOCIETY

The Rise of Surveillance Systems in Europe

Thomas Mathiesen

Towards a Surveillant Society
The Rise of Surveillance Systems in Europe
Thomas Mathiesen

ISBN 978-1-904380-97-9 (Paperback)
ISBN 978-1-908162-44-1 (Adobe E-book)
ISBN 978-1-908162-45-8 (Kindle /Epub E-book)

Cover design © 2013 Waterside Press. Design by www.gibgob.com.

Cataloguing-In-Publication Data A catalogue record for this book can be obtained from the British Library.

e-book *Towards a Surveillant Society* is available as an ebook and also to subscribers of Myilibrary, Dawsonera, ebrary and Ebscohost.

Printed by CPI Antony Rowe, Chippenham.

Main UK distributor Gardners Books, 1 Whittle Drive, Eastbourne, East Sussex, BN23 6QH. Tel: +44 (0)1323 521777; sales@gardners.com; www.gardners.com

USA and Canada distributor Ingram Book Company, One Ingram Blvd, La Vergne, TN 37086, USA. (800) 937-8000, orders@ingrambook.com, ipage.ingrambook.com

Published 2013 by
Waterside Press Ltd.
Sherfield Gables
Sherfield on Loddon
Hook, Hampshire
United Kingdom RG27 0JG

Telephone +44(0)1256 882250
E-mail enquiries@watersidepress.co.uk
Online catalogue WatersidePress.co.uk

TOWARDS A SURVEILLANT SOCIETY

The Rise of Surveillance Systems in Europe

Thomas Mathiesen

✹ **WATERSIDE** PRESS

With the support of the Fritt Ord Foundation

www.fritt-ord.no

DICTIONARY FOR BIG DATA

If a byte is a grain of sand with information:

1 megabyte = 1 million bytes = a teaspoon of sand.

1 gigabyte = 1 billion bytes = a box of sand.

1 terabyte = 1 trillion bytes = a sandpit of sand.

1 petabyte = 1000 terabytes = 1 kilometre of sand beach.

1 exabyte = 1000 petabytes = a sand beach from Oslo to Tromsø (714 miles).

1 zettabyte = 1000 exabytes = a sand beach around all of the USA.

1 yottabyte = 1000 zettabytes = enough sand to bury all of the USA under 296 feet of sand.

From Aftenposten, 8 November 2012

TABLE OF CONTENTS

2. ENEMY IMAGES — AND TERRORISM   61

3. THE SURVEILLANCE SYSTEMS   95

ABOUT THE AUTHOR

Thomas Mathiesen is Professor of Sociology of Law in the Department of Criminology and Sociology of Law at the University of Oslo. One of the leading international commentators on surveillance issues, he has long been associated with penetrating analysis of attacks on democracy and abuse of power. His acclaimed works include *Prison on Trial; Across the Boundaries of Organizations; The Politics of Abolition* and *Silently Silenced: Essays on the Creation of Acquiescence in Modern Society.*

PREFACE AND ACKNOWLEDGEMENTS

In 1997, and then again in 2000, I wrote two books in Norwegian on information and surveillance systems in Europe. Both are mentioned in the *Bibliography* at the end of this book (Mathiesen 1997a; 2000).

In other words, more than ten years have passed since the last of the two books in Norwegian was published. I have found that it is time to write yet another book, this time in English, on the information and surveillance systems in Europe, translating parts of the two Norwegian texts into English and updating them throughout. The basic structure of the information and surveillance systems outlined in the 2000-book is still valid, but an enormous amount of important information on them is now available to make updating possible and necessary.

Moreover, two additional topics have come up to make a new edition in English necessary: the development of the Internet, which has come much further than in 2000, and the development of terrorism. The present development of information and surveillance systems in Europe and elsewhere must be seen within the context of these features. The systems are "net-phenomena" based on the Internet, and they have the struggle against terrorism as their professed and most specific goal. The first two chapters, therefore, have the development of the Internet and of terrorism in our time respectively as bases for understanding information and surveillance systems.

The long middle chapters of the book, *Chapters 3* and *4*, deal specifically with the most important information and surveillance systems. *Chapter 4* was originally meant to be the concluding chapter. However, as I was about to finish the first draft of the book, a major terrorist attack on my own country, Norway, took place (22 July 2011). Also, the various surveillance systems which Norway was implicated in, were, as I had expected, of no help. They were totally unable to resist the terrorist attack. But they may become a threat to legal security and the Rule of Law in my country. I had to write an additional chapter, *Chapter 5*, relating the story of 22 July 2011 and some of its aftermath, and I did so during the following year.

I wish to express my sincere gratitude to Statewatch, which monitors the State and civil liberties in Europe, and which has provided me with masses of relevant information on the surveillance systems in Europe. In particular, I wish to thank Tony Bunyan, the director of Statewatch, and Chris Jones, researcher there, for reading and commenting on *Chapters 3* and *4* of this book, and in general for their constant willingness, helpfulness and guidance during the time of writing.

I also wish to thank Ole Kristian Hjemdal for reading and commenting on *Chapters 1, 2* and *5*, Tomas Wennström and Snorre Mathiesen for reading and commenting on *Chapter 1*, and Marie-Louise Berg for reading and commenting on *Chapter 2*. I also wish to extend my gratitude to Per Jørgen Ystehede, research consultant at the Department of Criminology and Sociology of Law at the University of Oslo, and to Vibeke Lagem, librarian in the same Department, for continual advice during the process of writing and for very efficient librarian assistance.

Many thanks also to Christian Fuchs, professor of media and communication studies at Uppsala University, for inspiring contacts; Linda Gulli for her careful proof-reading; and to Bryan Gibson along with the staff at Waterside Press. But I alone am responsible for any errors that the book may contain.

I wish to thank Mathieu DeFlem, editor of *Surveillance and Governance: Crime Control and Beyond* (Emerald, 2008), for permission to use some of the text included in my own article "Lex Vigilatoria: Global Control without a State?", and Phil Scraton, editor of *Beyond September 11* (Pluto Press, 2002), for permission to use some of the text included in my own article "Expanding the Concept of Terrorism?".

Finally, I would like to thank the Fritt Ord Foundation for their valued support.

Thomas Mathiesen
Oslo, June 2013

Thomas Mathiesen brings into the light the hidden effects of the surveillant society in the European Union (and beyond) and by doing so warns us all of the need for vigilance, informed debate and, which is currently absent, stringent democratic accountability.

Tony Bunyan, Director, Statewatch

A timely and highly troubling analysis of the rapid escalation of surveillance systems. While the focus is largely upon Europe and its institutions, the book reinforces alarm regarding a panoptical globe.

Andrew Rutherford

CHAPTER 1

THE SOCIOLOGY OF THE INTERNET: TOWARDS AN "INFORMATION SOCIETY"?

A World Wide Development

Definitions

Throughout the past 40 years or so, we have witnessed a worldwide development of various types of international *information systems* at the disposal of national and international law enforcement agencies. The development has been accelerating in Europe and the USA as well as in other parts of the Western world and elsewhere.

The information systems are *also surveillance systems* due to the fact that not only are data assembled and stored over long periods of time about individuals, groups and categories of people or whole populations, but in that the information stored may also, if needs be, be brought to the fore, through given technical procedures, about individuals as well as larger or smaller groups of people. This is my broad definition as far as surveillance goes.

The information systems often concern "big data", to use a term from Internet language. "Big data" means extremely large — almost limitless — quantities of data. To handle big data represents an important asset, as well as a major problem in as much as you may go wild in the data, especially when a crisis occurs. You — or better still, the police — may be unable to put the pieces together in a meaningful pattern. We will return to issues concerning big data quantities in later chapters.

Of course, by no means all of the Internet supply is intended for use in this way. Much of it is intended for and is used for transmitting information, education, building economies, earning money, communicating with others, friends and a whole host of other behaviours.

The definition of *an information and surveillance system* given here, is an "ideal type" definition — the information is gathered with the more or less explicit purpose of surveillance of people. But an information system may initially have another purpose, such as a census established for taxation purposes, but may be turned into an information *and* surveillance system, also exemplified by a census (see below).

History is replete with such examples. Even an old-fashioned telephone directory in paper form, produced with the goal of informing people of other people's telephone numbers, may be turned into an information and surveillance system. In the 1970s a socialist in Norway used the telephone directory as a source of information about addresses and the like of secret service personnel, which he threatened to publicise and which, incidentally, led to abrupt arrests and imprisonment of quite a few left socialists. The event spurred the establishment of a left wing organization among lawyers in Norway (which still exists). A further example would be the registration of Jews by the Norwegian Census Bureau in Norway before World War II. It was probably initially done for simple bureaucratic reasons, but as far as we know was actively used by the Nazis in tracking down and eventually exterminating Jews during the German occupation of Norway 1940-1945 (Mathiesen 2000, p. 16-17).

More recent examples are Facebook, Twitter and the like from the first decade of the 2000s, which probably were initially established for people's enjoyment and interaction (and earning money on them). But people leave behind electronic traces. There have been discussions concerning *inter alia* Apple's iPhone or iPad and their apps which may be used to provide "profiles" of users. As far as commercial use is concerned, we will return to that, but they may also in principle be used for surveillance.

In this book, I will largely stick to the "ideal type" definition given above, which looks at systems of gathering information about people with the more or less explicit goal of keeping track of them and undertaking surveillance of them. Law enforcement agencies regularly build such systems, and also did so before the Internet phase. They are today crucially important for the development of nations, regions of the world and—as a matter of fact—the whole world. Such are many of the systems now crisscrossing Europe, the West and the globe. But in the book, we will also make excursions to the "outer fringes" of surveillance, and look into the realm of the less clear-cut types of surveillance systems—activities which with time develop from something else into surveillance.

In this first chapter, we will at times go still further away from the "ideal type" and discuss aspects of the development of the Internet generally, without necessarily tying-up developments with surveillance in any form. We do this because the surveillance industry—and it is essentially an industry, at least in its "ideal type" form—lives its life within the context of the Internet generally, which today permeates all parts of society. Without the positive clamour tied to the Internet cultural and technical context, which is developing so rapidly, the information and surveillance systems would hardly have survived, at least in their present form.

The Digital Divide

On a general level, and whether we talk about information and surveillance systems in "ideal type" form or something else, a digital "divide" currently constitutes an issue of hot debate. It is a global divide, which in terms of the Internet heavily reinforces the already strong position of the advanced industrial economies as opposed to the developing countries. The cost of obtaining Internet access is still much too high for the poorest peoples of the world, who often do not even have access to a telephone service. To illustrate further, in North America 74.4 per cent of the population are online, while at the other end of the scale, only 5.6 per cent of Africa's population has Internet access (Jewkes, 1910 p. 240).

But there are exceptions even to this. An example would be China. The use of the Internet in China grew from 23 million users in 2000 to 162 million at the beginning of 2007. In 2008 the figure had increased to 210 million, only five million below the USA. China has six million new Internet users per month, which is more than ten times the speed of increase compared with the USA. The largest supplier of online video is Tudou, which has surpassed YouTube. The search engine Baidu has more hits than Google. And so on (information from Jewkes, 2010, p. 241).

The Great Fire Wall of China

All the more interesting is the fear among the Chinese authorities about the potential use of the Internet as a socially destructive and even revolutionary force. I don't know enough about surveillance in China to say off-hand how much of it is utilised for surveillance purposes as defined above. But I assume that information and surveillance systems in China are widespread. A catch-all term summarising and symbolising the various forms of Chinese political control and censorship is the "Great Fire Wall of China".

Expressions and words related to political activists, resistance movements against the Government and against censorship are at the greatest risk of being weeded-out from Chinese blogs and social websites. The Chinese "Fire-wall" expresses how the authorities in China block home pages and Internet traffic in and out of the country and expose them to censorship. Google and Facebook have, for example, been objects of censorship. A study undertaken by Carnegie Mellom University in the USA is among the first to investigate single messages, words and expressions.[1] The researchers found for example that world famous artists like Ai Weiwei and the name of Liu Xiaobo, Nobel peace prize winner some years ago, are in large measure blocked on Chinese web sites and micro blogs, because both are outspoken critics of the political system in China (Liu Xiaobo is perhaps more of an adherent of the USA than anything else). Messages containing politically sensitive information, for example the name of one of the architects of the Chinese "Fire Wall", Fang Binying, is frequently deleted.[2]

Our knowledge about surveillance in China has been significantly augmented by Norwegian professor of sociology Børge Bakken at the University of Hong Kong. In addition to having edited a book on *Crime, Punishment and Policing in China* (Bakken 2005), he has done extensive research *inter alia* in Guangzhow on closed circuit television (CCTV) on the Chinese mainland, entitled "The Chinese Surveillance State: The Rationalities of 'Social Management' in China" (Bakken forthcoming). He looks at what he calls the "surveillance camera craze observed over the last years". He goes on to say *inter alia* (manuscript p. 7-12):

> … The 510,000 cameras planned for Chongqing during Bo Xilai's reign would probably have left urban Chongqing with the highest density of cameras in the world. The 33 million figure for the population of Chongqing municipality is

---

1. Source: *Computerworld's* News Service on Google.
2. Same source.

referring to the administrative area, an area the size of Denmark. The urban area, however, has a population of about 5.4 million. The CCTV camera project was meant to cover the 400 square miles of urban Chongqing. It would have meant a density of one camera for 10.6 persons. I am not sure if the project is indeed being implemented in its original fashion.

The government is now setting up targets for the use of surveillance cameras. Every organization, work unit or institution has to submit to a certain procedure for the use of surveillance cameras. Kindergartens, primary and middle schools, and universities are involved. Massive expenses are incurred. The international capitalist world is involved:

> Since the expenses on policing are not engendering any profits for the local administration, and there is little central funding coming into the police stations, police units have started asking companies for sponsorship agreements through the local administration. It is well known that McDonalds is working as a sponsor for the local police in Guangzhou, and the traffic police in other cities in China (Like Xi'an). Kentucky Fried Chicken is a sponsor as well, but their commitments go even further since they do most of their packaging for domestic consumption in China in the Laojiao—the reform through labour institutions—a fact confirmed by former inmates.

The number of cameras varies widely in counts, but they are certainly many. London may no longer be the leading city in the world in terms of numbers of cameras. Bakken documents that international data clearly suggest that the effect in terms of reduction of crime is small, largely speaking. The same is most probably true of China, although the authorities contradict it. Another aspect is what the Chinese say they gain—in terms of happiness:

> "You Are Entering an Area Under Surveillance, Please Maintain a Smile!" The message we found on a banner covering the gate of a local hospital in central Guangzhou. This is exactly what many articles claim in China today, that the rapidly rising number of surveillance cameras will make you both safe and happy.

When, in 1785, he described a new prison design the eccentric philosopher and prison reformer Jeremy Bentham coined the term "panopticon" (literally, "all-seeing"). Bentham's panopticon allowed a few guardians to oversee and control large numbers of inmates by keeping them under constant and easy surveillance… Bentham never reasoned that imprisonment or panoptic surveillance would increase pleasure or happiness among those who were imprisoned or were under surveillance. In China today, however, it seems that the 24-hour "panopticon" is supposed to buttress happiness for all.

One of the recent campaigns has emphasised the task of increasing the "feeling of happiness" among people as a guiding principle for policy-making. So "You are entering an area under surveillance, please maintain a smile!" is really meant, not as a joke, but as a statement of "good governance".

We will return to the concept of the panopticon later in this chapter.

This Book

In this book, however, I will be more modest. *I will concentrate on conditions "at home", in Europe, especially within the European Union.* It deals with the accelerating development of information and surveillance systems, particularly in Europe.

The present chapter as well as *Chapter 2* place the development of European systems in a historical and sociological context. This chapter deals with some features of the development of the Internet which is specifically relevant to recent information and surveillance systems. *Chapter 2* deals with some features of terrorism, which is central to the variety of goals facing the systems.

Chapters 3 and *4* deal in detail with the most important of the European information and surveillance systems. The chapters concentrate to a considerable extent on the questions of why the systems fail to reach their expressed goals, such as fighting terrorism, and why they instead become dangers to legal security and the Rule of Law. The chapters also deal with attempts to integrate the various systems. Are we facing a trend towards integration of systems, coupled with a weakening of ties to nation states — a kind of frightening *Lex Vigilatoria* — operating of its own accord without controlling ties to the nation states?

Chapter 5 is essentially an Epilogue, dealing with a recent case of major terrorism in Europe (Norway). Though the future is uncertain, the case may lead to an alternative way of thinking about terrorism rather than increased surveillance and tougher sentences.

Beginnings?

Beginnings are often hard to assess. Information and surveillance systems have probably existed in some form in States in all ages. By an information and surveillance *system* I mean an organization with a specific leadership and specific functionaries, assembling information about people and keeping track of them by using the information for this purpose. Such systems may be more complex or less so — some are large with intricate connections and levels between the functionaries, others are small with very simple relationships between people. Past State formations have had such systems in the form of censuses — like the Chinese Hang dynasty some 2000 years ago, or the old Babylon, or the Egyptian State with its Pharaohs in the Egyptian realm 2000-3000 BC. Censuses were probably held among other things for taxation purposes, and were in other words a bit away from the "ideal type" of an information and surveillance system. But the idea of also using the information for surveillance purposes, keeping track of people whom the regime felt they could not trust, must have come early.

The Roman State, at the outset with its (partly mythical) kings, then its Republic and finally its Emperors, and with an empire even so far north as the distant province of today's Great Britain, had its censuses. A Roman Emperor who lived some 2000 years ago provides a well-known and dramatic example, containing a narrative of a far-reaching census which clearly also had surveillance purposes. Some people even had to seek refuge in another country far away. We all know that particular story, it was read to us by our parents and grandparents, but I summarise it here anyway:

> "In those days", at approximately 0 BC/AD, the Roman Emperor Augustus (63BC-14AD; ruler alone from 27BC until his death), grandnephew and adopted son of Gaius Julius Caesar, ordered "that a census should be taken of the whole world"—everyone in the Roman Empire. The people "all went to be registered, each to his own city". (Quotes from Luke 2).

This is one of the earliest examples of such a vast undertaking I have been able to find, in an Empire characterised by a tremendous amount of legal and cultural pluralism at that.[3] The order came from the very centre of the Empire. It was no doubt given for bureaucratic reasons, so that order in the widespread Empire would be maintained. It was important to know who was where. There were people who could be trusted, but in many places also many people who should be met with distrust.

But the census probably also had surveillance purposes on a different level in the Roman bureaucracy:

> During the reign of the local Roman Governor, King Herod, there arrived wise men at Jerusalem from the east, inquiring, "Where is the newborn king of the Jews? For we saw his star in the east and we have come to worship him". This disturbed King Herod and all Jerusalem greatly, and after consultations with all the chief priests and scribes Herod inquired of them where this Christ should be born. He also summoned the wise men to ascertain "just when the star appeared". He asked the wise men to search carefully for the young Child, since he also wanted to worship him. But what he actually wanted was to kill the Child, fearing he might become a threat to the Empire.
>
> However, the Child's would-be father Joseph was warned: "Then, because of divine warning in a dream not to return to Herod, they were sent back to their own country by a different route". Herod's people did not find the Child, because the Child's mother Mary, with Joseph and the Child, had fled to Egypt. Herod was furious and ordered the murder of all male children of two years and under in Bethlehem and its environs. The little family remained in Egypt until Herod had died. Coming back, they settled in Nazareth (Quotes from Matthew 2).

Also non-state societies, long before and after the large empires, have probably also had surveillance activities. People have kept track of each

---

3. See also Price and Thonemann, 2011, p.223. In their remarkable book on the early Greek and Roman empires, Price and Thonemann point out that several censuses were undertaken in the mid-second century BC. The most reliable one took place soon after the so-called "Social War", when the count was 910,000, "which should probably also be increased by 20 per cent". Adult male Roman citizens were counted. A number of people from allied States in Italy at the time, who first fought for independence, after a while became Roman citizens.

other in non-state societies—they have trusted some and feared many, and tried to keep track of those they feared. We may infer this from evidence concerning violence in non-State European societies, which probably, the archeologists and historically inclined cultural anthropologists tell us, was more widespread than some of us like to think (Armit 2011). Though the way of keeping track of those we feared may not have had the characteristics of "systems" — they may not have been organized with particular leadership and functionaries—keeping track of people at least implied retaining information through memory, bringing it to the fore if need be.

The Modern Computer

We will, however, begin much more recently, in a period when instantaneous messages in time and space became common. This means starting with *the modern computer.*

Let this be clear: The lines even here go far back: The telegraph is a good example. In the language of Morse, instantaneous messages could be sent far away to other populations and societies—as news, warnings, signals for attack, cries for help, or whatever. Everyone today who has seen the film *Titanic,* about the steamship which was unsinkable but sank, in 1912, four hours after having struck an iceberg, knows the importance of the telegraph, though it could save neither ship nor passengers. The quest for instantaneous messaging has gone ahead with the rise of modern capitalism. Capitalism created a need for instantaneous messaging.

As I said, we begin recently, with the modern computer. Also the modern computer was here earlier than our own time. In the beginning large and clumsy, as with IBM which in 1956 came up with the first magnetic hard disk, RAMAC (Random Access Method of Accounting and Control), which equalled two refrigerators in size, had a weight of ten tons, and a storage capacity of five megabytes.[4] Technologically speaking, then, it is even here possible to speak of evolution. But in spite of the hazy beginnings of the modern computer, a qualitative shift took place as it was becoming common property. The computer as common property represented a qualitative shift in that the personal computer appeared on "everyone's desk". It took place

---

4. Source: *Aftenposten*, 11 June 2011.

roughly between 1980 and the beginning of the 2000s. This is a remarkably short time for a remarkable invention.

Following or tied to the personal computer, a long string of other inventions readily came along. The Internet was originally developed for defence purposes — it was seen as so robust that it could also be used after a nuclear attack. This, we now know, turned out to be wishful thinking. From defence the technology spread to research and educational institutions in the USA, and then to the world in general. In the beginning of the 1990s the Internet was opened-up for commercial use, and developed like a fireball.

The Internet is an electronic medium which offers various services, like the World Wide Web. The Internet comprises a world-wide network of computers, a "network of networks", a coupling of thousands of smaller networks all over the world. When you look for information, physical distance is almost abolished, the information is accessed independently of where it is (or where you are) in the world.

From Industrial Society to Information Society?

One of the major issues confronted by social scientists for the last 20 or 30 years has been that of whether or not we are moving away from the industrial society and towards, or even into, an information society.

Daniel Bell

One of the first people to place the concept of "information society" on the public agenda sociologically speaking, was the sociologist Daniel Bell in his book *The Coming of Post-industrial Society* (Bell 1973, with a new preface 1976; here largely from the new preface).[5] Bell tried to describe the transition from what he called the industrial society to the post-industrial society. The post-industrial society was according to him characterised by two large dimensions (p. xix) — the centrality of theoretical knowledge, and an expansion of the service sector as against the manufacturing economy.

The first, the centrality of theoretical knowledge, means an increasing dependence on science as a means to innovate and organise technological change. The second change, the expansion of the service sector, means an

---

5.   Alain Touraine came slightly before Bell (Touraine 1969).

expansion in transport, trade, insurance, banking, public administration, medical, legal and other personal services, and so on.

The first transformation, with the centrality of theoretical knowledge, has made new inventions and organizations of technological change much more dependent on science, with an increased role of industries based on science. The second transformation — the increased role of service-oriented businesses — has led to a strong relative decrease of the industrial work force.

Bell mentions the possibility of calling the post-industrial society "the information society" or "the service society". But it must be added that he abstains explicitly from the temptation (p. ix) of doing so himself, and maintains that the post-industrial society does not come instead the industrial society, but constitutes developmental trends which place themselves on top of earlier trends, erasing some of them and condensing the societal weaving as a whole. "Broadly speaking," he argues, "if industrial society is based on machine technology, post-industrial society is shaped by an intellectual technology" (p. xiii).

Håkan Hydén

Bell's analysis did not have — and could not have — today's emphasis on information technology or new media as a point of departure (even if he touched on the significance of the computer). After Bell's book was published, scientists were above all preoccupied with the general importance of knowledge and education for the development of society.

Only in later years, towards our own time, has information — and communication technology dominated the debate, and the thesis of a transformation from industrial to information society has had increasing support. One supporter of the thesis is the Swedish legal sociologist Håkan Hydén (at Lund University), who points to the following in one of his books (Hydén 1997, p. iii, translated from the Swedish by me):

> Today we confront a transformation of systems. Industrial society has outlived itself, and is in the process of gradually being replaced by an information society, a society of knowledge or what you now choose to call the introduction to what is to become a cyber epoch. Historically we are therefore in the same phase as sociology and sociology of law were in when they were first established.

To be sure, there are indications that we are in such a transformation. In many Western countries the labour force has gone markedly down, and the service businesses and the IT technical — and consultant — personnel have gone equally markedly up. Hydén has emphasised the change from analogical to virtual communication.[6] At the universities throughout the West (my own university in Norway is a case in point) there are now whole armies of technical consultants teaching the professors how to use our personal computers. The various new systems and intricacies which frequently and without warning invade our computers and our work, make you highly dependent on the new class of consultants also residing in your department. Only a minority of us need all of the personal computer's many new functions, which frequently come. Catalogues become obsolete, if you ask for information the answer is that it is provided on the web (but the time is not "paperless" — paper is massively used for print-outs). Banks, insurance companies, State bureaucracies, medical doctors, dentists, social workers and a whole series of other services are dependent on doing the same.

Davidow and Malone

An account relevant to the recent growth of an "information society" is William Davidow and Michael Malone's *The Virtual Corporation*, which came as early as 1992. The book centres around "instantaneousness" as a core value, and instantaneousness, or at least rapidity, or speed, is of central importance. Instantaneous products and services are already becoming pervasive, "a regular part of our daily lives" (p. 4). "They are so remarkable", the authors go on to say, "so distinct from anything that came before that they deserve a special name". In their book they are referred to as *virtual products*. "The ideal virtual product or service is one that is produced instantaneously and customised in response to customer demand" (p. 4). Physical products and services are made virtual.

A perfect "virtual" industry does not exist, they say, but many come close. Japanese production of automobiles does. The Japanese are striving to put in place systems that will produce finished cars to domestic order in a very few hours. Dell Corporation producing computers is another example.

---

6.   Oral communication from Hydén.

Davidow and Malone imagine entirely new organizational types and differentiate (pp. 68-72) between four informational levels—*content information* (information about quantity, location, types of items); *form information* (shape and composition of an object); *behaviour information* (prediction of the behaviour of a physical object through simulation of its motion in three-dimensional space; and *action information* (the triumph of the information revolution; it instantly converts information into sophisticated action; computing power will increase still more but become "inexorably cheaper" as we build machines "that not only gather and process information but act upon the results" (p. 71)).

The most important information level is that which concerns action, and which provides a basis for machines to perform tasks. Davidow and Malone argue for a technology which even supplies machines with human-like sight—something which requires massive data power, but also an organization of neural networks which resembles the networks of the brain. The quest for such a technology may be somewhat outdated (their book is after all 20-years-old). But continually more sophisticated systems exist for automatic picture analysis. Polar Rose (bought by Apple in 2010), for example, is a world-leading company in face-recognition. Some years ago, a certain optimism could be seen for neural networks and "artificial intelligence". There is more scepticism now. But there are continual improvements in analysing great quantities of data (and pictures).[7]

Work places will be transformed, Davidow and Malone predict (p. 71-72):

> Work environments will also change. More and more factories will operate with "lights out", devoid of humanity except for the occasional passing guard or visiting repair person.

Another important part of the development is that even "ordinary people" today have access to the Internet and to data power (at least in the Western world). The cost of publishing and of data power have gone markedly down during recent years. Today, "ordinary people" may establish their own home page and express themselves, without having their views filtered by

---

7.   Information kindly received from Tomas Wennström.

the traditional media. Today it is much cheaper and simpler to market one's views than before. My son, in fact, has a home page and communicates with "the whole world".

Freedom?

Everything which I have said so far favours the view that we are approaching or even inside an "information society". But I am still not sure. We shall soon return to the vision of Davidow and Malone, but first a short injection on the "freedom" mentioned or inferred so far: I fear that strings are increasingly attached to this "freedom". An effect of how the Internet is constructed is that no State or business owns or controls the whole Internet. This seems to have been a conscious choice of design on the part of people at the universities who developed the Internet further during the 1970s and 1980s. Today, however, there is a struggle taking place regarding who controls the net and the information which is allowed to be public. Discussions concerning "net neutrality" are today lively all over the world.

Briefly, the question at the outset is whether the Internet suppliers may require payments for a given traffic on their net. For example, Telia in Sweden wishes to receive extra payments for Skype conversations on the mobile net. Other suppliers will demand payments from YouTube or Facebook for delivering their traffic more quickly. As the first country in Europe to do so, The Netherlands have recently produced legislation on net neutrality.[8] In short, and to put it bluntly, once more there is a development towards "net-competition" between the rich and the poor.

What is also important, is that there is a net competition between the repressor and the repressed. The "Arab Spring" in 2011 is a case in point. The net was used for the sake of freedom. Authoritarian regimes toppled due to protesters via Twitter and Facebook and by other information means, and this was heralded throughout the world as signifying a new era in which information technology alters the balance of power in favour of the repressed. But there are important counter forces. In an interesting paper, John Villasenor has done some thinking on the scenario (Villasenor 2011). He limits himself to authoritarian States (Iran, China and so forth), but his message

---

8. http://en.wikipedia.org/wiki/Network_neutrality

is more general, encompassing, also, so-called "democratic" states, if democratic policy alters just a little bit:

> The Arab Spring of 2011, which saw regimes toppled by protesters organized via Twitter and Facebook, was heralded in much of the world as signifying a new era in which information technology alters the balance of power in favor of the repressed, However... [p]lummeting digital storage costs will soon make it possible for authoritarian regimes to not only monitor known dissidents, but also to store the complete set of digital data associated with everyone within their borders. These enormous databases of captured information will create what amounts to a surveillance time machine, enabling state security services to retroactively eavesdrop on people in the months and years before they were designated as surveillance targets. This will fundamentally change the dynamics of dissent, insurgency and revolution.[9]

It is not easy to make a definitive choice between the two sides in this battle of predictions. I think in a way we shouldn't make a definitive choice, because both are true at different times and under different conditions.

To Bend, Creep and Crawl? A New Class Structure?

Back to Davidow and Malones' factory without labourers: Imaginative, but I for one find it very hard to think of all, or more or less all, production as being "virtual", like that word is understood and defined by them.

True enough, the production of hardware and other products may be run by computers, and robots may put products together. The tendency in this direction has increased. Again the automobile industry is a case in point. The vast State bureaucracy is planned to be digitised — the enormous number of forms which must be filled in by large masses of people will become the people's second choice — the first choice will, according to planners, be digitised and available on the net. The plan for this has already in part been carried out. Digitisation of tax forms is an example.[10] There are many other examples.

---

9. http://www.brookings.edu/research/papers/2011/12/14-digital-storage-villasenor
10. Source: *Aftenposten*, 7 December 2012.

But it is extremely difficult to imagine that this can become standard to all hardware and other products and services.

Think of all the varied and complicated *things* in our surroundings in everyday life. The factory (even if modernised), but also the shipbuilding yards, the automobile repair shops, the building and construction sites of various sorts such as those for railways and roads, the continual repairs of our city streets, our street car lines, our city sewerage systems deep underground, our water pipelines also underground, require and will require, even if automated, a very substantial labour force. So will the hiring of plumbers, the hiring of electricians, the hiring of painters, the hiring of various types of repairmen inside as well as outside your house. They have to be willing to bend, creep and crawl to do their strenuous work. I count them as a part of "industrial society", which I see as not consisting only of factory labourers hired in factories by owners of capital.

A partly new class structure may emerge. There will be comparatively high strata of more or less educated technicians and computer people who are responsible for the automated computer work which is needed. But there will also be a large underclass, comparatively speaking, preoccupied with the actual construction of railways, roads, ships and whatever, as plumbers, electricians, painters and repairmen, in our thousands of homes, who have to bend, creep and crawl to do their work.

The class structure suggested here is not yet fully formed, but it must be counted as a distinct possibility. If and when it is fully formed, and accounted for as classes with a modicum of class consciousness and social networks, a new social order will have been introduced.

These old occupations, crucial though they are, are washed away from our consciousness by the elegance of the new order — by the virtual and the digitised world. They don't "count" in a society presumed to be an "information society".

Outsourcing

We also *outsource* production to countries were labour is cheaper. In one sense this brings us closer to post-industrial society, but only if we do not take into consideration that the "purification" of our own industrial society is followed by labour, only *elsewhere and less costly.*

Also, outsourcing of data power is important today. The server which delivers home pages or calculation capacity may today be located anywhere in the world, where it is cheapest. I have no idea where the various parts of the production of this book will take place.

Are there no limits? Many products are simple enough to outsource, but complex enough not to outsource to societies where labour is cheap. An example: There are now three dimensional printers which may print out three dimensional objects in plastic. Today there are advanced three dimensional printers for industrial use, and there are cheaper and simpler three dimensional printers for personal use. A movement has grown up around these cheaper printers. Sebastian Gjerding (2012) says that

> The Internet economy has given us a new way of producing… Chris Anderson, who is author and editor-in-chief of the influential American technology magazine Wired [writes]… [i]n his new book *Makers: The New Industrial Revolution* [about]… 3D printers and 3D scanners…

The movement looks ahead to a future where many or most "everyday things" may be printed out in three dimensions and produced. Crowd sourcing and crowd funding are central concepts—groups on the average think better than the individual, and when groups decide to fund something, each does not have to pay much. You download the prints of say the spare parts of your bike and print them out at home or at the three dimensional print shop.[11]

But as far as outsourcing is concerned (or for that matter at home), is the time near when such printers may be used in societies where people are poor and labour is cheap?

Gjerding by implication says no (but perhaps in a distant future?), and I concur. First you have to know the mechanisms of the spare parts on your bicycle—and even more so—in your car. Second, you have to reckon with social strings, cultural values and norms, and so on. You have to be an economist, but also partly a sociologist. The thinking that everything may be outsourced, and quite soon at that, bluntly disregards that when outsourcing

---

11. http://en.wikipedia.org/wiki/3D_printing; http://iysn.org/2011/09/17/pushing-the-bounda-ries-3-d-printing/; Tomas Wennström has kindly provided me with this information.

takes place, it must also take place, in a cultural context which does not necessarily fit with outsourcing.[12]

Outsourcing — of Waste

As I have said, there certainly is a tendency toward virtual production. A possible sign is that modern products in many cases last for shorter periods of time. My mother's refrigerator lasted longer than my own much more modern one, and when something goes wrong with my fridge we buy a new one rather than get a repairman to mend the old one. In a sense we live in a "waste society" — and that may be because repairing old products is more or less as costly as buying new ones and takes a longer time — they are less "virtual".

But what happens to all the waste which we find too difficult or too expensive to transform into new products? It is to a considerable extent outsourced, and has to be handled by manual labour elsewhere. A growing business, especially in China and other parts of the Third World, is the retrieving and recycling of valuable components and raw materials from various products.

One of the "waste cities" is *Guiyu* in the Guangdong district of China, seen as one of the largest electronic waste sites in the world. In 2005, there were 60,000 e-waste workers in Guiyu who processed more than 100 truckloads that were transported to the 52 square kilometres every day. Many recycling operations are toxic and dangerous to workers' health, with 88 per cent of children suffering from lead poisoning. The labour there is largely manual, and health wise it is dangerous. The soil has been saturated with lead, chromium, tin, and other heavy metals. Discarded electronics lie in pools of toxins that leak into the ground water, making it so polluted that the water is undrinkable. Lead levels in the river sediment are double the

---

12. One fifth of the world's merchandise is produced in China. Chinese workers have up until about now produced merchandise which is sufficiently cheap to significantly decrease or even stop prices from going up all over the world. This may now be coming to an end. Chinese wages, especially in cities and towns, are increasing. This may make outsourcing to China from Europe and the USA less simple. An increase in prices on merchandise from China may make producers shift location to, for example, Vietnam or Cambodia, where wages are lower. Chinese industrial concerns may also outsource production to Vietnam, Cambodia, Bangladesh and the Philippines. But China may also compete with a view towards the Western world with greater quality and more secure delivery. The future of outsourcing as we see it today is a bit uncertain. Source: *Aftenposten*, 11 November 2012.

European safety levels, according to the Basel Action Network.[13] Guiyu is appropriately nicknamed the "electronic graveyard". The Chinese claim that cleanups are going on.[14]

Another waste town is *Agbogbloshie*, a suburb of Accra in Ghana, known as a "digital dumping ground". Millions of tons of electronic waste are processed each year in Agbogbloshie, and due to a high crime rate and other conditions the area is nicknamed "Sodom and Gomorrah". The Basel Convention prevents transfrontier shipments of hazardous waste from developed to less developed countries, but the convention is not ratified by several States, including the USA. More important is the fact that every month cargo containers arrive, often illegally, from the USA, the UK, European countries, Japan and other places. Unprotected people, often children, who work there searching for example for metals to sell, are often affected, and the waste processing emits toxic chemicals into the air, land and water.[15]

Conclusions So Far

Above I have discussed authors like Bell, Hydén and especially Davidow and Malone, and the strings attached to the freedom which the Internet provides. I have looked at the bending, creeping and crawling and, I might add, the stressful and hard lives which masses of workers face when they produce and repair the countless things with which we surround ourselves in our daily lives. I have even discussed general outsourcing as well as the outsourcing of electronic waste in the world. Outsourcing goes to others, farther away but certainly to workers. A provisional conclusion is that though there are arguments for our present entry into an "information society", I have grave doubts and think that important elements of an "industrial society" remain. Though the traditional labourer is becoming rarer, we still need him or her, in addition to everyone who bends, creeps and crawls. The class structure is in this way altered, the "working class" has certainly become "contaminated",

13. "Exporting Harm: The HighTech Trashing of Asia"; http://www.ban.org/E-waste/tech-notrashfinalcomp.pdf (pdf). Basel Action Network. February 25, 2002 http://www.ban.org/E-waste/technotrashfinalcomp.pdf.
14. Source: http://en.wikipedia.org/wiki/Electronic_waste_in_Guiyu
15. Same source.

but it is still there in a wider sense, including service men and women in large numbers who perform manual and menial labour.

Perhaps you could say that information technology and the Internet *promotes* industry and industrial life. IT and the Internet does not exist as a sphere separate from industry, as a boundary-maintaining system apart from industrial society, but has become part and parcel of the "methodology", the communications, of industry and industrial relations. From this point of view the separation of "industrial society" and "information society" is actually a misnomer—the two are integrated in the sense that the important or even vital steps ahead taken by "information", presumably makes "industry" all the more efficient.

How is this important as far as information and surveillance systems go? It is important in so far as it represents a context, a mode of life, which furthers the new information and surveillance systems. It also *greatly promotes* them, like it promotes other aspects of industrial/technological life. This perhaps especially occurs when the economies in the West face trouble, as they do now. We see this in the various riots which have taken place, or are taking place today (England and France are cases in point). When times are such, authorities like to have information and surveillance systems of the most modern kind in hand. Various summits and similar occasions during recent years have testified to this, and we will return to some of them later.

Panopticon or Polyopticon?

The Internet, and the use of the personal computer "on everyone's desk", has gone through phases. There are many of them; I will summarise them at two major points in time.

Panoptical Communication

The first phase of the Internet is the one which ideal-typically relied on "one-way communication". This was the high time of the "home page". It has received the symbol Web 1.0.

"Everyone" had a home page. In a wide sense of the word, "messages" were sent from centres, numerous centres, to receivers, more than numerous receivers. Businesses of all sorts relied on such one-way communication. Capitalism thrived on one-way communication. Merchandise was lavishly advertised. Receivers could reply, choose among various merchandise, and pay for their choice. So there was some two-way communication. But the bid and beginning came from the centre, the premises were defined there and the alternatives between which you could choose were largely set up beforehand from the centre. Power in this sense, and in the sense of income, came to the centres.

All kinds of other messages, such as messages from State bureaucracies, also had a more or less "one-way communication" profile with some structured possibilities for replies. Power also came from these centres.

In short: The early Internet business communication was a bit like the ordinary postal order catalogue. The one-way communication profile entered the Internet in the very first part of its life, at least of its life which was accessible to the public in general, in the late-1900s. It was an undemocratic one way situation, a one way communication with power located at the centres.

To be sure, there was a grass roots counter movement. In the chatroom called IRC, and at the discussion forum called Usenet, a worldwide distributed discussion system, there were lively exchanges. Some put up their own home pages, outside the control of commercial interests. A certain dualism did exist: on the one hand the conversation on many home pages was a one way communication. At the same time there was a parallel communication system where IRC, discussion forums and mailing lists were parts and where conversation was lively. Historically, communication has perhaps never been more democratic and accessible for the ordinary man and woman than during the first years of the Internet. But certainly, to many observers the grass roots movement was overshadowed by the one way communication trend.[16]

In a book from 1975 (Foucault, Eng. ed. 1979), Michel Foucault has used the concept of "panopticon" to characterise our (European) period in history. He used the prison for illustration.

The modern prisons had an important common form, they were organized so that a few could supervise or survey a very large number. The prisons were, in this sense, "panoptical", from the Greek word *pan*, meaning "all", and *opticon*, which represents the visual. Such a prison was first invented

---

16. http://en.wikipedia.org/wiki/Usenet; http://en.wikipedia.org/wiki/Irc; http://en.wikipedia.org/wiki/Discussion_forums#History; Tomas Wennström has kindly provided me with this information.

by Jeremy Bentham in 1799 (JB 1748-1832, a British philosopher and legal reformer). Bentham's Panopticon had several floors organized in a circle with a glass roof, a ring of cells on all floors, and a grid door towards the centre, so that all of the prisoners could be seen from a watchtower in the middle. In principle, one man in the tower could see all of the prisoners. Later on, the so-called Philadelphia prisons took over, which were organized differently with several wings but also based on the principle that a few persons could observe all or most of the prisoners in the prison from the centre where the prison's wings met. The wings had no floors but gangways along the wall and grid doors to the cells so that the guards in the centre in principle could see each prisoner on all floors from the centre.

But to Foucault this was not just a matter of prisons. His idea is well known: a new kind of society was implied. "In appearance", he said, panopticism "is merely a solution of a technical problem, but, through it, a whole new type of society emerges" (Foucault, 1979 p. 216). Panopticism represented a fundamental movement or transformation from the situation where the many see the few *to a new situation where the few see the many.*

He let the German prison reformer M H Julius describe the situation in 1831. Antiquity had been the civilisation of spectacle. "To render accessible to a multitude of men the inspection of a small number of objects", this was the problem to which the architecture of the temples, theatres and circuses responded. This was the age of public life, intensive feasts, sensual proximity. Rome's Colosseum was an archtype of antiquity.

The modern age poses, on the other hand, the opposite problem: "To procure for a small number, or even for a single individual, the instantaneous view of a great multitude" (Foucault, 1979, p. 216). Foucault formulates it this way: "Our society is one not of spectacle, but of surveillance... We are much less Greek than we believe. We are neither in the amphitheatre, nor on the stage, but in the panoptical machine, invested by its effects of power, which we bring to ourselves since we are part of its mechanism" (p. 217).

In my opinion, there is much to be said for Foucault's analysis. True enough, there were a great number of panoptical machines in earlier history, before modern times (the Inquisition from 1200 and onwards; the various great military "machines" through the centuries), where a few with power surveyed the many (people, soldiers). And true enough, there are many examples of communication lines having gone *both ways* (the great Inquisitor giving Grace up front, not only surveying the many but also seen by the many; the victorious Emperor coming back from battle, not only surveying the masses but also seen and evaluated by a multitude).

But, especially after his time, Foucault has been right in that the late-1900s and the beginning of the 2000s, have seen an upsurge of a multitude of surveillance systems of an *electronic kind*, where the few indeed survey the many but are unseen by the many; grand surveys which have important functions in our lives. There are many of these surveillance systems, and we will return to them in other parts of this book.

It is, in other words, important to emphasise that the late-1900s and early-2000s have in a way vindicated Foucault. The great electronic machines, which the surveillance systems under late modernity could be called, are basically panoptical. So has the initial phase of the Internet as such been.

Panoptical Funnels — One-Way Funnel, Star Funnel and Depth Funnel

Let us look more closely at the one-way communication on the early-Internet, which had a panoptical structure so that the few could see and survey the many. The centres in the one-way system saw the many through large surveys giving them knowledge of what the masses wanted, and of what and how to sell their merchandise. There were a number of varieties. A content analysis which I conducted in the late-1980s and early-1990s (Mathiesen, 1999a), concentrating on a number of case studies rather than generalised quantitative (and representative) data, showed that the *one-way funnel* was a typical case.

In commercial activity and seen when entering home pages, this tempting form seemed to be widespread. The one-way funnel was one of the most common routes to sales and income. Pornographic home pages constituted examples, but also home pages for magazines — for men, for women, for children and so on. I don't know how large the business sector was (and is), but it was large.

The point is that you were offered small samples free of charge and invited to move on, which you often did. You received further samples free of charge, and so on until it suddenly stopped: You had to choose all or nothing. By this time you were so excited and tempted that you might choose "yes", and if you did, you entered into the wilderness of new choices and payments for pornography. The same held, perhaps to a lesser degree, for example for magazines for men and for women.

The one-way funnel could be shorter or longer. A hypothesis might be that the more controversial the end product might be, the longer the funnel to create time for a rising temptation. I received some support for longer funnels to create temptation also from developments in non-pornographic home pages, such as in magazines for men, or advertisement for milk and yogurt for children (Borch 1998).

The second type would be what I would call *the star funnel*. In the star funnel you were brought from a centre of the business activity in question to the far away periphery, and perhaps across the border to several, or even many, other home pages. The star funnel might bring you from say pornography to home pages which were financially related to the original home page, for example magazines for men. Or if the two were not financially related, they were at least akin in terms of symbolism.

A third funnel would be what I would call *the depth funnel*. In the depth funnel you were led/tempted, again presumably through your own choices, still further into the very centre of specific material. The continually greater details in pornography are interesting from this point of view. So are the increasing details about good shoes, nice dresses or whatever as you move through those depth funnels. The point is that prices for the good shoes or dresses increase at the same time.

The one-way funnel, which brought you step-by-step forward towards a particular goal, gives the clearest picture of the expanding commercial sector of the early Internet. The one-way tract was interactive in the sense that you had to respond and click yourself forward. But communication both ways, "true communication" where replies had to be taken into account by the original centre so that messages from the centre had to be changed, were almost non-existent in my case studies, except in the moment you answered yes or no to an offer to buy. It did happen for some types of merchandise that you were asked to comment on your purchases, and say whether you were satisfied or not. That could initiate a reply from the centre. But this was not frequent and rarely led to a full scale "true communication", where new results and new initiatives came up.

The depth funnel and the star funnel were less clear-cut than the one-way funnel, but in reality they were also "one-way". Even if various routes could be chosen, the alternatives between which you could select were systematically constructed "from above": interaction from sender above and receiver below, where the receiver was invited to communicate back, and state his/her own preferences and point to his/her own demands which had to be taken into account, were rare.

This way we may elaborate on the panoptical structure, the structure where the few see and live on the many, in the first Web 1.0 phase of the Internet.

To be sure, all along there has been a living culture of debate and discussion on the net. But it has not been as visible, well-known and widespread as today's Facebook-like, Twitter-like and blog-like activity.

Polyoptical Communication

The second phase had a several/many way communication profile, and came a bit later, overlapping the first phase. It came for good with the so-called "social media" in the 2000s — Facebook, Twitter, YouTube and what have you. Facebook soared like a rocket, reaching hundreds of millions of users throughout the world. It now has 900 million users, almost one seventh of the world population.[17] Perhaps it is now receding a little, at least in Norway. But very many people are still with Facebook and its like. By these and a long string of related inventions, people and groups of people entered into what you might at first sight call "true interaction".[18] This is a phase symbolised by Web 2.0.

We may call this the *polyoptical* phase on the Internet. The *Polyopticon* is a platform technology — "a device offering a 360 [degrees] by 360 [degrees] that uses internal positioning to enable users to orient multiple information windows in contex..."[19] The "poly" part of the concept is from the Greek, and stands for multiple, many, as in "polygamy" (married to many), "polyandry", "polygyny" (one woman married to many men, one man married to

---

17. http://www.pcmag.com/article2/0.2817,2403410,00.asp
18. The two phases of the Internet are outlined in more detail in Mathiesen 3rd edn., 2002.
19. The concept is taken from "The Polyopticon–The First 4-Dimensional Computing Device", http://www.polyopticon.com/.

many women), "polyfon" (polyphonic, in music) and so on. In Polyopticon, the opticon part again has to do with the visual.

The Entry of the Forum — Flash Back as an Example

The most well-known word symbolising the polyoptical phase on the Internet is perhaps the word "forum" (from the *Latin*, plural "fora", but in Internet language the plural is "forums"). There is a countless number of "discussion forums" on the Internet. We find the beginnings in the middle of the 1990s, when they were less developed. They soared upwards in large numbers from 2000 during the web 2.0 phase, in the first decennium of the 2000s. They are possibly receding somewhat now, because Facebook has taken over much discussion. Attempts are sometimes made to create compromises via Facebook.

A good example of a forum is the so-called "Flash Back". It is a very large forum, not so much in Norway but very hot in Sweden. It was established in 2000. From 2010 it was owned by Flash Back International Inc., which is registered in New York. On 2 September 2012, Flash Back had 682,885 members, and it had increased to a total of about 37 million messages and replies.[20]

Flash Back has 15 to 20 broad categories of content. Each broad category is sub-divided into a number of sub-categories, each of them in turn containing a multitude of messages and replies. For example, a broad category on Flash Back would be "Politics". One of the numerous sub-categories would be "Terrorism". There are countless messages and replies in this category.

Everything may be discussed on Flash Back. There is a wide variety of content, and only limited censorship — Flash Back has a high tolerance for a broad range of statements; they say they *take freedom of speech seriously* — as long as the statements do not contain specific threats of violence geared toward specific individuals. If such statements are found, a "moderator" of the forum edits the statement. Complaints are sometimes sent in by members of the forum. Complaints are sent on to the owners, in New York, who finally decide whether the statements should be deleted. But again, a very wide variety of statements are fully allowed on Flash Back — also racism is tolerated as long as it does not include direct threats toward specific

---

20. http://www.flashback.org

individuals. However, posts expressing irrational hatred toward races and categories of people seem to be generally accepted.

Replies to statements and counter-statements are of course received. *Discussion* back and forth is the major point of a forum. Forums differ in their degree of stringency. Smaller forums often do not even have moderators — the administrators see to everything (often a moderator takes care of everyday decisions, while the administrator sees to the general framework rules). Forums also differ in terms of specificity of content — there is a great number of art forums, film forums, cartoon forums and what have you. There are various rules governing different forums. "Deviant-Art" accepts art which contains Nazi sympathies without the creator having to mark the works as "Mature Content", which means that there is an 18-years-of-age-limit. On the other hand, even the smallest inkling of "nakedness" must be marked "Mature Content". An art forum may accept nakedness as long as a new member is 18-years-of-age or over. But the same art forum may accept art which supports say Nazi inspired works. A person's page may be blocked if rules are broken, but he or she may move the activity to another forum with other rules or other interpretations of the rules. The importance of the interpretations of rules in crucial.

In both Internet phases, but in particular in the Web 2.0 phase, emphasis has been placed on the Internet's ability to be a method and wedge used by the less powerful against the powerful. We have touched on this before but it needs to be reiterated. Networks with criticism of aspects of society (Sabau and Thomas 1997, Atchinson 1997) on the agenda, groups lacking channels with which to influence political bureaucracies, groups established on Facebook with thousands of people supporting given causes, mass resistance among consumers (Andresen 1998), alternative evaluations (Statewatch in numerous noteworthy analyses and publications, and their continuous messages of important information about surveillance and citizens' rights in the EU), and international counter-power (the Falun Gong movement in China), are cases in point.

But as indicated before we should also realise that those in power do have ways of slowing down or even cutting short such initiatives (Falun Gong was forbidden in China in 1999). When the Mubarak regime was met by a revolution in Egypt in 2011, the falling Egyptian Government abolished all Internet access in the country.[21] Also, authorities may actively utilise the Internet for their own purposes. In a number of countries, democracy and human rights adherents have found their e-mails hacked into, or their computers infected with spy equipment which reports on developments.[22] Many leading, moderate bloggers have had to escape the country because of personal threats on the net, says Robert Guerra, the leader of the global internet programme Freedom House.[23] "There is a war of its own which takes place in cyberspace", says Wissam Tarif, leader of the human rights organization Insan in the Middle East.[24]

At the same time, and again, Internet activists far away from the borders of Egypt, Tunisia, Libya and Syria have helped democracy activists in those countries to get their messages out, despite the fact that the nets of these countries may have been turned off. Via satellite telephones which have been smuggled in, through private radio links crossing borders and via cell phone networks also crossing borders such assistance has been given. The organization *Telecomix*[25] is one example of an activist network which works at getting around Internet censure. In short: The Internet facilitates surveillance, but it may also make surveillance more difficult.

Panopticon Vindicated — In the First Sense

Is, then, the one-way structure, the panoptical form, gone from the Internet? The so-called "social media" have developed so fast and so as to involve so many people that we tend to forget the one-way profile. But the panoptical form has not disappeared. Power is still around. The blossoming of the several/many ways profile, the Polyoptical profile, has not supplanted the one-way phase, but has merged with — and you might say improved on — the one-way phase. One example is from the most modern of technologies, which gives you a glimpse of Panopticon vindicated — in the first sense:

The reading of news on "smart phones" has increased tremendously in Norway during the past few years. Their use for reading news was for several

---

21. Source: *Aftenposten* 24 May 2011.
22. Same source.
23. Same source.
24. Same source.
25. http://telecomix.org/ Source: Tomas Wennström.

years low, only 3-5 per cent of mobile users used them daily for this purpose. However, in the last couple of years something has happened: The number of daily users in Norway increased from 5 per cent to 19.3 per cent.[26] The prediction is that the increase will continue. Tor Axel Ødegård in THS Gallup says that urban men with a solid income in the age group 30-50 show the greatest interest. He thinks that the ordinary computer will be more work-oriented in the future. A further study (by Synnovate) among leaders shows that they are on top when it comes to reading newspapers on the mobile. Over half of the 480,000 Norwegians classified as leaders have already invested in a smart phones. To have access to a smart phone is of course decisive for people who read mobile newspapers.

You can use the smart phone for example when you are waiting in line for something. A top score is between seven and eight thirty in the morning: People read news in bed before they get up. The iPhone is a leading platform.[27]

Admittedly, mobile surfing is increasing because the new mobiles are better for web reading. Older phones are poorer for web reading or have no capacity for it. Smart phones are something that new generations want and buy.

A wide choice of smart phones is now offered. A Norwegian advertisement on the net from Nokia says the following: "Choose your smart phone—Nokia offers a long line of smart telephones which suits everyone's needs—here you can choose between our best telephones". A British add begins like this: "Group test: what's the best smart phone? The Top 5 smart phones reviewed". On 12 September 2012 Apple iPhone 5 was launched. A sale of ten million was predicted within a month. "Apple may sell ten million iPhone-telephones only in September following the new launch, thinks analyst Gene Munster at Piper Jaffray Cos, according to Blomberg. Compared to this Samsung used 50 days on selling ten million of its flagship Galaxy S III".[28] There is great competition and advanced marketing. The smart phone will probably become our first choice when it comes to consuming Internet traffic, regardless of content.

The smart phone competes with the hard copy versions of newspapers. After reaching a peak some years ago, the number of newspapers sold in

---

26. TNS Gallup — Forbruker & Media. The source here is *Aftenposten*, 5 July 2011.
27. Source: *Aftenposten*, 5 july 2011.
28. Source: *Aftenposten*, 12 September 2012.

paper form has fallen markedly, first internationally and then nationally (Norway).[29] But the media concerns in Norway also send news electronically, and the platforms are changing. The prediction is that the mobile phone will soon become the most important platform. For this reason alone, the profile of consumption of "analytical" news will perhaps, or possibly, become less clear, or maybe obsolete after a while. We always have the mobile phone in our pocket, and will use short breaks to find out what has happened to friends and the world.

Summarising: TNS Gallup reports for all of 2012 that 37 per cent of the Norwegian population read mobile editions of newspapers daily (as opposed to 3 per cent in 2005); 81 per cent read newspapers on the net (as opposed to 2 per cent in 1995) and 61 per cent read paper versions (as opposed to 95 per cent in 1995). The change is dramatic.[30] My point here is that despite the change, the tendency among the many to keep reading news manufactured and edited by the few still lives on. In fact, many more read news manufactured by the few than before.

What will not become obsolete though possibly subdued by Facebook and the like, is the fact that news in a general sense will be covered by the relatively few, and will be communicated to the many—whether the news is world news from far-away countries or from closer to home. Only very few of us ordinary people have the energy and above all the technological knowhow to employ the channels which are necessary and to compress the news to a manageable and understandable form, and to communicate the news to the many. We are consumers of news manufactured by others. An exception may be individual news of friends and so on on Facebook and Twitter. This will happen by people sharing their experiences with friends directly through, for example, Twitter.

It is interesting that not only the existence but also the power of one-way panoptical structures on the Internet is admitted and seen as worrying by young generations of Internet enthusiasts who follow the developments closely. Rasmus Fleischer is a young Swedish historian and public commentator mostly known for being a spokesperson for the Swedish organization

---

29. Source: *Mediebedriftenes Landsforbund* (The National Association of Media Concerns; having 324 members of which 181 are newspaper concerns), in *Aftenposten* 20 September 2012.
30. My source: *Aftenposten*, 20 February 2013.

Piratbyrån (Pirate Office), which is one of the actors behind the controversial and illegal file-sharing website Pirate Bay. Under the headline "Rasmus on the cyber-bum", the Norwegian university newspaper *Universitas*[31] says that Rasmus "thinks Pirate Bay belongs to the New Millennium and that *we are at a time when the big actors continually get more control over the Internet.*" He goes on the say:

> The tendency is in the direction of Google, Spotify, Facebook and Apple. Lots of power is concentrated in their hands, and that has heavy political consequences. The State which controls these agents has lots of power over the world… He thinks Pirate Bay belongs to the past, and that we now are into a new period on the net. According to [him] we have now fallen back to a kind of cultural consumption which is governed by a small number of large actors which govern what buttons we as users are to press… YouTube is so user-friendly that it is very easy to distribute information. But then you also lose control over what you make available.

The main point here is this: Even with the most modern of technologies the one-way profile is still standing, not alone but at least as important. The development is still at least partly *panoptical,* meaning that (relatively) few journalists/agencies/websites and other people send messages — though on new platforms — to many people or large masses of people who are not invited as equals to respond or not able to respond. There is a distinct unevenness in power.

Panopticon Vindicated — In the Second Sense

The above is the first sense in which communication is still in part panoptical, from the few to the many. But there is also a second sense in which communication is panoptical. We tend to forget that "social media" are not that social, but subject to conditions which also make people who participate relative victims of the power of others. In more detail:

The several/many ways profile, the polyoptical profile, is also in itself invested with the power of the relatively few over the many, though in a less clear-cut way. Christian Fuchs, currently professor of media and

---

31. 19 September 2012, p. 16.

communication studies in Uppsala (Sweden), is one who has brought our knowledge an important step forward regarding this. In a paper (Fuchs, 2012) he first tells us, by way of introduction (pp. 31), that

> Facebook, YouTube, MySpace, Blogspot/Blogger, Wordpress, Twitter, Flickr—these are just some of the World Wide Web platforms that have become popular in recent years… Scholars, the media, and parts of the public claim that the Internet has become more social, more participatory, and more democratic…

But Fuchs is bitingly critical of the view that the Internet (only) has become "more social, more participatory, and more democratic…" He follows up in this way (pp. 31-32):

> … [C]ommercial social networking sites are keen on storing, analysing, and selling individual and aggregated data about user preferences and user behaviour to advertising clients in order to accumulate capital. Google is itself a main player in the business of online advertising.

What we think is just harmless fun, pictures and preferences which we communicate to each other on, say, Facebook or Twitter or elsewhere, are transformed into hard business. There is a difference between Web 1.0 and 2.0 firstly in that Web 2.0 effectively hides the businesslike Web 1.0 which certainly still exists, and secondly in that Web 2.0 collects "huge amounts of personal data in order to work". Facebook and the like, with hundreds of million users, contain enormous amounts of personal data—personal interests, alternatives, whims, fads and foibles, in the case of Facebook everything from likes and dislikes in food to politics. Christian Fuchs broadens the picture with Google as an example (p. 33):

> Google's economic strategy is to gather data about users that utilise different Google applications in different everyday situations. The more that everyday situations can be supported by Google applications, the more time users will spend online with Google, so that more user data will be available to Google, which allows the company to better analyse usage and consumer behaviour. *As a result, more and more precise user data and aggregated data can be sold to advertising clients*

who then target users with personalised advertising in all of these everyday situations [My emphasis].

Here lies the power of Google, Facebook and many more: On the basis of the huge amounts of data from different everyday situations, *advertisements are analysed and presented which are individually targeted to (groups of) users, and sold to those who can afford it*. A strong economic incentive follows for Google's and other companies' analysis of the personal data they collect. In a sense they cut the personal data into small pieces, reorganize them as individually targeted, and sell them for a price to those who can afford them. "Given these empirical results", Fuchs therefore says that (p. 53)

> it seems feasible to theorise the contemporary "Web 2.0" not as a participatory system, but by employing more negative, critical terms such as class, exploitation and surplus value. Such an alternative theory of Web 2.0 can here only be hinted at briefly... It is based on the approach of the critique of the political economy of media and information.

Quoting Felicity Brown (Brown, 2006[32]), Brown and Fuchs call for a combination of critical political economy of communication and surveillance studies. Brown maintains that "in particular, the intense monitoring of cyberspace by private corporations seeking information on consumer behaviour is worthy of critique" (p. 54).

To summarise, in both Web 1.0 and Web 2.0 lie important possibilities for a political critique. In Web 1.0 a critique of its power is near at hand since it is performed by the numerous centres in State bureaucracies and business life, advertising for anything and everything from educational possibilities (in State bureaucracies) to automobiles and pornography (in business life), demanding replies to highly structured alternatives. In Web 2.0 lies a critique of power as power has developed in a more hidden fashion through the numerous platforms like Facebook, Twitter and, for that matter, Google, which in reality are less "social" and certainly less "democratic" than many people like to think. The platforms are less "social" and less "democratic" in

---

32. http://www.iamcr.org/component/option.com_docman/task.doc_download/gid.31/ (accessed by Fuchs 28 August 2009), later to be found in Fuchs *op. cit.* 2012 pp. 53-54.

that we are led to think and even feel that we are engaged in socialising and in democratisation, while we, without being made aware of it, are used in aggregated form for analysis and reorganization, and sold as categories to the highest bidder. Hiding knowledge and keeping secret how you are (ab)used by others, counters a basic value in a free society. It might be useful finally to turn once more to how this important fact is hidden and kept secret. In a major write-up on 18 February 2012 the Norwegian daily, *Aftenposten*, started with the following words, which Fuchs might have applauded:

> We bring it along to dinner parties, meetings, in bed and to the theatre. But the smart phone makes us more absent than accessible. It is a new and infinitely useful part of the body. We care for it as if it were a baby. With the smart phone we are always accessible, always on the net. Without it we are nothing. 57 per cent of Norwegians over two years have a smart phone, 93 per cent of the population has access to the Internet. Almost three million Norwegians are on Facebook, according to TNS Gallup. As a student said to me once: If what you are doing is not documented on social media, it has not happened…

Indeed, only the few see, survey, reorganize and cut to pieces the many for the purpose of advertising and selling goods to the many. Once more Foucault is vindicated, though in a different and unexpected way than before.

This is a pessimistic analysis, as is the analysis of surveillance which follows.

Institutions Clustered around Functions

A main point and overall conclusion is that the transition from industrial to information society *varies in degree between institutions*. Some are, in a sense, archaic and far removed from the information society whilst others are nearer, so that our society in this respect is many-faceted. This gives a context to an understanding of today's information and surveillance systems. We don't have "hard data" with which to support this general conclusion, this is an area of sociological speculation illustrated by examples which gives rise to future research.

Various Institutions

We concentrate on *institutions.* By "institution" is meant organizations and norms clustered around a specific and important function or set of functions in society. The concept of "function" is here used as a synonym for "task" or cluster of tasks. The family is an institution, so are religion, education, culture, sports, the various branches of public administration, criminal justice and other legal systems, surveillance systems and so on. They all have *organizations* clustered around them. For example, "the family" has organizations like social aid organizations, child welfare boards, kindergartens and what have you catering to the family. Religion has, with us, the Church as a key organization, but also other organizations, for example low-church movements. The surveillance systems have a number of official and unofficial working groups, in Europe and elsewhere in the world, which continually work for the development of those systems. Institutions also have *norms* clustered around them. The norms cluster around the specific and important functions in question and may be "directive norms", that is, giving directions concerning what is forbidden and what is allowed, or degrees of this. But the norms may also be "qualification norms", they may tell us, for example, what counts as a "corner" or "off side" in soccer, or what counts as "status" — is it education, income or glamorous cars (or perhaps a combination of these) in the family?[33] Various institutions may overlap in the sense that organizations and norms may be important and relevant to several of them, and types of norms — directive norms or qualification norms or other kinds of norms — may exist in parallel or fuse together.

The concept of "institution" defined more or less in this way runs through the whole of the modern history of sociology, and I have therefore not said anything new here. What is perhaps somewhat new, is the following:

Institutions in our Western societies today are in varying degrees absorbed by and carried out through Internet technology. I said earlier that the Internet and the related modern communication technologies *promote* industry, and not only industry. Here I am refining that notion further. Some institutions, like religion and the church, are — my guess is — only mildly or moderately absorbed, they are only mildly promoted by the Internet. The educational

---

33. This distinction between these two types of norms is taken from Sundby, 1974.

institution — our numerous elementary schools, high schools, university colleges and our universities — are more than moderately absorbed, more than moderately promoted by the net and net-related solutions. An example:

Teachers rely on Powerpoint. It is not a contrivance tied to the Internet. As a technology it is independent of the Internet. Still, it is related to the Internet in that it was invented and developed by the same or similar people at about the same time or a little later, and as such it was a part of the same technological movement. It is also promoted by the Internet: Powerpoint presentations are placed on the net for students after class, or for students who were not in class last time round. If you don't know how to use Powerpoint, you are barred from many activities as a teacher.

Another example:

Quite a few students use laptops for taking notes during class. Using a laptop in this way is just to use it as a very advanced typewriter. But at the same time, they fill their laptops with all kinds of information on the net. They save their notes partly or wholly informed from the Internet, and they use the net to find out about courses and a whole string of other events. The administration uses the Internet to send messages (e-mails), new reading lists, news to staff about last or next week's happenings, making individuals or groups aware of dates, times and appointments for guest lectures and a whole host of other matters.

New Public Management

Of course, we still talk and write at the universities. But the writing has changed greatly *in the direction of goal-oriented efficiency*: Four years lead you to an undergraduate degree. Two further years lead you to a Masters — if you have enough examination points to enter the line of study. Four more years may lead you to a Doctorate. Your department receives some money for a Bachelor, a little more for a Masters and quite a bit for a Doctorate. As a staff member, you have to report your writings — a book gives quite a bit of money to your department, an article in a refereed journal gives your department some money, an article outside the refereeing system gives your department nothing. This is a system which greatly favours middle of the road points of view — a deviant view which belongs outside the refereeing system does not belong. There may also be a gradation of money to the writer. In

Norway, academic journals are divided into two sections, Level 1 and Level 2. Level 2 is the highest level, and gives the researcher three times as many publication points as Level 1. Level 1 gives only one publication point per article. Level 2 may according to the rules constitute not more than 20 per cent of publications in an area. A researcher who gets his article published in a Level 2 journal is lucky. It gives his institution more prestige and more money than an article in a Level 1 journal would have given. Several institutions have introduced personal wages based on whether the researchers have attained publication on Level 2 or 1, with prizes for those who receive the greatest number of publication points.[34]

Mind you, much or most of this is again unrelated specifically to the Internet. But again, it belongs to the new modern technological movement of the times. It is inspired by (and perhaps also inspires) the development of the Internet.

The key word to cover these and other efficiency goals is that of New Public Management (NPM). Incentives have changed basically to measurement in terms of money, earned on production and time — students have to follow the master plan for timing, or else... The big question is whether this, which is essentially based on Internet support (at any rate, without the Internet it could not have been carried out), helps intellectual learning and production. I think not. It favours not originality but mediocrity — the middle of the road. The notion that the Internet and related technologies "promote" not only industry but also educational activities and organizations is therefore double-edged — it has its positive side — but definitely also its negative side.

There is a similar development in the various branches of public administration in general. From roughly 1980 onwards, the idea of New Public Management has invaded public administration. It is in general a concept used to cover a whole series of administrative reforms in public administration. They are all geared towards increasing goal efficiency. This is why I bring it into a book on surveillance systems. Though not directly related to modern surveillance, it represents one of today's most central cultural traits in administration, which in principle props up and strongly supports efficiency — but produces mediocrity. It also props up and is supportive of

---

34. Sources: Own experience, and *Aftenposten,* 24 September 2011.

surveillance. Together they are parts of a broad cultural stream, or collective understanding, favouring, or saying "yes" to "the development" rather than questioning it.

A larger measure of market thinking is thought to be instrumental in creating more cost-efficiency in offering public goods in the public sector. Strong criticism has, however, met new public management in administration, both professionally and ideologically. There is also criticism concerning our universities. Unlike in the private business sector, the goals are not clear cut and countable (How do you measure "creating learning" or "providing care"?). Indeed, it is maintained that in the public sector, efficiency should not necessarily be a general and superior goal. It does not "fit well". The lawyers, for example, maintain that business profitability cannot be used as a criterion when treatment or procedure is geared toward creating legal security or equality.

At the universities and elsewhere we have not yet reached Davidow and Malone's "instantaneousness", and hopefully we never will in full or on a complete scale, but *institutions have in varying degrees reached "the information society"*. Some are far away from it, others have reached further. In general, public administration is developing in the direction of goal-oriented efficiency similar to the private sector — but reaches mediocrity. That is the main content, as far as public administration goes, of "information society".

· · · · · · · · · · · · · · · · · ·

I see the counter argument: Could not the drive towards New Public Management and efficiency have occurred for other reasons, without the Internet and without communications technologies specifically unrelated to the Internet? Perhaps it could, and other features such as an independent change in the culture of institutions has probably been important. But two points make it likely that the Internet and the Internet-related technologies are important. Firstly, the new technology on the one hand and the new drive towards efficiency on the other *have occurred roughly at the same time*. Secondly, the technology opens-up fresh avenues to efficiency in a new sense, above all *in the sense of speed and presumed accuracy*. Decisions made are communicated via the net which goes around the globe in seconds. Earlier it took days or weeks.

The Max Weber-like bureaucratic ideal type was certainly efficiency-oriented (at least in Weber's mind),[35] and aspects of it remain in actual practice today, but classical "bureaucracy" is something we now believe is slow and full of rules, hierarchical levels and other stop signs making efficiency problematical. Whether the decisions which today so easily spread with the speed of light also wash away scholarly reflection, maturation and maturity, is another matter. I reiterate that I think the latter often happens, and the New Public Management endangers reflection and maturity, in addition to organizational life being cut to pieces rather than remaining whole.

Major Conclusion: Varying Degrees of "Information Society"

I consider the above, the variations between institutions, a nuanced statement about our society. It is *a major conclusion about our society, and the transition from industrial towards information society.* Some institutions are rather far away from it, others are closer. By the same token, I reject the many facile generalisations about "the information society" which are so trendy in modern sociology.

A whole panorama of research projects, hypotheses and problem areas follow in the wake of this conclusion.

But what about our main concern in what follows, the institution of surveillance systems? I venture a second conclusion:

In contrast to many other institutions in society, which have only in varying degrees reached the level of an "information society", *our surveillance systems have fully entered the information stage, and are moving rapidly on to new refinements of it.* Other systems, such as science/the natural sciences, are also far along toward an information society, but in surveillance almost everything is now net-based. The findings may be used in different ways by people in flesh and blood, but the findings as far as surveillance systems go exist wholly or almost wholly in digital form.

They did not back, say, in the 1940s or 1950s. At that time, and even up to the 1970s, findings existed in archives, reports, notes. One example:

---

35. Gerth, Hans H. and C. Wright Mills (first published in English in 1948). *From Max Weber: Essays in Sociology*, Oxford University Press, Chapter VII.

In Norway a major report from a commission appointed by Parliament concerning illegal surveillance methods, the so-called Lund Report (headed by the then Supreme Court Judge Ketil Lund), was made public in 1995-96.[36] Those who had been objects of illegal surveillance during the Cold War could demand to see what was "in their files". The State was required to pay damages for illegality if demanded. I was not paid damages (and did not demand any), but my own file contained a series of clippings of newspaper articles I had written and several brief memoranda (written by people who had followed me without my knowledge) on my contact with prisoners in the Norwegian Association for Penal Reform (KROM), and on my communication with Polish researchers in social science from behind the Iron Curtain.

Today, my "file" would largely have contained electromagnetic signals.

Framework of Interpretation — The Technology of Political Control

The issue of information and surveillance systems may be discussed more concretely within several frameworks of interpretation. One framework is the development of the European Union as a State. The slogan here is "Policing the New Europe". When the police and police activities transgress national borders within the EU, it is, at least to a Norwegian, a sign of the beginning of a State formation of the EU.

Another framework is the development of the inner market based on the principles of free movement of persons, goods, services and capital. These principles imply that labour may move across national borders and that goods and services may be sold in all Member States. This in turn presupposes that ordinary border controls between countries are abolished, while a common border control is erected along the boundary facing external third countries. The Schengen cooperation in particular, but also other parts of police cooperation, has the abolition of internal borders alongside the development of external border control as an important dimension.

---

36. Document No 15 1995-96, with the long title "*Rapport til Stortinget fra kommisjonen som ble nedsatt av Stortinget for å granske påstander om ulovlig overvåking av norsk borgere (Lund-rapporten) avgitt til Stortingets prresidentskap 28. mars 1996*" (Report to Parliament from the Commission Appointed by Parliament to Investigate Alleged Illegal Surveillance of Norwegian Citizens (the Lund Report) Submitted to the Presidency of Parliament, 28 March 1996).

The abolition of internal borders together with the erection of the common external border may be seen as yet another sign of State building. In the chapters which follow I will touch directly or indirectly on both of these ways of interpreting what goes on in terms of information and surveillance. There is, however, a third framework which is of primary importance in Europe and perhaps beyond. This turns around the conflict in Northern Ireland in the late-1970s. This conflict was central for pushing ahead the Internet and other very modern inventions for surveillance purposes. Other conflicts—for example the Vietnam War in the 1970s—were important for European development and certainly for development in other parts of the world, notably the USA. Here we concentrate on the conflict in Northern Ireland, important as it was for Europe.

Close to 40 years ago the British Society for Social Responsibility in Science (BSSRS) warned against a technology which was being developed in the conflict in Northern Ireland. In 1977, members of BSSRS published a book on the development, entitled *The Technology of Political Control* (Ackroyd *et al,* 1977). The role and functions of technology as a result of research and development during the conflict in Northern Ireland, Great Britain's last colonial war, were analysed. Critics from non-Government organizations in the USA at the same time pointed to how this technology was developed further within the "military-industrial complex" in the USA, certainly during the Vietnam War.

The BSSRS was the first group of scientists and technologically-oriented personnel in Europe who, in an outspoken fashion, said that we were here confronted by a type of technology which had social and political control as its main target. In Ackroyd *et al,* the expression "the technology of political control" was launched, signifying "a new type of weaponry". It is the product of the application of science and technology to the problem of neutralising the State's internal enemies. It is mainly directed at civilian populations, and it is not intended to kill (and only rarely does). "It is aimed as much at hearts and minds as at bodies" (p. 11). The authors went on to say:

> This new weaponry ranges from ways of monitoring internal dissent to devices for controlling demonstrations; from new techniques of interrogation to methods of

prisoner control. The intended and actual effects of these new technological aids are both broader and more complex than the more lethal weaponry they complement.

As time has passed, what Ackroyd *et al* as well as others anticipated and predicted during the 1970s has come true. A report 20 years later, from January 1998, by Steve Wright from the Omega Foundation in Manchester had the following to say about "Developments in Surveillance Technology", one of the many new types of weaponry (Wright 1998, p. 2; in a report referred to as a "working document" to the European Parliament):

> This section addresses the rapid and virtually unchecked proliferation of surveillance devices amongst both the private and public sectors. It discusses recent innovations which allow bugging, telephone monitoring, visual surveillance during night or day over large distances and the emergence of new forms of local, national and international communications interceptions networks and the creation of human recognition and tracking devices.

> The EU is recommended to subject all surveillance technologies, operations and practices to: (i) procedures ensuring democratic accountability; (ii) proper codes of practice consistent with data protection legislation to prevent malpractice or abuse; (iii) agreed criteria on what constitutes legitimate surveillance targets, and what does not, and how such surveillance data is stored, processed and shared. These controls should be more effectively targeted at malpractice or illegal tapping by private companies and regulation further tightened to include additional safeguards against abuse as well as appropriate financial address. The report discusses a massive telecommunications interceptions network operating within Europe and targeting the telephone, fax and e-mail messages of private citizens, politicians, trade unionists and companies alike. This global surveillance machinery (which is partially controlled by foreign intelligence agencies from outside of Europe) has never been subject to proper parliamentary discussion on its role and function, or the need for limits to be put on the scope and the extent of its activities...

Even more recently, some 12 years after Wright—*Statewatch*—which monitors the State and civil liberties in Europe (and which for 20 years on end has published and brought to the attention of a large internet public, massive data on the surveillance activities in Europe and elsewhere[37]) has for example commented on the UK National DNA-database in the following words (*Statewatch Bulletin*, 2010 p. 1):

> The UK national DNA database is the largest in the world containing the biometric samples of approximately 5.1 million people. It owes its record size to the fact that, since April 2004, anyone aged ten or over who is arrested in England and Wales for a "recordable offence" (which includes menial offences such as begging and being drunk in a public space) automatically has a DNA sample taken, usually by a mouth swab, which is then used to create a profile (a string of numbers based on parts of the genetic sequence of the individual) to be entered into the database. Both are retained indefinitely regardless of a person's age, the seriousness of the offence for which they were arrested, and whether or not they are eventually charged and convicted of a crime. No legal right to be removed currently exist…

This was the situation as of 2010. The example goes to the heart of surveillance systems and activities in Europe. We envisage an accelerating string of events, from Ackroyd *et al* in the 1970s through Wright towards the end of the 1990s, up to Statewatch in our own time.

With this as a background, we could now start digging into the great number of information and surveillance systems which are developing on the European continent. But we must first say something about terror and terrorism and related dangers, which the surveillance systems are meant to stall.

---

37. Statewatch celebrated its 20th anniversary in 2011.

CHAPTER 2

ENEMY IMAGES — AND TERRORISM

Too Much of a Simplification

It is frequently maintained that the terror incident on 11 September 2001 against the Twin Towers in New York and Pentagon in Washington DC was a main point of departure for everything that happened in terms of surveillance after that time. It is true that an important part of the official aim for establishing the surveillance systems was the struggle against terrorism as well as what is called organized crime across the borders of the European States. There was also a concern with the control of the EU's common border against third countries.

It is, however, an overstatement and too much of a simplification to say that it all began with 9/11. The literature we have referred to earlier testifies to this. Developments began long before that. The main information and surveillance systems were already in the making or (in some cases) implemented when the attack against the Twin Towers and Pentagon took place. Old and strong interests were behind the development. As I have said, in 1997 and 2000 respectively, it was possible for me to write two books (in Norwegian) on the various surveillance systems existing at that time. Even today they are counted as the most important of such systems in Europe (Mathiesen 1997a, 2000).

Three Enemy Images

In other word, three official aims — *the struggle against terrorism, the struggle against organized crime, and the effective control of the EU's common external borders* (and particularly the first two, terrorism and organized crime) were salient goals long before 9/11: Three new enemy images replaced the enemy image of communism when this vanished or lost its impetus towards the end of the 1980s. As the Swedish historian Mattias Gardell formulated it in 2011 (Gardell 2011, p. 10, from the Norwegian edn.): "In the 1990s terrorism was picked up as a term signifying the anti-Muslim attitudes which began to assert themselves in the public discourse after the Cold War, when the green danger substituted the red as a collective enemy picture".

Not only Muslims, but terrorism, organized crime and foreign cultures with various Muslim populations up front were three images which grew and developed among politicians, in the media and in some parts of the peoples of Europe.

The fact that they could be seen as enemy images does not mean that the images contained no reality. They were not pure fiction, established as such for example by the media. Terrorism and organized crime were actually problems, and so were the increasing number of foreigners knocking at our—Europe's—door. But around the realities were developed images which constituted serious exaggerations of their dangers. For this reason it makes sense to use the term *enemy images*.

Neither does it mean that terrorism, organized crime and foreigners in general, and especially from outside the Western world, were, or are, the only enemies, or the only enemy images presumably threatening the globe. The world is increasingly meeting problems, and new problems at that, which large segments of the population are concerned with—poverty, the dangers of atomic energy, tsunamis, mass killings, widespread revolts and so on. And if the world is not *increasingly* meeting major problems, problems are much more easily communicated in our own time than before.

There are, however, three reasons why we here point specifically to terrorism, organized crime and foreigners pressing to enter our territory.

Firstly, the point is that terrorism, organized crime and foreigners queuing up at the borders are singled out as the enemy images discussed in this book. Up to a point that is legitimate in itself.

Secondly, the point is that the surveillance systems discussed in later chapters of this book, which constitute the core of the book, are to a large extent, or even primarily, geared towards these three enemy images. In the context of this book it would therefore be a mistake not to highlight them. Europol has terrorism and organized crime as two of its most important explicit goals. The Schengen Accord and the Schengen Information System (SIS), in its simpler SIS I form and more complex SIS II form noted later in this book, explicitly have as their goal the control of unwanted aliens and other foreigners at the EU's common borders. The other information and surveillance systems — the PNR, the EU PNR, the API, the VIS, the Eurodac, the Data Retention Directive, the Prüm Treaty and so on (all these acronyms and terms will be explained as we go along) have also — through their daily decisions and activities — the three enemy images as their goals.

Thirdly, I wish to add that *the presumed dynamics* of the three enemy images we have singled out are partly different from the dynamics we find in other areas.

Tsunamis occur as *natural disasters* and they are terrible. Accidents in coal mines on land and oil wells at sea are formidable killers. They are *unwanted occurrences* even if someone in the end is made responsible. Riots, revolts (such as those we have seen in the Middle East), or for that matter minor or major wars, are *more clearly intentional*. They are gruesome whether you are for or against those who are responsible for the killings.

But terrorism, organized crime, and foreigners at our borders are partly different in that they are presumed to have different dynamics. Unlike natural disasters, unwanted occurrences and intentional wars, however terrible they may be, *they are presumed to develop secretly and insidiously until they overtake us*. Terrorism, organized crime and foreigners on the road are insidious, hidden, presumed to develop secretly, finally striking at the core of our nations.

In more detail: The terrorist may be everywhere and anywhere before he or she strikes, and may strike again, though we don't know when or where. The individual in an organized criminal network likewise is hidden and unseen, money is laundered and seems to be legitimate, sex slaves are paid for in terms of travel and earned on for profit. The foreigners are uncanny — they are not what Georg Simmel wrote about in *Der Fremde* (Orig.1908/1950) but closer to what Sigmund Freud concentrated on when he coined the term *Das Unheimliche* (Orig.1919/1963, though my usage is not identical to Freud's).

The uncanny—the eerie, the creepy—sneaks upon us until *Eurabia*—the end product where we are overtaken by foreigners—is one day established.[1]

The three enemy images to a considerable extent represent a *belief system,* emphasising hidden and insidious threats. Surely, there are degrees involved here. It would be dangerous to conceptualise our enemy images in ideal-type form as fully different from other issues. Other issues may also have degrees of presumed insidiousness. There are also other "occurrences" which make us fearful or downright scared than those mentioned in the sketch of a classification brought forth here. But there is a difference in emphasis. The sketch at least makes us conscious of some features common to the three fears we are going to be concerned with.

Below we will, in the first place, briefly bring out some salient points concerning the grounds for exaggeration on each of the three enemy images. We will begin with terrorism and move on to organized crime and foreigners in general, ending with an interaction perspective on foreigners (Muslims) and terrorism, which is crucial to this book.

Next, we will discuss in some detail various understandings of "terrorism" before and after the 9/11 onslaught, ending with the Framework Decision on Terrorism adopted by the EU back in 2002.

In other words, most of our time will be spent on various aspects of "terrorism". The reason is that irrespective of "objective" importance in the form of risk of becoming a victim of a terrorist attack, "terrorism" is probably the most important popular scare in Europe today.

---

1. I owe this important semantic point—about the "uncanny"—to Per Jørgen Ystehede. Sigmund Freud wrote *inter alia*: The uncanny "is undoubtedly related to what is frightening—to what arouses dread and horror; equally certainly, too, the word is not always used in a clearly definable sense, so that it tends to coincide with what excites fear in general. Yet we may expect that a special core of feeling is present which justifies the use of a special conceptual term. One is curious to know what this common core is which allows us to distinguish as 'uncanny'; certain things which lie within the field of what is frightening" (translated from the German by, as I understand it, Laurel Amtower at San Diego State University, and made available to a certain Mark Taylor's course on the Psychology of Religion. I find Freud's comment cited here to be to the point concerning that which is presumably threatening in refugees, immigrants, foreigners. But then he goes on to say that the concept stands for an instance where something can be familiar, yet foreign at the same time, resulting in a feeling of it being uncomfortably strange or uncomfortably familiar. This does not fit quite so well. The Internet site reports that the item cannot be found, but I received a print on Google.

Terrorism

The exaggerated danger of terrorism is documented or may be inferred in many places. This especially concerns the danger of terrorism in the Western world.

Certainly, there have been certain bloody occurrences in the West which should be recognised. This includes the internationally well known Norwegian terrorist attack on 22 July 2011 (discussed in the *Epilogue, Chapter 5* of this book), by a right wing white Norwegian citizen, where Government buildings were hit killing seven people, and where also 69 young people were shot to death (and many wounded) in a Norwegian summer camp for social-democratic youths. The white extremist's plan was to warn the population of what he saw as the Muslim threat to Norway and Europe.

It also includes The Oklahoma City bombing in 1995, which claimed 168 lives and injured more than 680 people, destroying or damaging 324 building within a 16 block radius. It was carried out by an American militia movement sympathiser and Gulf War veteran and an American co-conspirator who assisted in bomb preparation.

It likewise includes the London blast in 2005. It may be instructive briefly to compare the Oslo case of 2011 with the Oklahoma case of 1995, where there are comparable data (Wollebæk *et al,* 2011, p. 18; we will return to that study towards the end of the book and from another angle). Right after the Oklahoma bombing, 38 per cent of a national sample said they were very worried about terrorism, and 40 per cent a little worried. Two-and-a-half per cent and 16.6 per cent respectively of a representative sample said the same in Norway right after the Norwegian events. Wollebæk *et al* (2011) also report other data which go in the same direction.

Maybe the difference in results is founded on a difference between the two countries in degree of vulnerability. The USA seems more vulnerable than Norway as far as the future goes. But maybe it also has to do with a difference in degree of confidence and trust in various authorities, who give a different view in Norway than that given in the USA of the stakes involved, and a difference in social arrangements generally. This would be in line with reasoning followed up later, in *Chapter 5* of this book. There is, in other words, presumably a generalised exaggeration of the terrorist threat throughout the Western world, probably constructed by mass media coverage, but there may be differences related to cultural background and social structure.

This concerns "abstract" or generalise worry. Concern or worry (*bekymring*) with respect to becoming a victim of terrorism is also generally speaking relatively low in Norway. But there are variations between groups which probably are important. Concern or worry varies with the amount of time spent using various media. There is a clear, and significant, relationship between the extent of TV consumption and worry. The relationship is somewhat weaker, but still significant, with regard to social media. The relationships are also robust when controls for age are made. High consumption of blogs is likewise significantly related to concern or worry.

Another large study from the USA confirms this picture, but is perhaps more important in that it reports on the *increase in news reports* rather than peoples' opinions. As such the study may be taken as an indicator of concentration on the issue, and of the creation of a terrorist *image*. David L Altheide (2006) examines how news reports about terrorism in five nationally prominent USA newspapers reflect the term and the discourse associated with the "politics of fear", which means the decision-makers' promotion and use of audience beliefs and assumptions about danger, risk and fear to achieve certain goals.

Qualitative data analysis of the prevalence and meaning of the words "fear", "victim", "terrorism "and "crime" 18 months *before* and 18 months *after* 9/11, shows that terrorism and crime are, during the latter period, linked closely with the expanding use of *fear*. There was a dramatic increase in linking terrorism to fear, while coverage of crime and fear persisted but at a very low rate (the latter is consistent with media studies in general). There was also a large increase in news reports linking terrorism to victims.

I wish also to mention a Norwegian study which compares two "worries" that people have in modern times, by way of example of what becomes and what does not become an "enemy image". Joakim Hammerlin has asked the simple question: Why do traffic accidents (and a number of other accidents and incidents), though of course far more prevalent and certainly much more risky than terrorist onslaughts or even attempts, receive far less attention than terrorist acts in Europe and North America (Hammerlin 2009)?[2] On the face of it, it may seem obvious, but I think it is not all that simple. It probably has to do with the intentions of the perpetrators — the driver did not "mean" to kill, while the consequences of terrorism are certainly intentional. It may also have to do with the fact that the perpetrators of terrorism constitute a small minority of individuals rather than potentially all of us. And it may have to do with the fact that there are sometimes many victims of a single terror act, but normally relatively fewer victims of a single traffic accident. It may, finally, have to do with the fact that the unpredictable and insidious terror acts, which you don't know where and when they will come next, stand in contrast to the predictable and in that sense mundane and "regular" traffic accidents, making them more scary despite their rarity.

And the terrorism which exists is only to a small extent curbed by the various surveillance systems which have been developed, while at the same time there is good reason to believe that the systems constitute important threats to legal security and protection of privacy.

Hammerlin is among those who have argued that we have to consider the possibility that our political system may be affected by the surveillance systems. Even marginal changes in political affairs may make the various surveillance systems become much more repressive than they are today. Repression concerns the freedom to congregate, the freedom to debate and discuss openly, and to have majorities win by elections while minorities are protected by legal rights decided by a democratically elected Parliament.

Organized Crime

The exaggerated danger of organized crime is also documented or inferred in a number of publications. One presentation a good way onto the critical side of the spectrum sees "organized crime" as "first of all a construct, a *notion vulgaire* in the Durkeimian sense…, which mirrors social reality just as much as the feelings, prejudices and ideologies of those involved in the construction process" (Lampe, 2009, especially pp. 165-166; see also van

---

2. In 2011 there were 170 deaths on Norwegian roads, the lowest number in 58 years, let alone all of the wounded. For a Norwegian study of traffic accidents, at least in the 1970s, which were far more prevalent but received far less attention in newspaper write-ups than the relatively few violent crimes, see Simonsen, 1976.

Duyne, 2009). The area is filled with individual and atrocious stories of, or rumours about, abductions or trading in women (and men) who are brought into prostitution or have become sex slaves throughout the world. Sicilian mafia stories have been romanticised or told as shoot-out stories (or both) in best-selling movies, stories of the exchange of billions of dollars on black or grey markets across nations and continents flourish on TV, and so on. A serious overview of research just on trafficking in human beings (Bruckert and Parent, 2002) found that research had identified

> 22 definitions of the concept of trafficking and present[ed] them as an attachment to their study…Aside from the lack of consensus on a definition, there is no consistent theoretical framework that structures analysis and empirical research on this question… Motivated by the stark lack of knowledge on their particular research subject and by indignation, may have confined them to the basics in describing the phenomenon…

I have gone though some of the (vast) literature and found a similar degree of unclarity concerning definition. It is important to keep in mind that the wider a definition is, the more "organized crime" there is, and, the other way around, the narrower the definition is, the less "organized crime" there is. It follows that the field is open for conjectures and political claims and opinions. Close to 25 years ago one author wrote, "…[P]erhaps organized crime does not exist as an ideal type, but rather as a 'degree' of criminal activity or as a point on the 'spectrum of legitimacy'" (Albanese, 1989, pp. 4-5).

We might ask how *the authorities of a State* define "organized crime". The opening sentence of a statement made by the Norwegian White Paper NOU 2009:15 (*Skjult informasjon — åpen kontroll*), the committee in question says the following: (translated from the Norwegian by this author) "'Organized crime as a concept has existed for a long time, but has received increased attention in recent years". Whether this implies that "organized crime" has become more of an enemy image also to the committee or the Ministry, or whether it implies that organized crime in fact has increased, is hard to say. Maybe the unclarity is intentional. The committee goes on to say, in a careful ministerial tone:

> The concept does not have an unambiguous content, something which *inter alia* has led to its not being seen as a legal concept… Because the concept in later years has come to signal a central evil in criminal policy, and is actively used as one of the reasons for an extension of the Norwegian rules concerning the application of coercive means in criminal investigation and prevention, the commission will nevertheless say something about the content and functions of the concept, as well as the development of crime which we must assume belongs to the core content of the concept.

If we disregard the polished language, the concept perhaps says something about the concept's status as providing a kind of exaggerated enemy image. The committee follows up by discussing the definition of the concept, ending up with a "limited" definition. Organized crime is "limited to punishable acts performed as part of an organized criminal group". An "organized criminal group" is further defined as "three or more persons who have as a main goal to commit an act which may be punished with three years' imprisonment, or where a considerable part of the activity consists of committing such acts". This also became the definition of an "organized criminal group" in section 60a of the Norwegian Penal Code. The committee adds that

> … even if the concept "organized crime" does not have a clear and unambiguous content, there appears to be agreement both in a Norwegian and an international context that there are some elements [enkelte elementer] which characterise organized criminal activity.

In the EU there is agreement to criminalise a series of acts related to "criminal organizations". There is agreement on a list of eleven points which are seen as characterising organized crime. Cooperation between more than two persons, over a long or indefinite period of time, suspected of carrying out serious criminal acts, guided by the goal of profit and/or power, are four mandatory points out of the eleven.

Two points may be made: First of all, the definition as well as the elements mentioned or listed by Norway or within the EU are still quite vague, to say the least. This is, in fact, admitted by the Norwegian committee. The vagueness makes "organized crime" dependent on time, place, political winds,

winds favouring or disfavouring control, and so on. Large headlines point-ing to "organized crime" in general, to "organized crime" behind the Roma beggars coming to Norway and other countries in Europe from Romania and Bulgaria (a craze in Norway at the time of writing), escapes from Nor-wegian prisons committed by "organized criminals" (in a TV report some time ago, as if the prisoners were members of some "trade union") — these are only a few examples of the enlargements of the concept following from its vagueness.

Secondly, the vagueness of the concept of "organized crime" easily if not automatically leads to a conception of such crime as an enemy image. Since the concept appeared on the agenda it has become continually and greatly expanded as one of the main threats of European States and the USA, if not by academic people and in research, at least in the popular press, in films, on TV, and so on. The doubts of academic people and researchers are so to speak washed away by the array of exaggerations and catch-all phrases indicating or implying that "organized crime" is a main threat to the world.

Let this be clear: Organized crime based on a relatively clear definition does exist. It is not a total lie, or a total construction. But around a core of truth, painstakingly unravelled by researchers and others, there is a great amount of bewildering confusion, on TV and amongst others in the press, which suggests images that very greatly enhance the phenomenon.

Foreigners

For a presentation of *the exaggerated danger of people coming from outside the Western world,* see for example Banakar, 1994; Woon, 2008; Gardell, 2010. A fine word for it is *xenophobia.* A reasonable definition of it is "an unreason-able fear of foreigners or strangers or of that which is foreign or strange".[3] It comes from the Greek words *xenos,* meaning stranger/foreigner, and *pho-bos,* meaning fear.

"Foreigners" (from beyond Europe) in the West have increased by leaps and bounds during the past decades, and this opens up a wide selection of issues — employment and other economic issues, family issues, cultural contributions to Western societies, refugee and migration issues and so

---

3. http://en.wikipedia.org/wiki/Xenophobia

on — but may, in the context of this book, fruitfully be discussed in relation to the issue of terrorism. The above-mentioned attack on Norway on 22 July 2011 — "the Norwegian 9/11" — was, to repeat, carried out for the purpose or goal of cleansing Norway and Europe of the "Muslim threat". Extremely few if any Norwegians agreed with the extremist's method — the killing of as many Norwegian social democrats, presumably the main advocates of "multiculturalism", as possible. But the occurrence brought forward the view that a minority of Norwegians, perhaps a sizeable one, advocates keeping a certain distance from Muslims. We will return to that.

There are probably variations concerning the extent to which xenophobia exists or is strong in various countries. As a general picture, *Muslim terror* seems still to be the main enemy image. Even after 22 July 2011, Norwegians authorities have maintained the view that there have not been changes in the threats facing Norway — or for that matter, the world. It is still Muslims. They are *the terrorists*.[4]

Are all Terrorists Muslims?

Actually, the background of those who are called terrorists is much more complex. The right wing Norwegian politician Carl I Hagen once commented, some time before the terrorist attack in Norway on 22 July 2011, that "if not all Muslims are terrorists, then all terrorists are Muslims". Right after 22 July he reiterated this comment, only introducing an "almost" between "then" and "all", because this was after 22 July. Also after 22 July, the Norwegian Secret Service expressed the same view during its "threat report" for Norway in early January 2012. The main threat presumably came from Islamism.[5]

To be sure, during the early and late-autumn of 2012, newspapers in Norway and other countries increasingly focused on small groups of extremist, and partly criminal, Islamists who were — presumably — threatening and more or less on the verge of committing actual terrorist acts. The police in several States reacted strongly, following the groups closely, shaking them up and arresting people at short notice. The question of whether a confrontational line such as this was wise, or whether it just instigated further trouble, was largely left untouched. In Norway and perhaps other Western countries

---

4. On NRK Television, 10 September 2011.
5. Source: *Aftenposten*, 21 January 2012.

a debate ensued over whether the threat only concerned a few and small groups, or whether aspects of Muslim culture were in conflict with Norwegian values and therefore a basis of more widespread terroristic attitudes or even actions. Syria was a country where "terrorists" were presumably gathering, being trained in terrorist actions.

The facts bring us rather far away from this. Europol, the European organization for police cooperation (for more about Europol, see *Chapter 3*), published its yearly TE-SAT Report on the EU-terrorism situation for 2010 in April 2011. Of 249 unsuccessful, prevented and successful terrorist attacks in ten EU states during 2010, the great majority were caused by separatists (160 or 64.3 per cent, mainly from Spain and France; only a total of two from other States). Forty-five or 18.7 per cent were classified as "left-wingers". Forty or 16.1 per cent were classified as "not specified". All of the latter were from the UK. *Only three attacks against targets in the EU States were performed by Islamist groups* (two attacks in Denmark and one in Sweden; p. 26 in the Europol report).

Add one so-called single issue attack and you end up with the total of 249.

The TE-SAT report for 2012 shows a similar trend for 2011. Unsuccessful, prevented and successful attacks in 2011 amounted to 174 in seven States in 2011 (p. 36 in Europol's report), a total reduction compared with 2010. The great majority, 110 or 63 per cent out of the 174, were caused by separatists from France and Spain. There were no separatist actions in other States. Thirty-seven or 21 per cent out of the 174 attacks in 2011 were carried out by so-called left-wingers. Twenty-six or 15 per cent were not specified; all of them were from the UK. Religiously inspired attacks amounted to zero in the seven Member States. Add one right winger, and you end up with a total of 174 (p. 36 in the Europol report). "In 2011, religiously-inspired attack plots included al-Qaeda-directed groups, homegrown cells inspired by al-Qaeda and self-radicalised and self-directed lone actors. *However, Member States have not reported a single al Qaeda affiliated or inspired terrorist attack actually carried out in 2011*" (TE-SAT report, 2012, p. 15, my italics).

The report repeats this twice: "In 2011, no al-Qaeda affiliated or inspired attacks were carried out in EU Member States" (TE-SAT, 2012, p. 15).

Islamist Groups in More Detail

The three attacks performed by Islamist groups in 2010 are worth looking at in more detail. They are not only very few, but they have some common traits. All three caused minimal damage to the intended targets (though according to Europol they could have caused massive damage; TE-SAT report, p. 15). All three attacks concerned Western ridicule of an extremely important Islamist symbol, the Prophet Mohammad. The Danish cartoonist Kurt Westergaard, who had drawn cartoons of the Prophet Mohammad, and the Swedish painter Lars Vilks, who had made cartoons of the same prophet, were targets of two of the three attacks. Both were retaliatory attacks (a second explosion in Sweden took place close by, ten minutes away, the only fatality being the suspected suicide bomber). The third attack consisted of a "minor and apparently premature explosion" (terminology from TE-TAT report, p. 15) caused by a Russian national of Chechen origin in a hotel toilet in Copenhagen, close to the offices of the newspaper *Jyllands Posten* which had published Westergaard's cartoons some years earlier. The target of the attack was most probably *Jyllands Posten.* The three attacks could most likely have been avoided had the cartoons not been published.

In my opinion (views in the West regarding this are varied) this would not have meant giving in to a restriction on expression of opinion. Rather than "expressing an opinion", the cartoon drawings were consciously intended to ridicule and hatefully stigmatise religious believers, and to provoke reactions. Compare this with what would have followed in our society if homosexuals had been ridiculed and hatefully stigmatised by cartoons containing a variety of open and direct sexual symbols?

The three attacks at targets in the EU (and a fourth attempted attack) "underline", according to Europol (TE-SAT, 2011 for 2010, p. 16), "that the threat of Islamist terrorism by al-Qaeda inspired groups and affiliations remains high". I question this summary evaluation. Note again that in 2011 there were *no* such attacks (see above).

Arrests

Figures regarding arrests are different, and higher. Arrests have to be higher: A number of people are arrested who are simply released or acquitted. One-hundred-and-seventy-nine of the 611 who were *arrested for terror-related crimes in the EU in 2010 — 29.3 per cent — were categorised as Islamist.*[6] To be sure, a higher figure than the three attacks performed by Islamist groups, but still a clear minority. Note that arrests for "terror-*related* crimes" (p. 9 of the report) is a much broader category than terror "attacks" (however unsuccessful, prevented or successful they may be).[7]

A much higher number of arrests for terror-related crimes were of "separatists". They showed 349 arrests — 57.1 per cent. The great bulk of them were, expectedly, from France (123), Spain (104) or the Republic of Ireland (57). So-called "left wingers" showed 34 arrests (5.6 per cent) and 45 arrests were "not specified" (7.4 per cent). Again, the "not specified" were all from the United Kingdom. Add one right winger, and the total adds up to 611.[8]

It is of some interest also to look in further detail at Islamists who were arrested. Europol (in TE-TAT, 2011 for 2010, p. 16) stated:

> Compared to previous years, a relatively high number (89) of individuals were arrested for the preparation of terrorist attacks. This emphasises the ongoing planning of attacks by Islamist terrorist groups in the EU.

> Reasons for arrests, other than for direct preparation of attacks, include propaganda and recruitment activities and facilitation, raising the possibility that channels for legal and illegal immigration will be increasingly used by those seeking to engage in terrorist activity in the EU.

Apparently the arrests do not concern actual attacks, but various forms of preparation or recruitment activities and so on. Elsewhere in the report (p. 17) various networks and media outlets are noted, featuring propaganda of different kinds. Few figures are given, and, to repeat, actual attacks are not mentioned.

---

6. Not 47% as the report itself claims (p. 9 of the report).
7. "Arrests" are probably based on number of individuals, whereas "attacks" will, except for so-called "lone wolves", be based on groups which have several members.
8. The total number of arrests in 2011 was 484 for the 18 States, compared with the 611 in 2010 (see above). In other words, again there has been a reduction. *Islamism is, however, not a category for the data on 2011.* Neither is "terror-related crimes" used as a concept.

Civil Use of the Internet

Over and above this, various scientific discussions give a different picture of Muslims on the net, to a large extent emphasising the *civil* use of the Internet. For example, Shaheen Sardar Ali has studied a sample of fatwas concerning women and sex on three net platforms. She provides a wealth of information on women's use of the Internet, and religious leaders' answers even to very intimate questions from women (Hellum *et al,* eds., 2011), such as dress codes, women's reproductive rights, and so-called Halala marriages. Of course, would-be terrorists would tend to use less open channels of communication, but it goes at least to show that not all Muslim activity on the Internet is geared toward terror.

The Europol TE-SAT report of 2011 for 2010 adds that threat statements by terrorist organizations have been recorded. The threat statements have focused on the EU as a whole, on individual Member States or European interests abroad. It is maintained that the vast majority of these statements have had the form of general communiqués addressed to EU Member States. Altogether 46 threat statements were recorded in 2010 (43 in 2009). It is maintained that "[t]he vast majority of these threat statements had an Islamist terrorist background" (p.10), and that in most cases, the threats refer to issues perceived as expressions of Western anti-Islam sentiments, such as the Mohammed caricatures published in Denmark or the banning of veils in France. Though threat statements may have various functions, the recording of cultural/ethnic or religious background does not provide hard data on prevalence. For example, one individual group may produce a large number of threat statements. The figures given earlier appear much more reliable as far as prevalence of attacks go. Islamists are in a distinct minority. A doctoral dissertation from 2011 by Lena Larsen (Larsen, 2011; in Norwegian only) gives a similar impression.

Multiculturalism

In Norway, at any rate, "multiculturalism" has partly become a derogatory term signifying the country's general and negative development. In several large and small European countries, heated debates are taking place concerning the role or roles of people from outside the Western world in these countries. In Europe, the many positive contributions of immigrants from the

Third World, cultural as well as practical (what would we have done without their work force?) tend to be played down in segments of the populations, while their presumed threats receive attention. Violent demonstrations have occurred in several places, against for example cartoon representations of important, symbolic figures like Mohammad (see above). The important point would be to realise that those among them who are *violently* inclined in their response are small minorities, as well as to realise the importance of not engaging in cartoon provocations and what have you, which have little to do with "freedom of expression".

Overly restrictive policies on immigration of people from non-Western countries (and the handling of legal and illegal refugees) constitute, on the other hand, serious problems which should be debated. It is also important to realise that the exaggeration of danger connected with non-Western individuals is in part created by ourselves: We have broadened the definition of those who are "dangerous" from the small minority of hardened violent people to those who are more or less critical of parts of our Western values — certainly a large category of people who are largely peaceful and not violent.[9]

· · · · · · · · · · · · · · · · · ·

The three enemy images were (and are) not sharply separated, but constitute a diffuse totality. People from foreign cultures are supposedly seen as the foremost actors in the development of terrorism. They are seen as largely the most responsible, those we presumably first of all have to defend ourselves against. Altogether, the enemy images thereby constitute a partly unclear, partly clear type of racism in Europe. In part, the racism may be called structural in that it is deeply rooted in public administration and State agencies in Europe (Diesen *et al*, 2005).

To a large extent due to the exaggeration of enemy images, the nation States of the EU took several initiatives long before 9/11. For example, on 30

---

9. In *Statewatch News Online*, No 2 of 2: 13 July 2011, Statewatch emphasised this by writing: "However, the component of Prevent [a particular policy under discussion] that had given rise to concerns over excessive surveillance, known as the Channel project, has now acquired a greater emphasis in the revised Prevent strategy. The new strategy has *also widened the definition of extremism from support for violence to any rejection of 'British values'*; this is likely to mean a wider range of individuals are identified as potential radicals" (My italics).

July 1996, 25 measures with which to combat terrorism were recommended by the leading industrial countries (G7) and Russia at a meeting in Paris (Council Framework Decision, 13 June 2002). On 5 September 2001, only a few days before 9/11, the EU Parliament adopted a recommendation on the EU's role in the struggle against terrorism (same source). During the years before and at this time, concentrated attempts to use the new technology to establish large information and surveillance systems suited to the "new" enemy images came along.

Certainly, the establishment of new large information and surveillance systems also had other underpinnings, notably the closing and secretive and semi-secretive character of a good measure of the debates, documents, reports, memoranda and what have you about the images as if they were realities. Once the enemy images were established as such on the political level and in parts of the population, such underpinnings found fertile soil — important parts of the political establishment gave support to the underpinnings creating a vicious circle out of it. Again this does not mean the enemy images had (or have) no reality behind them. It did/does mean, however, that they were exaggerated even more, out of proportion, and perhaps most importantly met with by dysfunctional reactions, somewhat like the reactions discussed in Stanley Cohen's famous account of the creation of moral panics back in the 1970s (Cohen, 1972).

The particular "underpinning" we have referred to here, an increasingly secretive State and State bureaucracy in the Western and certainly the European context, has in turn become one of the main attack-points of those defending human rights in the age of terrorism. They have coined the word "democratic deficit" to cover the phenomenon. The "democratic deficit" constitutes an important part of the struggle.[10]

The Framework Decision on Terrorism

We turn now to the important Framework Decision on Terrorism and related issues. As I have said already, the question of terrorism as well as the two questions of organized crime and foreigners in general, which the information and surveillance systems also addressed early on, were in the making

---

10. See for example Statewatch at http://www.statewatch.org/analyses/no-64-secret-trilogues.pdf

long before 9/11. They provided a much earlier start than 9/11 to the rise of modern surveillance in Western (European) societies.

But admittedly, the development of the systems before then was relatively slow. With the attack on New York and Washington on 11 September 2001, events moved into a much faster gear. The bureaucratic inertia was quite suddenly lifted.

Concomitant to the shift of gears, that is, concomitant to the much more rapid development of a number of surveillance systems after 9/11, has come an even stronger belief that Islamists/Muslims were/are behind most if not all terrorism. The fact that al-Qaeda on 11 September 2001 were behind three successful attacks by large passenger planes (the Twin Towers and Pentagon) and only one abortive attempt (the crash landing of a fourth plane where nothing vital was hit), presumably became proof of this.

The frantic quasi-legal activity which followed during the days, weeks and months after 9/11 implied a *dramatic widening of what we usually understand by "terrorism", "organized crime" and even of what we know as "foreigners".* Terrorism became an everyday threat, pursuing organized crime became something like the organization of witch-hunts in the late-middle-ages, and foreigners, especially from "the Third World", a threat to the very fabric of Western society. This is a widening of concepts which is still with us, though perhaps slightly subdued by rationality during the years which have followed 2001, especially as far as terrorism is concerned. Towards the very end of a dramatic string of political events which we are going to deal with, the concept of "terrorism" was given a somewhat more limited use.

A few further words on the very concept of terrorism are first in order.

Various Understandings of "Terrorism".

"Terrorism" is a complicated concept. So also it was before 9/11. As far as definitions go, it is in considerable measure dependent on a political view. Palestinian actions in the Middle East are defined as "terrorist" by Israel and many Western States, while they are defined as legitimate and necessary political actions by many Palestinians. Palestinians, on the other hand, define Iraeli actions as "terrorist". Frequently an important part of the political struggle consists of winning the battle over definition.

What is defined as "terrorist" may also change through history. The demonstrations and actions of the Norwegian labour movement in the early 1900s were frequently defined as terrorist, while in retrospect they are seen as having been legitimate and necessary attempts to change Norwegian politics and social structure.

Despite variations like these, the question of definition cannot be seen as an entirely relative matter. Some core activities are commonly, but perhaps not always, seen as "terrorist", at least by a majority, more or less regardless of political view and historical phase. *Violent and arbitrary actions consciously directed towards civilians, with a political and/or ideological goal more or less clearly in mind, constitute such a core.* But those who commit such acts may at the time not consider them terrorist. From this core emanate several — popular, quasi-legal and legal — understandings of terrorism. The mass bombing of the city of Dresden during the closing months of World War II, followed by the indiscriminate shooting of civilians (from allied fighter planes) who tried to flee from the demolished city, are such acts.[11] Though the professed aim was to shorten the war, the war was obviously coming to an end anyway, Dresden was of no military importance, and the bombing was a violent and arbitrary slaughter of tens of thousands of civilians. The carpet-bombing during the Vietnam war, the slaughter of civilians in My Lai, the attacks on Somalia, the actions against the World Trade Center in New York and the Pentagon in Washington DC on 9/11, the attacks in London in July 2005 and the attacks on Oslo and its vicinity in Norway on 22 July 2011 are other cases in point.

Other types of action may also be included in the concept of "terrorism". For example, damage to or demolition of important institutions such as oil installations, symbolically important physical structures or structures with important practical functions for civilian populations (Norwegian oil rigs, Buckingham Palace, the WTC and Pentagon once more, electricity and water supplies, would be cases in point).

There is also an admittedly hazy "outer parameter" of the concept, comprising activities which may or may not be included, depending on the circumstances. Even if consciously targeted against military goals, the

---

11. The mass bombing of Dresden was perhaps, in today's strict legal terminology, a crime against humanity, but it is frequently referred to as a terrorist act.

incessant USA bombing of Afghanistan in 2001 in response to 9/11, leaving craters as large as five football stadiums and killing an unknown number of civilians, would be called terrorism by many people. Perhaps fewer would include the united air attacks, backed by a unanimous vote in the UN Security Council, against Libyan dictator Gaddafi's infrastructure. But the killing of numerous civilians took place during the Government's attack on civilian protesters and demonstrators in 2011. [12] A more obvious case, *not* backed by the UN, is Syria in 2012. I have noticed that the word "terrorists" has been used on TV by the parties involved, and that the nuance between "crime against humanity" and "terrorism" is blurred indeed. A particularly clear example is the use of the term "terrorism" during the uprising/civil war in Syria in the fall of 2012. One example:

In November 2012 the Syrian leader was interviewed on Russian TV — in itself a rarity. The interview was relayed to Norwegian TV (8 November 2012). It was done in English, and the leader several times used the terms terrorism/terrorists about the dissidents. Once the words "from abroad", that is, travelling to Syria, were used, a notion also expressed by Western (Norwegian) authorities, but it was never explained how a few travellers to Syria with terrorist attitudes could manage to instigate such a broad and popular uprising. Again on 30 November 2012, Syria's Minister of information commented on the absence of the Internet and mobile telephone communication throughout the country, maintaining that "terrorists" had cut off net communication. The examples also show that the legal limitations placed on the concept "terrorism" are actually quite shaky, and may be significantly broadened by those in power who need the concept to defend their interests.

· · · · · · · · · · · · · · · · · ·

In short, there are various understandings of "terrorism", within and beyond the core activity outlined above. The concept is more carefully defined in Article 3 (later re-numbered as Article 1) in the EU Commission's first proposed Framework Decision on combating terrorism briefly referred to

---

12. The bombing of Libya, again in today's strict legal terminology, probably did not qualify as "terrorism", but people generally are not lawyers and frequently think beyond a legal definition, e.g. to "mass terror".

earlier, which became public only a few days after 9/11. But even the first proposal of a Framework Decision comprised activities which without doubt went far beyond any reasonable definition.

The Offences

A list, vaguely referred to as "offences under national law", was produced. The offences were not defined according to any concrete stipulations in any criminal Act (the proposal was to cover all EU States).

A number of offences were listed, from murder to attacks through to interference with information systems. Several of the offences, including theft and robbery are not necessarily associated with anything particularly terroristic. More important is the fact *that acts covering regular civil disobedience — Gandhi's time-honoured* approach — were included. "Unlawful seizure" of "places of public use" arouses strong associations with environmental protests such as those in Northern Norway in the early 1980s, which were considered so serious that they were met with by secret (but unleashed) military operations from the Government.[13] Thousands of people participated in major peaceful sit-down demonstrations to prevent irreversible damage to nature in connection with the use of a particular river (in the Alta Kautokeino canyon) for electricity.

Likewise, the demonstrations at summits in major European cities like Gothenburg (a Swedish city; EU summit June 2001, visited by the then president of the United States George W Bush) and Genova (an Italian city; G8 summit July 2001) are relevant. Note that both events occurred before 9/11 and the publication of the first draft of the Framework Decision on Terrorism. The inclusion of "unlawful seizure" of "places of public use" was probably inspired by the largely peaceful sit-down actions of civil disobedience which took place at the symbolically important square *Järntorget* (the Iron Square)[14] at the Gothenburg summit. Civil disobedience in Genova was probably also important.

---

13. A number of military trucks painted in order to cover up their actual character were secretly driven through Sweden to reach the Norwegian *Alta*. A large passenger ship in the harbour served as headquarters for the police.
14. *The Iron Square*: Between the years 1785 and 1892 there was an iron weighing machine at this place, where all iron was to be weighed and controlled. This gave the square its name. Historically the square and the buildings around it was a centre for the labour movement.

"Damage" to such places of public use and facilities was likewise included "Damage" is in itself a highly subjective category, open to wide discretionary interpretations. Even in terms of krona, or pounds sterling, the concept is open to interpretation, as everyone who has a car knows. Some years ago I accidentally bumped into another car, leaving a small scratch in the other car's door. Repairs cost 10,000 krona, a little under 1,000 pounds, an enormous amount for such damage.

There is wide disagreement on the extent and seriousness of the damage which occurred in Gothenburg and Genova. The authorities and the courts in Sweden argued (especially in the beginning) that the events as a whole were two enormous "damage occasions", while demonstrators and others argued that, despite some damage, the demonstrations were largely peaceful, the damage being partly provoked by police intimidation and brutality. This goes to show how much the concept is subject to interpretation. These activities could well have become a basis for legal action against "terrorists" had the stipulations as discussed here been in force at the time. The expressions "terrorists" and "terrorism" were in fact consciously used by many people, including a number of police officers against many of the demonstrators. We will return to this.

"Unlawful seizure…of State and Government facilities" was also in the package of concepts in the Framework Decision. State or Government facilities were not seized in Gothenburg in 2001. But municipal schools were "seized" (but allowed) and subject to minor destruction as living quarters for demonstrators. The concept opens the way for thoughts about the protests of environmentalists against nuclear power plants.

We sense the difficulties of the authorities in drawing the line, if they think a line should be drawn, between such illegal protests and acts of terror. "Unlawful seizure" as well as "damage" are very general concepts, and may be the focus of wide interpretations depending on how panicky the situation is. In Gothenburg in June 2001, a wide variety of interpretations of "damage" could be heard.

It is important to realise that both "seizure" and "damage" were integrated in the relevant sentences of the Framework Decision, and that *the word "or" was used between the words "seizure" and "damage"*. This connotes that "seizure" — sit-down actions — could or would be enough for terrorism to be a legitimate word.

Especially "seizure of public places" but also damage to public places" represented a serious widening of the concept of terrorism, which certainly might have been used to contain and stop entirely demonstrations such as those in Gotheburg. [15]

The Purposes of Terrorism

But the offences in and of themselves, as listed in the Commission's proposal, were not enough. The *purpose* must be terroristic, the Commission said, and in the proposal a terroristic purpose was given a broad definitions indeed: If the offences which were listed were "intentionally committed by an individual or a group against one or more countries, their institutions or people with the aim of intimidating them and seriously destroying or altering the political, economic or social structures of those countries, [they would] be punishable as terrorist offences". Note once more that there is an "or" between seriously "altering" and "destroying". Think of that — seriously destroying *or altering* the political, economic or social structure. The demonstrations against electrifying the major Northern Norwegian river mentioned above, or the Gothenburg demonstrations in June 2001, and numerous other peaceful actions or demonstrations by ordinary people in our society, have precisely had this aim — of "altering" social structure. So do environmental protests of various kinds. So does the organization Attac. They all want to "alter" social structure.

The first response of the Justice and Home Affairs Council of the European Union (JHA Council) to the proposals of the Commission is interesting: the JHA Council *widened* the definition of terrorism. Most significantly, in

---

15. After June 2001, a large number of books and articles were produced on the demonstrations which had taken place in Gothenburg. See for example Dahl *et al*, 2001, Wijk, 2002 and 2003, Oskarsson, 2005, and the official report SOU, 2002: 122. A detailed description and analysis of the events belongs outside this chapter; such descriptions and analyses may be found (though only in Swedish or other Scandinavian languages) in several of the works listed. I was in Gothenburg for part of the time during the demonstrations, and base my comments on personal observations, interviews with demonstrators (Dahl 2001), an evaluation of a PhD dissertation written by a police officer (Oskarsson 2005) as well as partly SOU, 2002: 122 and other literature. SOU, 2002: 122 was to a considerable extent critical of the line taken by the authorities, and the police were criticised for their various actions.

the definition of a terrorist purpose, the JHA Council changed the word *"altering"* political, economic and social structure to *"affecting"* such structures. "Affecting" is even wider, and includes almost anything. Also, in its response, the JHA Council did not wish to limit the issue to altering the political, economic or social structures of countries, but *added international organizations*. As Statewatch noted in a significant submission to the House of Lords Select Committee on the European Union, such a "broad definition would clearly embrace protests such as those in Gothenburg and Genova". In addition, Ireland and the UK apparently proposed to delete the word *seriously* in the definition of a terroristic purpose, broadening the scope even more. In view of this, it was of little help that the Council on the other hand in its response added the word "serious" to the description of the offence called "unlawful seizure of or damage to places of public use" (see above).

Consultations

The European Parliament was consulted — without introducing significant changes. In a draft report from the European Parliament's Committee on Citizens' Freedom and Rights, Justice and Home Affairs, the Commission's definition of a terrorist purpose was not changed, and the extremely broad definition of purpose was retained. In the final report it was somewhat altered, but not in a way which changed the content greatly. Among the offences, "unlawful seizure" of "places of public use" was only delimited in a vague and discretionary way in the draft report from the Committee — "unlawful seizure *of control* of, thereby endangering person…" (emphasis added by the Committee to indicate the changes). The word "serious" was added to "damage", and "serious damage" would have to be performed "by means of arms or dangerous acts". The purpose of these formulations was, according to the Committee, not to confuse a terrorist offence "with unlawful occupation, which may constitute a form of protest which is tolerated in the context of public demonstrations". Probably well-intentioned, but in actual practice hardly enough to limit the target area of the provision. What does "endangering persons" mean? Resisting the police, such as in Gothenburg? What are "dangerous acts"? Throwing cobblestones, as some did in Gothenburg? The content of formulations such as these is dependent on the political climate of the time, and may under the circumstances be stretched far beyond intent and recognition. In times of panic over terrorist attacks, and in times when the authorities wish to control demonstrations from the "grassroots", as in Gothenburg and Genova, they may be stretched very far indeed.

In the End

What, in the end, became of all this? The JHA Council came to a "political agreement" on 6-7 December 2001, very quickly in view of the bureaucratic context. It agreed on the following definition of a terrorist purpose:

> i) seriously intimidating a population, or ii) unduly compelling a Government or international organization to perform or abstain from performing any act, or iii) seriously destabilising or destroying the fundamental political, constitutional, economic or social structures of a country or an international organization.

The concept of "destabilising" is perhaps slightly narrower than "altering" (the Commission) and "affecting" (the JHA Council's first response). But the difference is small. What does "seriously intimidating a population" mean? Were demonstrators who probably intimidated people in Gothenburg , or for that matter Council members who were present there, terrorists? What does "compelling a Government… to execute or to abstain from executing *any act*" (my italics) refer to? Certainly, the demonstrators in Northern Norway in the early-1980s tried to compel the Government to abstain from something, notably using a large river for electricity. What does "destabilising" a structure mean? Certainly and whether we like it or not some demonstrators in Gothenburg had "destabilisation" in mind. Were they for that reason terrorists? I can think of many legitimate groups or people who wish to destabilise given economic or social structures, for example structures where some people at the top run the whole game, and the rest of society is characterised by destitution and poverty. Today, structures of this kind often develop and thrive on the basis of global capitalism, a major goal of the attention of demonstrators at summits. The definition of purpose is wide open.

Glimmers of Light

If you search hard enough, you find some glimmers of light. Three, in fact, of varying strength. It is important to bring them out.

First, the JHA Council apparently scrapped the concept of "seizure… of a public place" as an offence which, if coupled with the broad definition of terroristic purpose, would have made a person a terrorist just by sitting in the middle of a street or on a square during a demonstration (as many did on several occasions at *Järntorget* in Gothenburg). The formulation was now limited to "causing extensive destruction to … a public place… likely to endanger human life…" (the reader may consult the list of "offences" in the Framework Decision). This could be viewed as a victory on the part of the civil society groups (such as Statewatch) and others (lawyers, independent writers) who had struggled ardently to narrow the EU concept. It goes to show that struggle pays.

I believe this is the most important limitation which has been introduced in the area of terrorism… The limitation has led to a public and political awareness of the fact that illegal protests such as straightforward civil disobedience are different from outright terrorism.

But we should not open champagne bottles, for the simple reasons alluded to earlier: (i) "destruction", even "extensive destruction", *is open to varying interpretations depending on the interpreter, on time and place*; (ii) almost any "destruction" may be interpreted differently by police and demonstrators; it may certainly be interpreted by the police as "likely to endanger human life"; (iii) at almost any mass demonstration or protest of the kind we are discussing here (again with Gothenburg as an example), a certain amount of "destruction" will almost inevitably take place. And not only destruction to "a public place", but also to "a Government or public facility", to "private property", and the like. In addition, "likely to endanger human life", probably meant to be limiting, is a highly subjective category, keeping in mind how the police will interpret it. In short, the definition still covers the political summit demonstrations which are our concern here, and it certainly covers the activities of various other protest movements and action groups which we normally do not view as terrorists.

Certainly, there are offences on the list which may only, with difficulty, be interpreted as anything but "terrorist" if a terrorist purpose is in place; see for example letters f, g and h in the Appendix later in this chapter. The crucial point, however, is how several offences on the other hand may frequently be interpreted as referring to widely different acts, depending on the circumstances.

Second, Recital 10 of the preamble stated that

> …Nothing in this Framework Decision may be interpreted as being intended to reduce or restrict fundamental rights or freedoms such as the right to strike, freedom of assembly, of association or of expression, including the right of everyone to form and to join trade unions with others for the protection of his or her interests and the related right to demonstrate.

As an expression of generalised values this is fine but, at least to a Nordic ear, expression of such values sounds rather empty and as something you put at the beginning of political statements without attaching too much significance to it. Significantly, the reference to "the related right to demonstrate" explicitly refers to demonstrations related to ordinary trade union work, and *not* to demonstrations and protest movements such as those we are concerned with here. The latter kinds of activities are not well protected by Recital 10.

The third glimmer of light is the JHA Council's addition of a Council Statement to the Framework Decision:

> Nor can [the definition of terrorism] be construed so as to incriminate on terrorist grounds persons exercising their legitimate right to manifest their opinions, even if in the course of the exercise of such rights they commit offences.

The formulation may be a further recognition of the need to exclude regular illegal demonstrations, civil disobedience, from the concept of terrorism. As such, it strengthens the first point of scrapping the formulation "seizure of a public place". But we should also note that the wording is vague--what is a "legitimate right to manifest their opinion" depends on interpretation, which again varies with time, place, context and who the interpreter is — and that exclusion of a series of *other* kinds of acts from the concept of terrorism are more crisply stated, even with reference to concrete historical examples which makes relatively precise comparisons possible: "It … cannot be construed so as to argue that the conduct of those who have acted in the interest of preserving or restoring these democratic values, as was notably the case in some member states during the Second World War, could now be considered as 'terrorist' acts". The authors were probably thinking first and foremost of the activities of liberation forces during World War II, but by the same token, essentially everything the Western alliance is or has been doing is excluded — even the bombing of Dresden in 1945, My Lai and other atrocities during the Vietnam war, USA bombing in other parts of the world after World War II. Those in power decide what is "terrorism". The point is that in incidents during World War II, people on the side of the allies had presumably acted in particular ways *"in the interest of preserving or restoring ... democratic values"*. In addition, we should note that a Council Statement is only a political and not a legal statement, and has no legal force.

Let me add to all of this that on the eve of 2002, notably on 27 December in the quiet week between Christmas and New Year, the Council of the European Union by "written procedure" adopted a so-called Common Position on combatting terrorism. A Common Position, made under Article 15 of the Treaty on European Union, does not have to be submitted to the European Parliament (or any parliament) for scrutiny. The Common Position stated among other things that measures *"shall be taken to suppress any form of support, active or passive, to entities or persons involved in terrorist act…"* This was confirmed as *decided* on the following day (*Official Journal*, L 344, 28 December 2001). No line was drawn between those who actively support and those who merely agree with the political aims of terrorists.

· · · · · · · · · · · · · · · · ·

On Wednesday 6 February 2002 the European Parliament voted, by a large majority, to support the Framework Decision on combating terrorism, with it accepting the definition of "terrorism" discussed above. On 13 June 2002, the text on terrorism was finally adopted by the EU Council (*Official Journal*, 2002/475/JHA). The whole affair took nine months from beginning to end.

The Gothenburg summit before 9/11 set an agenda. The Swedish journalist and writer Lars Berge on 11 June 2011, almost to the day ten years after the demonstrations in Gothenburg of 14-17 June 2001, made the following comment in *Svenska Dagbladet* (a liberal/conservative Swedish daily) on what happened (my translation from the Swedish):

The violence [in Gotheburg] eventually overshadowed everything. After Swedish State Power for the first time since Ådalen[16] fired with live cartridges against demonstrators, wounding two and almost killing one of them, a TV study was made on the home page of TV4. A large majority now demanded harder measures. They received what they wanted. Under the G8-meeting in Genova the following month the activists were exposed to meaningless violence. At the protests against the summit on free trade (FTAA) in Miami two years later the police literally made preparations for war.

Appendix

Article 1 in the Framework Decision of 13 June 2002 on Combating Terrorism

Terrorist Offences and Fundamental Rights and Principles
I. Each Member State shall take the necessary measures to ensure that the intentional acts referred to below in points (a) to (i), as defined as offences under national law, which, given their nature or context, may seriously damage a country or an international organization where committed with the aim of:
    — seriously intimidating a population, or
    — unduly compelling a Government or international organization to perform or abstain from performing any act, or
    — seriously destabilising or destroying the fundamental political, constitutional, economic or social structures of a country or an international organization, shall be deemed to be terrorist offences:
    (a) attacks upon a person's life which may cause death;
    (b) attacks upon the physical integrity of a person;
    (c) kidnapping or hostage taking;
    (d) causing extensive destruction to a Government or public facility, a transport system, an infrastructure facility, including an information system, a fixed platform located on the continental

---

16. Ådalen, a Swedish valley known for a battle in 1931 between the military, called in by the owners, and the labourers, and where the military shot and killed five labourers.

       shelf, a public place or private property likely to endanger
       human life or result in major economic loss;

(e) seizure of aircraft, ships or other means of public or goods
       transport;

(f) manufacture, possession, acquisition, transport, supply or use
       of weapons, explosives or of nuclear, biological or chemical
       weapons, as well as research into, and development of, biologi-
       cal and chemical weapons;

(g) release of dangerous substances, or causing fires, floods or
       explosions the effect of which is to endanger human life;

(h) interfering with or disrupting the supply of water, power or
       any other fundamental natural resource the effect of which is to
       endanger human life;

(i) threatening to commit any of the acts listed in (a) to (h).

II. This Framework Decision shall not have the effect of altering the obligation to respect fundamental rights and fundamental legal principles as
enshrined in Article 6 of the Treaty on European Union.

The 2002 Framework Decision still provides the overall legal framework for countering terrorism in the EU. In 2008 it was somewhat amended and enlarged. The amendment introduced three new offences — "public provocation to commit a terrorist offence", "recruitment for terrorism" and "training for terrorism".[17] The Council of Europe and other human rights organizations have been particularly critical of the "public provocation" clause. This clause has the aim of "… reducing the dissemination of those materials which might incite persons to commit terrorist attacks" (Point 6 in the Preamble). This may run counter to the notion of freedom of speech. "Recruitment for terrorism" and "training for terrorism" are, however, just as dangerous or more so because they may contain a broadening of concepts — recruitment and training are wide concepts which may take in a variety of facts rather than recruitment and training "for terrorism".

---

17. The full text of the measures is at: http://eurlex.europa.eu/LexUriServ/LexUriServ.do?uri=OJ
    :L:2008:330:0021:0023:EN:PDF.

The EU Framework Decision — A Model for Europe
All over Europe and the rest of the Western world (especially the USA) similar developments took place. It goes beyond this chapter to describe the details. However, a few short remarks on what happened in my own country, Norway, will indicate continuity with the EU development and variations.

Before 9/11 the emphasis on terrorism as a phenomenon and concept was developing slowly. For example, in Norway the relevant authorities were not particularly preoccupied with terrorism. In fact, the so-called *Security Committee* in 1993 (established in 1990 to evaluate whether the rules regarding criminal law and process were adequate and efficient as far as terrorism goes) as well as the *Ministry of Justice* in 1999 turned down a proposal on a particular "Terror Act", on the grounds that this would just lead to an increased focus on terrorism. In addition, terrorism was difficult to define, and the *de facto* offences in question were criminalised anyway.

After 11 September, the climate of opinion in official quarters abruptly changed in accordance with the UN Convention of 9 December 1999 on combatting terrorism (signed by Norway 1 October 2001) and by the unanimous adoption of resolution 1373 on combating terrorism by the Security Council. Suddenly a stipulation on terrorism was in great need. By 5 October 2001 a Provisional Regulation on prohibiting the financing of terrorism etc. was decided by Royal Decree. The haste was such that Norway could not wait for the regular procedures of Parliament, which would take longer: The argument was that, though Parliament was convened, it was not yet formally opened after the summer vacation by the King. Therefore a quick Royal Decree could be used.

Right before Christmas 2001, when people were preoccupied with matters other than debating terrorism, a proposal on stipulations concerning terrorism was presented by the Ministry of Justice. A heated public debate followed. Amongst others the Attorney-General, the Judges' Association, the Lawyers' Association, Amnesty International, the Data Inspectorate, the Department of Human Rights, the Prisoners' Organization KROM and others went against much of what had been proposed by the Ministry. The proposal contained many of the vague and widening aspects in the Framework Decision of the EU Commission. The vagueness of the concept and types of terror and terrorism were major points of attack from left to right.

Norway's "legal culture" and emphasis on legality became something of a watershed.

A formal Bill from the Government was issued on 12 April 2002. The final proposal taken by Parliament was modelled after the EU Framework Decision, but with some moderations forced upon a weak Coalition Government. The definition of terroristic purpose was still wide and vague, but the offences which were listed were closely tied to crimes already defined by law.

Similar developments—with the EU Framework Decision as a model but variations—came in other European countries. Alterations also came as the first decade of the 2000s developed.

The definitions of terrorism and types of terror were a most important sounding board for the developments of the information and surveillance systems which we now turn to. As I have said, they began to develop long before 9/11. But their development took on much greater speed its wake.

Epilogue for Chapter 2

In this chapter we have *inter alia* reviewed the history and conditions of "terrorism" before, during and after the creation of the EU Framework Decision on Terrorism. The influence of the Framework Decision has been great. Two points should be made.

First, the expansion of the concept has led to an increased concern over terrorism throughout the region and the world. Notably, terrorist occurrences in themselves have also increased the concern. But it is common knowledge in the sociology of law that legal formulations of a concern may in themselves inadvertently stimulate the concern. Proof of the existence of witches in earlier times was the fact that there were laws against them.

Secondly, on the other hand the limitations of the rules against terrorism may also have limited the use of the concept as such. The scrapping of the concept of "seizure of a public place" is such a limitation, in that it excludes regular civil disobedience. This is important. But other concepts easily come to mind, and are used to characterise events. Recent uproars in French and English city districts characterised by poverty and destitution, are perhaps not conceptualised as "terrorism", but instead as uproars allowing for extensive police brutality—perhaps more brutality than a concept of terrorism would have allowed.

The Framework Decision on Terrorism and the rules therein have latent functions that require continued attention.

Also, we have to remember that the concept of terrorism is always subject to interpretation, especially in acute situations, when the concept is useful as a defence and legitimation against opposition and threats to power. Remember how the Syrian leaders, in the autumn of 2012, used concepts like "terrorism" and "terrorists" against uprisings created by their own dictatorial rule.

CHAPTER 3

THE SURVEILLANCE SYSTEMS

A Case

On 22 May 2013, a British Army soldier was attacked by two men in Woolwich in London. According to media reports, the two men, since charged but not convicted, killed the soldier with knives. The men were of Nigerian Christian descent. Both were converted Muslims, who apparently had had contact with radicalised Islamic milieus. The two alleged killers stayed on at the scene, one of them showing a large meat knife on a video taken by a private person there. They told people who came to the scene that the murder was in revenge for the killing of Muslims by the British military.

The killers were shot at by the police before they were taken into custody. They were wounded but alive when taken.

The story created a flurry of banner headlines across the world. On 4 June 2013, the major Norwegian daily *Aftenposten* carried a big front page headline saying, "Norway must count on revenge attack". The quote was from an influential Islamist who referred to the war against Muslims and Norway's expulsion of a particular Islamist and a certain Mullah Krekar, who actually could not be sent out of Norway because of international regulations—among other things against the possibility of torture in the country it was planned to send him to.

What is the trigger importance of this particular story in the context of this book? It may be summarised in one word—surveillance. In Britain the call for more surveillance was loud and clear. The story has various strands which may be unravelled later, and public opinion polls will no doubt show the extent to which British people called for more surveillance (to anticipate, in *Chapter 5* I will show that Norwegian public opinion studies did not show a great increase in people's desire for more surveillance after Norway's 22 July massacre). But we can already observe a clamour for more surveillance on the political level in Britain. On 25 May 2013 the *Irish Times* carried the headline: "We must not overreact to Woolwich terror act, warns Clegg". Nick Clegg was Deputy Prime Minister at the time, and a Liberal Democrat. His reference to over-reaction was against the tidal wave of references to more/more intensive surveillance. The *Irish Times* went on to say that

> The Liberal Democrats leader has come under renewed attack for his decision to block the passage of legislation that would store details for a year about the internet habits of the population. His decision infuriated Conservative Home Secretary Theresa May and led to a bitter row between them before the Woolwich atrocity, though she now sees an opportunity to push for the legislation once more. Former Labour Home Secretary John Reid and the British government's one-time independent reviewer of terrorism legislation Alex Carlile have insisted the so-called snoopers' charter is needed to tackle British-based terrorists. Mr Clegg yesterday said knee-jerk security reaction is exactly the response wanted by Islamic terrorists, who wish to "sow that corrosive seed of fear and division".

Of course, we do not yet know how this particular debate will end. But that there is a political call, however mixed due to the Liberal Democrats, for more surveillance, a political call for a "snoopers' charter", is inescapable. Around the hard fact of a murder of a British soldier, a moral panic (Cohen 1972) is in the making.

The genesis of a surveillant state does not only lie in a moral panic, or in several such panics. Various political and technological channels are activated and provide the birth and development of surveillance systems. The technology of the Internet, partly outlined in *Chapter 1*, is one of them. But moral panics illustrated by the Woolwich case are certainly important.

The important lesson in this and the next chapter, is that despite the great abundance of advanced surveillance systems outlined there, and despite their meagre results in finding terrorists *before* terrorist actions are carried out, the Woolwich case illustrates well the tendency to call for more surveillance when atrocities occur. An illness leading to the administration of a medicine that does not help, leads to exactly that—more of the same medicine.

We turn now to the drier story of the structure and functions of the large number of surveillance systems in Europe.

A Plethora of Systems

Despite the relative rarity of terror cases, a whole plethora of surveillance systems and principles are developing or have developed in Europe. A great rush is on. The most important systems and principles we will discuss here are:

SIS—The Schengen Information System and SIS II; the latter an advanced version of SIS which has been in the making for a long time;

SIRENE Exchange—Supplementary Information Request at National Entries;

TECS—The Europol Information Systems;

EURODAC—the European Dactyloscopy—A large database of fingerprints of applicants for asylum, and fingerprints of illegal immigrants found within the EU;

Data Retention Directive—Which stores information for a given length of time (six months to two years) about everyone's use of telecommunications equipment—mobile telephones, fixed telephones, Internet and so on. Everything—names, start, termination, place, date, and so on—is stored, except the content of communication;

PNR—Passenger Name Record—Data provided by all travellers by air who cross USA borders, which is subsequently analysed and processed by law enforcement agencies, ostensibly for preventing, investigating and prosecuting serious crimes. The USA requires any flight entering its territory (and perhaps any flight near its territory) to supply PNR data to the USA Department of Homeland Security. An agreement between the USA and the EU was reached in May 2012, the EU also having agreements with Canada and Australia, and there is a proposal on the table for an EU PNR system for all flights coming into the EU. The UK is very involved and in favour of extending the system to sea and rail travel as well as air;

API—Advance Passenger Information—This is in many ways similar to the PNR and the EU PNR, and built on the same logic of using information from passengers for law enforcement purposes;

ECHELON—an international spy system, stemming partly from outside Europe but highly relevant to Europe, using advanced technology for industrial spying and related activities;

The Hague Programme—which rather than a system or treaty as such is a programme adopted by the European Council, *inter alia* advocating a particular *principle* in a number of states—the so-called *principle of availability*. As it was adopted by the European Council[1] (essentially summit meetings where EU leaders decide on broad political priorities and major initiatives), there was no vote in the European Parliament or national Parliaments—who were only generally informed and discussed it. The principle says that information lodged with law enforcement agencies in different Schengen States is to be made readily available across borders, *between* law enforcement agencies in various Schengen States. The Prüm Treaty (below) is based on the principle of availability—specific data stored nationally are to be made readily available to law enforcement agencies in the other participant States to the treaty. The expectation is that the principle will expand to many or perhaps all surveillance systems.

The Prüm Treaty—mentioned just above—Which opens access for law enforcement agencies in one Member State to have access to *DNA data, fingerprints and vehicle data* in one or more other Member States and vice versa. Prüm Decisions also permit the exchange of personal data for the prevention of terrorist offences and joint operations by police forces of different Member States (Jones, 2012).

---

1. It is not necessary here to go into the complexities of the EU political system. But a few salient points should be made: Meetings in the *European Council* are essentially summit meetings where EU leaders decide on broad political priorities and major initiatives. The European Council should not be confused with the *Council of the European Union* (sometimes just called "the Council"), which is the institution in the essentially bi-cameral legislative body of the EU. The other legislative body is the European Parliament. The Council is composed of several configurations of national Ministers (one per state). The European Commission is the executive body of the EU, responsible for proposing legislation, implementing decisions, upholding the EU's treaties and day-to-day running of the EU. The Commission operates as a Cabinet government, with 27 members (at the time of writing: informally known as "commissioners"). The *European Parliament* is directly elected by EU voters every five years. The Parliament is one of the EU's main law-making institutions, along with the Council (above).

In short, there are a number of surveillance systems, treaties or principles of information exchange between European States, either in operation or in the making. Other systems in the making will either be discussed in between the main systems mentioned above, such as VIS or the Visa Information System, as a supplement to the Schengen Information System, furthermore the Hague Programme and the Prüm Treaty (see above), which are examples of the opening of information channels "horizontally", between systems and States. Are we moving towards one large surveillance system, altogether with an enormous power potential, in the European Union?

As time passes, the surveillance systems in Europe take on a *dynamic pattern*. Internal mechanisms in the systems will increase their speed and efficiency. Even SIS II, which has been slow in developing, will in due course most likely follow such a pattern.

New norms are being established inside the systems — norms that emphasise a future-orientation involving control patterns over whole categories of people and which develop risk profiles for entire groups.

Because the systems develop fast and are continually widened, there is a great need for continuous updating and revisions of presentations. I give here a fairly quick run-down of the main systems, some relatively new data on them and, as mentioned, other less well known systems related to the main systems. I then go on to a theoretical idea which may possibly become useful for a deeper understanding of the systems and what happens to information exchange and surveillance in Europe — perhaps in the West — today.

Before we go on, let me say that the information and surveillance systems which are discussed here all have greater or less detailed rules concerning data quality and data security, which are related to personal privacy matters. I and others have discussed the rules in several places earlier (Mathiesen 2000; in English see Karanja, 2005, 2006). There is an Article 29 *Data Protection Working Party*, which *inter alia* comprises all the Data Protection Commissioners from Member States.[2] *The European Data Protection Supervisor*, EDPS, is set up by a regulation and is charged solely with the activities of

---

2. The Article 29 Data Protection Working Party was set up under Directive 95/46/EC of the European Parliament and the Council of 24 October 1995 on the protection of individuals with regard to the processing of personal data and on the free movement of such data.

EU institutions, not those at a national level.[3] There are ongoing negotiations between the EU and the USA concerning data protection.[4]

The existing rules concerning data quality and data security are not discussed in detail here. First, the most important rules concerning data quality hang on the person's right to know, delete and correct information about himself or herself. These rights are subject to important limitations as explained at appropriate points in what follows. Going into the details about rules therefore easily becomes a play on words. Secondly, the use of the rules is generally dependent on national practice followed in the various countries, which may differ greatly. Thirdly, even EDPS is confronted by active and powerful agencies, and frequently appears to struggle with its back against the wall. In the fourth place, even the most precise of regulations may lose force due to the speedy development of the systems and of technology in general, which makes control extremely complicated. Taken as a whole, rules of this kind are fraught with problems. Indeed, the idea that surveillance systems are so large and numerous that they constitute a "cloud" has been followed with interest among computer-minded professionals. Allegedly the USA Patriot Act may in fact obtain data from European surveillance systems through the "cloud". In this book, we do not enter into these allegations, but they may represent a development which the future will want to monitor carefully.[5]

---

3. The EDPS is an independent supervisory authority devoted to protecting personal data and privacy and promoting good practice in the EU institutions and bodies. It does so by "monitoring the EU administration's processing of personal data, advising on policies and legislation that affect privacy, and cooperating with similar authorities to ensure consistent data protection" (from the EDPS home page).

4. Negotiations on data protection in 2011 between the EU and the USA, Brussels 3, February 2012, from Commission Services to Justice and Home Affairs (JHA) councillors.

5. Cloud computing is the use of computing resources (hardware and software) that are delivered as a service over a network, typically the Internet. Cloud computing entrusts remote services with a user's data (from Wikipedia). The data is not located at a specific point, but may be anywhere on the net, hence the word "cloud". For the Patriot Act's obtaining data from European sources stored in the cloud, see http://www.cbsnews.com/8301-205_162-57556674/patriot-act-can-obtain-data-in-europe-researchers-say/

The Systems

I concentrate on Europe. The systems have in common that the information which is generated is spread regionally, in our case within the EU, but also across the borders of the region and even globally. As mentioned, they are heavily dependent on the expanding modern data technology.

SIS and SIS II — Schengen Information System

A bit of history

Schengen Information System, the SIS, had in 2007 close to 895,000 persons (aliases not included) and over 17 million objects in their central database.[6] In many ways the SIS is the "mother system" — the Eve which so many of the other developments in Europe started from. In 1985, five European States (Belgium, France, Luxembourg, The Netherlands and (the then) West Germany) entered into an agreement (in the little town of Schengen in Luxembourg) on the principle of abolition of border controls between the States in question, and a parallel fortification of the common borders surrounding the States.

The origin of the Schengen agreement in 1985 is often traced back to the European Coal and Steel Community (ECSC) proposed by the French Foreign Minister, Robert Schuman on 9 May 1950 — five years after World War II. The plan of such a community was formulated by the Frenchman Jean Monnet. All German and French coal and steel production was to be placed under a common administration, presumably in order to prevent war from breaking out again in the future on the European continent. The merging of coal and steel production also fitted nicely into the energetic industrial capitalism of the time. The institutional framework of the ECSC contained clear tendencies towards supranationality, foreshadowing the later European Economic Community(EEC)/European Union (EU) arrangements and goals. The six countries involved in the European Coal and Steel Community were the five signatories to the first Schengen agreement in 1985, plus Italy.

A detailed convention called the Schengen Convention was signed, also in Schengen, in 1990.[7] Instead of internal control between the States, measures

---

6.   Source: House of Lords, European Committee 2007a, p. 22.
7.   Convention of 19 June 1990, with later amendments.

were introduced which increased substantially the border controls along the external common border. For this reason Schengen has been referred to as *Fortress Europe*. Originally, the Schengen accord was outside the European Union, but certainly part of a more long term EU goal, and at the EU summit in Amsterdam in 1997, Schengen, with its whole *acquis*, its accumulated legislation, body of rights and obligations etc., was incorporated lock, stock and barrel into the EU (in force in 1999).[8]

By 2001, there were 13 full EU Member States in Schengen. The UK and Ireland, also EU Member States (giving the EU a total of 15 Member States at the time), participated in police cooperation, but wished (and wish) to maintain their own border control of the islands. On the other hand, Norway and Iceland, non-members of the EU, fully applied the provisions of the Schengen *acquis*, and were given associate membership in Schengen. Altogether, then, by 2001 there were 15 states participating in Schengen, 13 EU Member States and two states having associate membership.

The EU currently has 28 members which have transferred parts of their sovereignty — or law-making authority — to the EU (on 1 July 2013 Croatia became the latest member; there is a drive towards getting more members from Eastern Europe).[9]

Also Switzerland, another non-member of the EU, has decided to join the Schengen area. This took place on 12 December 2008. By that time, 22 of the EU states were full members of Schengen also, in addition to the non-EU members Norway, Iceland, Switzerland — and Liechtenstein, which became a member on 19 December 2011, giving a total of 26 Schengen members. In Justice and Home Affairs (JHA) there is the EU JHA Council of Ministers and the so-called Mixed Committee, which discusses Schengen issues and includes Norway, Iceland, Switzerland and Liechtenstein.

---

8. The term is French, meaning "that which has been agreed upon". http://en.wikipedia.org/wiki/Community_acquis
9. http://euobserver.com/enlargement/117769 The European Commission's new enlargement strategy says that corruption and organized crime are the biggest obstacles in Western Balkan countries' path to EU membership.

Still debate

There is still debate and controversy around Schengen. At the time of writing the first draft of this chapter (in August 2011), Bulgaria and Romania were not yet members of Schengen, though the two states had become members of the EU. A decision was delayed at the insistence of France and The Netherlands, apparently citing corruption worries.

The Schengen area covers about 400 million people. Also, in the beginning of 2011, Italy received thousands of refugees from Tunisia (via the little Italian island of Lampedusa in the Mediterranean), due to the revolts which took place in Tunisia. With many of them being French speaking, a natural destination was France. But Italy being their first country of entry into the EU (see the Dublin Convention below) the arrival of thousands of Tunisian refugees in Italy created overwhelming consequences for Italy. Their passage to France was made easier by Italy not keeping them in detention centres but granting them temporary residence permits so they could travel to France. In reaction, France reinforced its "spot checks" at the border, with riot police boarding trains and checking the papers of persons on board. The Italian Prime Minister and French President proposed all round reform of Schengen.

At the time of writing the debate is not over. A document produced by *Associazione di Studi Giurici sull'Immigrazione* on 12 August 2011 raised several concerns over the treatment of migrants who arrived in Italy as a result of the political turmoil in the Northern African countries of Egypt, Libya and Tunisia after December 2010. Under the title "The Law of France Must be Respected", it was emphasised in a document by Statewatch on 22 August 2011 that the prefecture of Gironde had proved keen on chasing irregular migrants, sometimes with little respect for the legal procedures and judicial decisions made. This had been criticised by the magistrates' trade union.[10] On 10 May 2011, a parliamentary debate took place in the EU; the vast majority of those who took the floor supported the Schengen arrangement as a great achievement which should not be jeopardised by 25,000 refugees

---

10. Information from Statewatch, 24 August 2011.

from Tunisia to Italy. But there was also an expressed interest in tightening the control, and increased solidarity between Member States.[11]

On the political level in the EU, the free movement of people is viewed as the Union's key achievement. On the other hand, the view is that it would be necessary to spell out a mechanism allowing a State to re-open border posts in case of a sudden surge in migration or inability of another EU State to control its frontier with non-EU nations.[12] There is an ongoing debate concerning possible changes in the Schengen Borders Code.[13] A proposal for a regulation in order to provide for common rules on the temporary re-introduction of border control at internal borders in exceptional circumstances (revised draft compromise text) is on the table.[14] There is also a draft regulation amending a council regulation listing the third countries whose nationals must be in possession of visas when crossing the external borders and those whose nationals are exempt from that requirement.[15] The Council has recently discussed *inter alia* the rules concerning Frontex in connection with the Southern neighbouring states.[16] There has also been discussions of how to counteract radicalisation and engagement in terrorist activities.[17] Taken together, these various initiatives indicate that the EU and Schengen

---

11. Source: http://www.statewatch.org/news/2011/may/ep-schengen-debate-10118-11.pdf In another note on conditions in Italy, Statewatch wrote *inter alia* (*Statewatch News Online*, No. 2 of 2: 13 July 2011 (19/11): "A number of the measures introduced as part of the so-called 'security package' adopted in May 2008, in the wake of an election campaign dominated by the law and order agenda and by criticism of migrants and Roma people by members of the coalition led by Berlusconi, have been quashed in a series of recent decisions by the Italian Constitutional Court and the European Court of Justice in Luxembourg." Italy sees itself as a victimised country.
12. Source: http://www.eubusiness.com/news-eu/immigration-travel.9x9
13. See Press Release 3,162nd Council Meeting 26-27 April 2012.
14. See document 27 March 2012 http://www.statewatch.org/news/2012/apr/eu-council-schengen-controls-6161-rev1-12.pdf See also Proposal for a Regulation of the European Parliament and of the Council amending Regulation (EC) No. 562/2006 in order to provide for common rules on the temporary reintroduction of border control at internal borders in exceptional circumstances, revised draft compromise text 5 December 2012 http://www.statewatch.org/news/2012/dec/eu-council-schengen-reintrod-controls-6161-rev5-12.pdf
15. http://www.statewatch.org/news/2012/apr/eu-council-visa-list-amendments-8218-rev1-12.pdf
16. Source: http://www.statewatch.org/news/2011/may/eu-jha-council-12-may-press-release.pdf
17. Press Release "Council Conclusions on De-radicalisation and Disengagement from Terrorist Activities" 3,162nd Justice and Home Affairs Council Meeting, 26-27 April 2012. http://www.consilium.europa.eu/Newsroom

are threatened by the Tunisian affair and the actions of the French and Italian President/Prime Minister. But too much is dependent on Schengen to expect a full scale change. We will return to Frontex's role and functions later.

The worries mentioned above have led to an interest among several actors to strengthen the political governance in the Schengen cooperation. A meeting took place on 8-9 March 2012, where procedures were planned to be adopted.[18]

It should perhaps be added that Great Britain, which is only a half-hearted member of Schengen and wants to keep control of its own borders, is perhaps the most critical partner (at the time of writing: among several others) to the EU on the governmental level. In October 2012, British Home Secretary, Theresa May said that the British want to opt out of the EU's police and justice collaboration and to regain national sovereignty of a number of laws and regulations in the justice sector. It became an issue at a two day meeting of EU justice and home affairs ministers on 25 October 2012, where reactions appeared to be sarcastic but also worried.[19] For example, the British no longer want to be bound by the European Arrest Warrant, and they are considering whether to pull out of Europol as well as Eurojust. This has received write ups in several of Europe's main newspapers.[20]

A development of 2012-2013 is a movement towards the UK pulling out of the EU altogether, through a referendum on membership status. This is happening at the time of the critical economic situation of the EU, particularly in the south of Europe. Such a withdrawal would imply a great blow to the EU structure and common policies. If it really becomes a threat, the main function of the Schengen Accord will possibly become that of bolstering the rest of a unified EU, which the UK is partly outside anyway.

The general purpose
The general purpose of SIS is stated in Article 93 of the 1990 Schengen Convention, and runs like this, *in extenso*:

---

18. Brussels 16 February 2012, 6332/112 Rev. 1, Draft Council decision on the establishment of a procedure for strengthening political governance in the Schengen cooperation.
19. http:www.euractiv.com/future-eu/uk-op-raises-eyebrows-home-affai-news-515655
20. See for example Norwegian *Aftenposten*, 19 October 2012.

> The purpose of the Schengen Information System shall be in accordance with this Convention to maintain public order and security, including State security, and to apply the provisions of this Convention relating to movement of persons, in the territories of the Contracting Parties, using information transmitted by, the system.

The general purpose of this Article may be seen as the "core purpose" of the Schengen Information System. The point is to *"…maintain public order and security, including State security…"*. The wording is dangerously vague. It is open-ended, making associations with controls crossing boundaries, including political control. The stipulation is wide and diffuse, and quite open to interpretation. It may pertain to a wide category of people — on the one hand to categories of foreigners who are more or less vaguely suspected of instigating public disorder and insecurity to, on the other hand, individuals suspected of transnational crime and even terrorism with a low degree of suspicion. The Presidency Programme on Police and Judicial Cooperation of 22 December 2006 made the following telling statement concerning asylum seekers and foreigners (quoted in Wiig, 2007, p. 67, my *italics*): "*Frequently, asylum-seekers and foreigners who are staying in the EU unlawfully are involved in the preparation of terrorist crime…*".

A detour to Norway

As we shall see shortly, Norwegian law enforcement agencies have clearly used Schengen for political purposes. Norwegian critics have not been happy with this. How could the Norwegian political establishment, in view of it, hide the explicit and written politicisation of Schengen? In the following way: In the Norwegian Bill for implementation of the Schengen Information System in Norway, Bill No. 56 (1998-99), it is stated that the Schengen Convention operates with stipulations of goals on two levels: On one level by the statement of purpose in Article 93 cited above, which is called "the superior purpose", and on a different level through the concrete descriptions, in Norwegian, in other Articles. The descriptions in the latter Articles (Articles 95-100 in the Convention, see below, as written in the Norwegian legal text) regard "the conditions for registration and for what purposes registration may take place…". "In practice", it is maintained, the latter conditions/purposes will be decisive regarding the question of whether registration can take place or not. If a report does not have a legal base in one of the latter stipulations, it may not be registered even if it actually fulfils the superior purpose of maintaining public order and security.

This way the overall, general and dangerously political purpose of the Schengen Information System is more or less wiped out by couching politics in descriptive terms which are seemingly objective and politically neutral.

On a single day in 2003, there were 125,000 access terminals (computers) monitoring the SIS (Hayes 2004). By 2009 that figure had increased tremendously, no doubt partly due to the increased number of Member States: Over 500,000 terminals were located in "the security services" of Member States. The reference to "security services" refers to police, immigration, customs and internal security agencies.[21]

Below we shall look more closely at the individual Articles 95-100. They are less carefully worded than the parallel Norwegian texts. First the important Article 96.

Article 96

A majority of the 895,000 *persons* on the database at the beginning of 2007, 84.1%, are "unwanted aliens", entered pursuant to Article 96 of the Schengen Convention. This means, in absolute numbers, *a little over 752,500 persons.* The decision to refuse entry "may", as stated in Article 96 and in line with the general goal of SIS quoted above, vaguely "be based on a threat to public policy or public security or national security", which the presence of an alien presumably may pose. This is one point where political demonstrators may come in. Conviction of a custodial sentence of at least a year, which may mean entirely different degrees of seriousness in different countries, is a further criterion. "[S]erious grounds for believing" that the alien has committed "serious criminal offences" is another. "[S]erious grounds for believing" are in practice beliefs based on police hunches.

At this point it may be of some interest to take a glance at more recent data from SIS statistics. Assembled data show[22] that the number of hits on

---

21. See EU doc no. 13305/09. p. 3.
22. http://www.statewatch.org/news/2012/jul/eu-council-sis-sirene-statistics-11970-12.pdf

foreign alerts registered with the Sirene offices increased by 512% between 1997, when registration began, and 2011. Hits on the different categories of SIS alerts since the start until 2011 show that by far the largest category was "refusal of entry/stay", which was almost 40% of the total number of hits. The next highest category was "vehicles", with 17.8%. The third highest was "locating", with 13.3%. The fourth was "documents", with close to 12%. Other categories were under 10%. Only a little over 5% had to do with "arrests". Summing up, it appears clear that the major bulk of the data also recently indicates that hits based on foreign alerts have to do with *travel*, first of all refusal of entry or stay. This roughly corresponds with the first set of data given above, from 2007, showing that over 84% of individuals registered in the SIS were unwanted aliens, though "cleansing" would be too strong a word, aliens are to be kept out — Europe is to remain for Europeans.

One of the problems with the statistical records over time, however, is that they are not controlled for the increase in the number of Member States, especially in the 2000s. The number of hits based on foreign alerts conse-quently indicates a wavering but relatively stable curve between 1998 and 2006. Then, and only then, do the figures really increase. Another problem with Article 96 is that it appears to be interpreted differently in different Schengen countries, creating variations in the degree of restrictiveness as far as entry into Schengen territory as a whole is concerned. In my judgement, the Article allows for the shutting out of political demonstrators, and for entering them in the Schengen database. Can we document that the stipula-tion has ever been used in this way, or used as a threat of extradition?

Demonstrators and extraditions

Yes, we can.
In September 1998, it became known that a Greenpeace activist, who had demonstrated against French testing of nuclear weapons in 1995, was declared unwanted in France. For this reason she was not allowed into Schengen ter-ritory at Schiphol Airport in Amsterdam. The decision was made pursuant to Article 96.[23]

---

23. Source: *Statewatch Bulletin*, September-October 1998.

A number of Norwegian demonstrators were arrested and expelled during and after the EU summit in June 2001 in Gothenburg, Sweden. They had done nothing wrong but to participate in the demonstrations. Many were addressed by Swedish police officers with a gleeful "Welcome to the Schengen register!" Note that this was before 9/11. It is uncertain whether the demonstrators were actually entered in the Schengen database, but at any rate this was used as a clear threat. One of the demonstrators related the following:

> And they followed up with threats. They said that I was now in the Schengen register. They said they would evaluate continuously whether I would be able to enter a Schengen country again. I asked them how they thought they would do that, since Norway was a part of Schengen. They had to do some thinking at that point. They appeared not to know this. But they could tell me that the Schengen database now enabled them to cooperate across country borders to stop people like me.[24]

Another demonstrator related that she had been viewed as a *terrorist* and that she belonged on the Schengen database:

> He also told me what kind of a devil I was, because I did not respect decent people. In addition he could inform me that I was a terrorist, and that they did not want to have people like me in Sweden. When I asked him what he meant by "people like me", and who "they" were who didn't want me in Sweden, I got no answer... He addressed me by saying welcome to the Schengen register!
>
> Suspicions were very vague and diffuse, this involves limiting free speech because it prevents people from participating...[25]
>
> Early in December 2001 (notably after 9/11) a Swedish citizen and a member of a legal Swedish left-oriented party helped a Belgian friend to paste up anti-EU posters in Brussels. The posters advertised an anti-capitalist meeting which was to take place before the EU summit in Laeken. To paste up posters without permission is illegal in Belgium, and for this he was arrested and expelled from the country, and

---

24. Source: Dahl *et al*, 2001 p. 18, 21 and 27. The quote is from p. 27.
25. Source: Dahl *et al*. 2001 p. 18 and p. 21.

in addition prohibited from entry into all Schengen countries except Sweden. He was not permitted to travel through any of the other Schengen countries (which were 14 at the time). The Belgian police gave two reasons for the expulsion order and the general ban on travel through Schengen territory. Firstly, the Swede did not bring a passport (a passport is not mandatory for travel within Schengen territory). Secondly, and pursuant to Article 96 of the Schengen Convention, he had caused "serious problems for public order". The Swede had done nothing but paste up political posters. People responsible for Swedish cooperation in Schengen were "surprised" at the fact that the general Schengen ban had no time limit.[26]

Article 2.2 of the Schengen Convention provides a possibility for closing national borders at short notice when there seem to be reasons for it, that is, when "public order and state security warrant it". This happened during the Nobel Peace Prize celebrations in Oslo in the autumn of 2001, and again during the World Bank meeting in Oslo in June 2002. The background was a fear of demonstrations. During the latter meeting a large and peaceful demonstration was organized against the World Bank. A number of foreigners who wished to participate in the demonstration were stopped at the Norwegian border. The police admitted that it could "well be" that foreigners were checked for entries in the Schengen database. In the newspaper *Klassekampen* (Class War) it was stated in an interview:[27]

> We base ourselves on concrete suspicion against people that they may carry out criminal acts, says head of section NN to Class War.
>
> Does that mean that the police are in possession of concrete information about foreign citizens?
>
> Yes, it does, says NN.
>
> Have you obtained information on this through the Schengen Information System?

---

26. Source: *Dagens Nyheter* (The Daily News, a major Swedish newspaper), 11 December 2001.
27. Interview 24 June 2002.

That may well be, says NN.

Several top level lawyers also implied that the Schengen Information System was actively employed. XX, attorney for "Oslo 2002" which was behind the demonstration, said the following to *Dagsavisen* (Daily News, a major Norwegian daily):[28]

> After these arrests Norway should demand reservations with regard to the Schengen agreement and restrict the Immigration Act. Clearly the police relied on the most far-reaching interpretation of the Act that they could find. The police move in a minefield from the point of view of legal protection when they ground the arrests in the prevention of criminal acts in the future.

The director of the Data Inspectorate at the time said *inter alia* this during an interview to the same newspaper:

> How much does it take to end up in a database, YY asks. Before Norway joined Schengen last year, the Data Inspectorate warned that the police data network, the so-called Schengen Information System (SIS), contains detailed personal information, and not just information concerning punishments. Information which counts as trifles in one corner of Schengen may be seen as threats to security in other parts of the territory. From this it may follow that people who have just been spectators during a demonstration may be seen by the police as potential threats, says the Director. It is a little too crude to call this a threat to democracy…. [But] suspicions were quite vague and diffuse, which implies gags on free speech because people are prevented from participating …

After the demonstration the police were praised for their considerate and withdrawn behaviour during the events (they were mainly located in various sidestreets), but strongly criticised for their actions at the national border ahead of time. Demonstrators who participated maintained that several or all of those who were checked for entries in the SIS could not be found in the database. Nevertheless they were refused entry into Norway.[29]

---

28. Interview 26 June 2002.
29. I have not been able to verify this piece of information.

Whether you can get access to what the SIS stores about you depends on national legislation. If national law allows it, this will be followed, pursuant to Article 109.1 of the Schengen Convention. But the Convention also stipulates major exceptions which national law cannot override. Article 109.2 states:

> Communication of information to the data subject shall be refused if this is indispensable for the performance of a lawful task in connection with the alert or for the protection of the rights and freedoms of third parties. In any event, it shall be refused throughout the period of validity of an alert for the purpose of discreet surveillance.

The vagueness of the first sentence combined with the preciseness of the second, makes access to what SIS stores dwindle into almost nothing of any significance. The same, incidentally holds for Europol's TECS, see below.

Articles 95 and 97-100.
Let us move now on to Article 95 and Articles 97-100. One point eight per cent of the 895,000 persons were entered in Schengen's database in 2007 for arrest and extradition (Article 95); 4.8% were entered as missing persons or persons who could not take care of themselves (Article 97); 5.7% were entered because they were wanted as witnesses, accused persons, or for enforcement of judgments (Article 98); and 3.7% (33,000) for so-called "discreet surveillance" (Article 99).

Article 99 is particularly interesting. Three point seven per cent, 33 000 individuals, are entered in the database for so-called "discreet surveillance". In the Norwegian version "discreet surveillance" is euphemistically called "observation". The measure is devised as a preventive action. A police prognosis holding that the person in question may commit a crime in the future is sufficient grounds for inclusion in the database (Statewatch Analysis, 2007a, p. 2). The number of persons entered for "discreet surveillance" has almost doubled between 2005 and 2007.

Article 99.2 stipulates that an entry may be made for the purposes of prosecuting offences and for the prevention of threats to public safety:

(a) where there are real indications to suggest that the person concerned intends to commit or is committing numerous and extremely serious offences, or

(b) where an overall evaluation of the person concerned, in particular on the basis of offences committed hitherto, gives reason to suppose that he will also commit extremely serious offences in future.

Article 99.2 (a) is a fairly precise stipulation ("where there are real indications"), but 99.2 (b) is open and vague ("an overall evaluation", "gives reason to suppose"); the stipulation is relevant to possible future, quite hypothetical acts.

Adding to this, Article 99.3 opens up the possibility of discreet surveillance on the basis of political behaviour. Article 99.3 states that

> In addition, a report may be made in accordance with national law, *at the request of the authorities responsible for State security, where concrete evidence gives reason to suppose* that the information referred to in paragraph 4 *[which provides a list of information which may be collected in connection with discreet surveillance: author's addition]* is necessary for the prevention of a serious threat by the person concerned or *other serious threats to internal and external security* [My emphasis].

"[T]he authorities responsible for State security" means, in plain Norwegian, the Police Security Service (earlier called the Police Surveillance Service). Article 99.3 in effect allows for discreet surveillance of political behaviour—it states, to repeat, that "a report may be made in accordance with national law, at the request of the authorities responsible for State security" which means the intelligence services of the various States (Mathiesen, 2004a, pp. 438-439). Not a word in this passage indicates that it has to do with criminal acts. The procedure which is to be followed by "the authorities responsible for State security", when discrete surveillance is required, is provided in a Sirene handbook (about Sirene, see below).

Clearly, there are important problems attached to the use of Article 99. A report from the Schengen Joint Supervisory Authority (2012) finalised a follow up to its 2007 inspection concerning the use of Article 99. It focused on three recommendations made in 2007: By various means authorities responsible for Article 99 alerts should ensure that data are accurate, up to date and lawful; authorities should better control these alerts and inspect them every six months; and it should be ensured that all conditions allowing an Article 99 alert are in place.[30] The last point is of course vital.

Objects are registered on the database pursuant to Article 100: "Data relating to objects sought for the purposes of seizure or of evidence in criminal proceedings shall be included in the Schengen Information System". A list of categories of objects is given. One might suppose that the most frequent category related to dangerous weapons and so on. This is not the case. On a specific day in the beginning of 2007 over 13.7 million of the objects were typically identity documents. Next there were vehicles (over 1.7 million), blank documents (less than 400,000), firearms (less than 300,000) and bank notes (over 250,000) (information about persons and objects is taken from House of Lords, European Union Committee, 2007a, p. 22).

Figures on "hits", indicating the "usefulness" of the SIS for narrow police purposes, are of course far fewer. Statistics show "successful" controls in the sense of hits that the police of the Schengen States have had inside the EU on the basis of alerts issued by other Schengen States. In 2005 there were altogether 20,600 hits on persons, the majority of them concerning unwanted aliens pursuant to Article 96 (in addition, there were 11,000 hits on objects; information from Statewatch Analysis 2007a) . To be sure, since then, figures have gone up: The number of Member States has increased, and from 1 January to 15 April 2008 the total number of hits was 33,819 regarding home alerts, and 42,832 regarding foreign alerts. Compared with the same period in 2007 (the new Member States came after this period, toward the end of the year), the increase was 79 per cent based on home alerts, and 216 % based on foreign alerts.[31] But we should note that given the tasks of the border police forces, the majority of hits most likely still concerned unwanted aliens — refugees and the like.

In short, the Schengen system is to a large extent, though not exclusively, a system for border control, and risks to "public order and security, including State security", which Schengen is supposed to advance, are intimately tied to foreigners as presumable risks. This is *the political or semi-political*

30. http://www.statewatch.org/news/2012/oct/eu-council-sis-art-99-alerts-13851-12.pdf
31. Source: 17327/SIRIS 167 COMIX 917, Staff Shortage and Work Load SIS II, 19 February 2009.

aspect. Many of the stipulations are open and vague. This is an aspect *going against the legal security* of individuals.

A main point is that once you have been denied entry to one Schengen State, you are also denied entry to all other Schengen States. As a point of departure each state is responsible for control of its own part of the common external border (see the role of "Fortex" later in this chapter) — Norway for the country's over 20,000 kilometres of coastal line with deep fjords, rugged mountains, icy waters and scattered fishing communities (admittedly not the best access points for migrants from the Third World) — though integration of policing between the various States is developing. The internal borders, between the Schengen countries have been lowered according to plan: normally there is no passport control (though notably, exceptions may easily be made at short notice pursuant to Article 2.2 of the Schengen Convention for political reasons, see above, and carrying a passport is essential for a variety of controls by airlines, hotels and hostels in the Schengen States to which you travel). Data may only be entered according to national legislation, but by the same token, information may also be abstracted according to national legislation.

Kinds of information

What kinds of *information* may be registered about persons in the Schengen Information System? This may be found in Article 94.3 and is today fairly limited, but important: name and forename, aliases, particular observable and physical features, first letter in second forename, date and place of birth, sex, nationality, whether the person concerned is armed, whether the person concerned is violent, reason for the report and action to be taken. Several of the types of information are very wide and open to interpretation ("reason for report" and "action to be taken"). Furthermore, in the not so distant future a series of other types of information, including biometric data, will be included. Plans for this are moving ahead:

Towards SIS II

Firstly, up until now SIS has had a central database located in Strasbourg, with a database identical to the one in Strasbourg in each of the participating countries. As the SIS grew larger, it had to be updated to "SIS 1+".

A so-called SIS II, with a new structure, far greater capacity and a greater number of items of information included (such as biometric information; Hayes, 2004; Karanja, 2005), was first announced to go online in 2007. But political as well as technical and even legal aspects prolonged the waiting period, and implementation of the plan was postponed. But a lot of money had already been invested in it (and for this reason the Commission has been severely criticised particularly by Austria and Germany),[32] but developments occurred as this book was going to press and it has been possible to include a note about these later in this chapter. SIS II "not only offers new technological functions, but it will also fundamentally change the police practice based on the system" (Statewatch Analysis, 2007a, p. 4). The British House of Lords has characterised the system as planned to "store an enormous volume of sensitive personal data", and went on to criticise it for lack of transparency in the following words (House of Lords, European Union Committee, 2007a, p.16):

> A project of this importance and magnitude needs to be developed openly and publicly. It potentially affects not only EU citizens, but also hundreds of thousands on non-EU citizens who may wish to travel to or reside in the EU. Information must be readily available, not just to EU institutions and national experts, but to all those affected.
>
> It is unacceptable for a project with such cost and resource implications to be developed without a prior full impact assessment, and a full legislative explanatory memorandum.

SIS II does not stand alone in this; the House of Lords generally attacks the lack of openness in the EU internal security contemplations — for example regarding the Standing Committee on Operational Cooperation on Internal Security (COSI): "There should be greater openness about COSI's activities

---

32. The cost rose by 1,000% from 15 million euros to 143 million euros between 2001 and 2010, and the Commission's new plans envisage that SIS II will be "far beneath the capacities of SIS 1+". Yet the Justice and Home Affairs Council in April 2010 by a majority of EU Member States decided "to continue the development of SIS II on the basis of the current project." http://www.statewatch.org/news/2010/jul/05aust-ger-sis-II.htm

so that it does not appear to be secretive and lacking transparency", writes the House of Lords Select Committee on the European Union in May 2011.

Concretely, in 2007, the transformation of SIS into SIS II was expected to be enlarged to the following in 2007 (Statewatch Analysis, 2007a):

— The alert categories will be differentiated and extended-
— Alerts can be linked, so that SIS II will be able to carry out true investigative actions.
— More authorities will be able to access SIS II data (in addition to Europol, which already can access the SIS), Eurojust,[33] national public prosecutors, immigration authorities and the like.

Stephen Karanja, who is a lawyer, has in an academic paper demonstrated that in a few ways SIS II is a "gain" in the sense of improving the legal safety or security of persons, but mostly represents "losses" in this respect (Karanja, 2005).

Alerts relating to persons will contain biometric data—fingerprints, pictures. At the time or writing, pictures and fingerprints are exchanged as auxiliary information through Sirenes, see below. In SIS II they are likely to be included in the SIS proper, which provides for more widespread and efficient exchange and search (see Wiig. 2007 p. 20).

On 29 June 2011, the European Commission released a "Progress Report on the Development of the Second Generation Schengen Information System (SIS II) July 2010-December 2010".34 By mid-June 2010 the scene was set for "significant progress achieved" in the SIS II project. SIS II will provide a system "about five times the size of the system originally envisaged (from 15-22 million alerts in the initial contract to 70-100 million alerts now required)... "The procedure for completing and testing SIS II was set at 35.95 million euros. The Commission had by autumn 201235 set aside 149 million euros for the development of SIS II, of which nearly 110 million had

---

33. Eurojust's stated primary goal is to stimulate and make more efficient coordination of police investigations and prosecution, when two or more EU states are involved, see Wiig, 2007 p. 14; Council Decision, 28 February 2002 (2002/187/JHA).
34. COM (2011) 391 Final.
35. http://www.statewatch.org/news/2012/oct/09sis-II.htm

been spent by the end of June 2012 (an EU with serious economic problems found no difficulty in raising money for this). Following a period of almost two years of technical difficulties, the conclusions adopted at an appropriate JHA Council meeting "provided a clear, realistic and widely shared roadmap for the SIS II project's finalisation".

Joanna Parkins has commented that SIS II will add a number of new features to the current SIS that may "have serious consequences for fundamental rights". They include the insertion of biometric data into the system; interlinking alerts on people and/or objects, and potential inter-operability with other European databases such as the Visa Information System (VIS).

The last estimate for finalisation (the coming into operation) of SIS II was planned for the first quarter of 2013.[36] It will be administered by the new Agency for Large Scale IT Systems (see later). Information exists on a proposal for amending the Schengen Borders Code which is under discussion. The amendments concern the reintroduction of border controls at internal borders.

Visa Information System

Secondly, with the Visa Information System (VIS) visa information will be collected. VIS is especially interesting in being a fairly direct "parallel" to the great information systems discussed in this book. VIS is a database containing information, including biometrics, on VIS applications by third country nationals requiring a visa to enter Schengen territory. The system was established in 2004 by a Council decision.[37] VIS was rolled out on a regional basis. Every member state must

> [N]otify the Commission that they have made the necessary technical and legal arrangements to collect and transmit alphanumeric and biometric data for all applications in the first region.[38]

---

36. Press Release 3162nd Council meeting 26-27 April 2012 www.consilium.europa.eu/Newsroom P. 18.
37. 2004/512/EC. The main source about VIS is Wikipedia: http://en.wikipedia.org/wiki/Visa_Information_System
38. Working Party on Frontiers: Summary of Discussions, 6885/11, 1 March 2011. Quoted from Statewatch.

While "2010 saw numerous technical and organizational problems, with the main contractor fined 7.6 million euros for delays incurred in 2009",[39] the EU Commission notes that the "project is in line with the new global schedule".

Two types of search are possible using VIS — verification and identification. *Verification* consists of a check, carried out by the Separate Biometric Matching System, BMS. Fingerprints are scanned at the border crossing point and checked to see that they correspond to those associated with the biometric records attached to the visa. All EU-states except Belgium[40] now comply with the obligation to issue biometric passports. The check takes about two seconds. *Identification* consists of comparing the fingerprints taken at the border crossing-post with the contents of the entire database. This takes about ten minutes. The database is expected to contain some 70 million biometric records at full capacity. The control function of SIS in relation to non-EU citizens will be greatly enhanced by the parallel creation of VIS. It is claimed that the two will have a common technical platform.

In short, Schengen with SIS II and VIS constitute a European *buffer* in relationship to third countries, as well as a structure which has important internal *political functions* for the EU. The lowering of internal borders as well as the fortification of external borders constitute strong support of "the four freedoms" in the EU, and are thus in turn strongly supportive of the neo-capitalist spirit and system within the union. SIS II with VIS will lead to a fundamental increase in restrictions, repression and control over non-EU citizens. SIS II with VIS may have grave political implications for large populations inside and outside of the EU — just minor changes of a political kind may lead to seemingly minor but important changes in the use of the system.

According to Statewatch, SIS II and VIS are "back on track". In a memo with the main title "Small Steps to Big Brother", Statewatch claims that

---

39. European Commission: Report on the Development of the Visa Information System (VIS) in 2010 (COM (2001), 346 final, 14 June 2011.

40. Press release from European Commission 29 September 2011. Ireland and the UK are exempt from the Regulation. Associated States (Switzerland, Norway, Iceland, Liechtenstein, the latter invited to join the Schengen area 19 December 2011) are obliged to adapt their legislation.

though there are controls in the making, they are more legitimising than actually controlling. To be sure, says Statewatch, both SIS II and VIS

> will soon come under the scrutiny of the newly established EU Agency for Large Scale IT Systems, which… is intended to start work in the summer of 2012. This new agency will also be responsible for Eurodac, the database containing the fingerprints of applicants for asylum in the EU. While this will provide greater scope for oversight of the use of the systems, *it can do nothing to question the assumptions upon which they are based* [My emphasis].

SIS II was opened for use in the 26 Schengen states as this book was going to press. The predictions about the contents of SIS II were largely correct. SIS II contains biometric information (photographs, fingerprints); after "Action to be taken" it mentions "Links to other alerts issued in SIS II" — this was not possible with SIS I and significantly changes the way the system works as it gives it an investigative function; after "The type of offence" it mentions that "Supplementary information" can also be entered. Alerts can be entered in SIS II for a number of reasons; access to SIS II and the right to search in SIS II is "reserved exclusively" for border control and police and custom authorities, *but* "the right to access data in SIS II and the right to search such data directly may also be exercised by national judicial authorities, including those responsible for the initiation of public prosecutions in criminal proceedings and *for judicial inquiries prior to charge*, in the performance of their tasks, as provided for in national legislation, *and by their coordinating authorities*" (My italics). Information is kindly supplied by Chris Jones, Statewatch. From this sample of contents it is clear that SIS II is very wide scaled, and that it in several important ways threatens legal safeguards and protection of privacy. An open debate is to be expected.

The EU Agency for Large Scale IT Systems
A little more about the newly established EU Agency for Large Scale IT Systems. Articles 8 and 9 in the regulation of the agency (1077/2011) cover "research" and "pilot projects". The agency should monitor research and can undertake pilot projects at the request of the Commission, which should inform the Council and Parliament at least three months in advance. The

press release accompanying the agreement on the agency's legislation noted that "the Agency may also be invited to develop and manage other IT systems in this policy area in the future".

The Commission's page on the agency states that "At a later stage, after gradually building up its expertise, the Agency will develop into a centre of excellence for the development and operational management of other future systems in this policy area".

The head of the agency has not been announced at the time of writing, but the current head of the Commission, DG Home Affairs Unit for Large Scale IT systems and Biometrics, believes that "in an ideal world" 13 types of biometrics are required to secure "identity management". The new Agency may well, like Frontex and Europol (see later in this chapter), be quite aggressive and flexible with regard to its competencies and tasks.[41]

The Sirene Exchange

So much about the SIS, and the related VIS and the new agency. The Sirene Exchange of Information is a further main system. As with SIS, and SIS II, it is intimately related to the Schengen Information System but of a different order: A so-called "Sirene Office" — Sirene meaning "Supplementary Information Request at the National Entry" — is established in each participating country, and is responsible for registration in the Schengen Information System and the administration of the SIS.

We may assume that the Sirene offices store a vast amount of auxiliary information about individuals registered on the SIS. In Norway, information in national police databases was available early on to the Norwegian Sirene Office, and could be communicated to other Sirene offices throughout Europe. The information was to a large extent of a personal character. A single example from *one part of one Norwegian national police base,* concerning police data on foreigners, at one point included the following (the information is taken from the relevant police manual in 1999): Registration number; registration date; police office code; identification (birth) number; citizenship; passport number; ethnic group; country of origin; sex; name/alias; address;

---

41. http://www.fiercegovernmentit.com/story/eu-official-says-identity-management-must-be-based-multiple-biometrics/2012-02-02 Information on the Agency for Large Scale IT Systems has kindly been provided by Chris Jones.

telephone; height; age; bodily features; hair; language/dialect; spouse (with name and identification number); occupation; position; employer; information about automobiles; information about close acquaintances; other individuals who are closely tied to the person; the person's history (".. should provide a brief history of the person's escapades; … supplementary information should be entered as time passes …"); as well as "soft info" ("information we don't wish others to see") and other information concerning where the person comes from (this "in order for us in the future to take out information on a whole national group").

The Sirene Offices communicate information to other Sirene Offices in other Schengen States, The operation of the Sirene Exchange is detailed in a secret manual, which is continuously updated. An early copy of the manual, which has been made available to me, placed a major emphasis on means of communication of information between the Sirene Offices which are quick and as traceless as possible.

The national Sirene Offices may exchange non-standardised information, "soft info", also about individuals who are not under suspicion. The head of the Portugese Sirene Office said the following to Norwegian TV (NRK 1) early, on 10 March 1997:

> It's the Convention which tells you who has access to the system. But generally the police have this. They are at the airports, in the harbours, and may monitor mobile phones. It follows that they have access to masses of information all the time. They don't need to fetch faxes. This is a rapid system. It is updated. There is lots of information. And it's natural that the efficiency is much better than in the traditional Interpol system.[42]

Maybe the Portuguese head of Sirene was tempted to boast a little. Early on the Sirene Exchange was discussed in detail in the Sirene Manual, which the authorities for a long time tried to keep secret. The information exchange of the Sirene Offices may be said to be a formalisation and thereby a legitimation of exchange of information between police agencies, and thereby a strengthening of it.

---

42. Statement written down by me in Norwegian on the basis of the Norwegian subtitles, then translated into English.

Sirene was not mentioned in the Schengen Convention when it was signed in 1990. However, the Sirene Offices were working energetically when the Schengen Information System became operative in 1995. The Sirene Exchange was not mentioned in the Convention until a change was made in 2005, when a new Article 92.4 introduced Sirene.[43] Though restrictions are partly made in other Articles or paragraphs, the new Article, which is not added to the original Convention but as an added document to the Schengen *aquis,* clearly shows the widespread and diffuse character of the information which may be exchanged:

> Member states shall, in accordance with national legislation, exchange through the authorities designated for that purpose [Sirene] *all supplementary information necessary* in connection with entry of alerts and for allowing the appropriate action to be taken in cases where persons in respect of whom, and objects in respect of which, data have been entered in the Schengen Information System, are found as a result of searches made in this system. Such information shall be used only for the purpose for which it is transmitted [My emphasis].

In Article 108, which is somewhat different, the concept of "authority" refers directly to Sirene. The Article says, *in extenso*:

1. Each Contracting Party shall designate an authority which shall have central responsibility for its national section of the Schengen Information System.
2. Each Contracting Party shall issue its alerts via that authority.
3. The said authority shall be responsible for the smooth operation of the national section of the Schengen Information System and shall take the necessary measures to ensure compliance with the provisions of this Convention.
4. The Contracting Parties shall inform one another, via the depositary, of the authority referred to in paragraph 1.

---

43. Council Regulation 871/2004 and Decision 2005/211/JHA in force from 13 June 2005. The initiative was apparently taken by Spain.

Article 108 is somewhat more restrictive; words like "all supplementary information" are not used. Is the Article an attempt to make 92.4 easier to swallow? Does the convention speak with two tongues as far as Sirene goes?

The Europol Computer Systems

Then there are the Europol Computer Systems (TECS). The Council Decision of 6 April 2009 establishes the European Police Office, or Europol. It supplants the Council Act of 26 July 1995 drawing up the Convention establishing the office. In the description and analysis provided here, I rely primarily in the Convention of 1995, and less on the Council Decision of 2009. The reason is that the Convention goes into greater detail, whereas the Council Decision seems to hide important details. The details are interesting from the point of view of this book.

The Europol Convention is based on Article K3 of the Treaty on European Union, on the establishment of the European Police Office.[44] It started in 1993 with the Europol Drugs Unit (EDU), it got its Convention in 1995,[45] became operational in 1999; and started operating the information systems in October 2005 (initially with only three of the 25 Member States — Sweden, France and Germany — involved, see Statewatch Analysis 2007a). At first, its aim was that of combating drug crime. According to one self-description;[46] Europol today has the aims of combating organized drug trafficking; immigration networks; vehicle trafficking; traffic in human beings, including child pornography; forgery of money and other means of payment; trafficking in radioactive and nuclear substances; and terrorism.

According to a different self-description, Report on Activities 2010,[47] "[t]he biggest security threats come from terrorism, international drug trafficking, trafficking in human beings, counterfeiting of the euro currency and payments cards, fraud, corruption and money laundering as well as other activities related to the presence of organized crime groups in the economy" (p. 7). Europol's 2011 report was released in May 2012. Statewatch's brief

---

44. Official Journal C 26, 30/01/1999 P. 0021.
45. Convention of 25 July 1995.
46. http://europa.eu/agencies/pol_agencies/europol/index_en.htm
47. General Report on Europol's Activities 2010, obtained with gratitude from Tony Bunyan, Statewatch.

write-up of it,[48] dated June 2012, has the headline "Europol Boosts its Reach, Scope and Information Gathering". Statewatch, e.g. writes that

> [t]he statistics provided in the report demonstrate increases on every front. Europol provided operational support for over 13,500 cross-border cases in 2011, an increase of over 17 % on 2010.

> 2011 saw growth in forensic and technical support; financial support to operational meetings; financial support to investigations; the hosting of operational and coordinating meetings; and deployment of Europol's mobile office, which increased to 84 in 2011, up from 31 in 2010.

We will return to Europol's Report for 2011 later. The Organized Crime Threat Assessment (OCTA), since 2006, is considered by Europol to be the most important strategic analysis document produced by Europol. It is the document on which the EU Council bases its priorities and recommendations for fighting against organized crime in Europe. In 2013 it is to be superseded by an improved publication — the Serious and Organized Crime Threat Assessment (SOCTA). As we shall see (this is not a self-description), Europol controls widely and diffusely defined categories, and partly relies on low degrees of suspicion. Europol has three important computer systems:

- A central information system (Articles 7- 9 of the Europol Convention) with partly standardised, partly less standardised data (Articles 8.2 and 8.3) about convicted people and suspects (Article 8.1.1), as well as about possible future offenders within Europol's competence (Article 8.1.2; "persons who there are serious grounds under national law for believing will commit criminal offences for which Europol is competent"). "The information system thus unites convicts, suspects and not-yet-but soon-to-be suspects" (Statewatch Analysis 2007 a, p. 2). We should notice the diffusely future-oriented character of the system.

---

48. At the time of writing, I did not have the report itself in hand. For Statewatch's summary, see http://www.statewatch.org/news/2012/jun/03europol-powers.htm

- Work files for the purposes of analysis (Articles 10 and 12). These are special, temporary work files set up for the analysis of specific areas of activity. The work files may contain extensive personal data, not only about persons registered in the central information system (Article 8.1.), but also about (quotes are from the Europol Convention): possible witnesses ("persons who might be called on to testify"); victims or persons whom there is reason to believe could be victims ("... with regard to whom certain facts give reason for believing that they could be the victims ..."); "contacts and associates", and informants ("persons who can provide information on the criminal offences under consideration"); in short, a very wide circle of individuals loosely tied to persons who have been sentenced or are under suspicion. In December 2004, Europol operated 18 or 19 files, altogether holding data on 146,143 persons. Approximately 10,000 people were registered in the work file "Islamic terrorism", 22,500 were registered in a file on Turkish, 14,000 in a file on Latin American organizations involved in drug trade, 2,200 persons were registered in a file on illegal immigration of Iraqi Kurds (a file created while the US was still bombing Iraq). The largest work file, with tips from financial institutions on financial transactions pointing to money laundering and cross-border cash transfers, contained information on 68,870 persons. In view of the open definitions stated in the Convention, the figures indicate a kind of "mass suspicion" which is likely to lead to concrete investigation results only in a minority of cases (information from Statewatch analysis, 2007a).

- An index system which enables one to find one's way around the vast amount of information (Article 11).

A bit more about the second of these levels, the work files. The kinds of personal information which may be stored in the work files are not specified in the original Convention, only in the so-called implementation rules, given pursuant to the convention. As an example of the kinds of personal information which the work files were designed for, mention should be made of a proposal presented in 1996, concerning supplementary information of a highly personal and intimate kind:[49]

> It shall be forbidden to collect personal data solely on the grounds that they relate to racial origin, religious or other beliefs, sexual life, political opinions or membership of movements or organizations that are not prohibited by law. Such data may be collected, stored and processed only if they supplement other personal data stored in the analysis file and only where they are absolutely necessary, taking into account the purpose of the file in question (Emphasis supplied by me).

The important word here is "solely". It will be seen that the proposal in fact opens-up the way for the inclusion of data about "racial origin, religious or other beliefs, sexual life, political opinions or membership of movements or organizations that are not prohibited by law".

Later, the proposal went through various new versions, following criticism by the European Parliament amongst others. But the final formulation still allowed the inclusion of such intimate personal data. The implementation rules applicable to analysis files stated:[50]

> Europol shall also specify in this order whether data related to racial origin, religious or other beliefs, political opinions, sexual life or health may be included in the analysis work file,…and why such data are considered to be absolutely necessary for the purpose of the analysis work file concerned. .[51]

---

49. Proposal for rules applicable for work files, 4 January 1996 4038/93 Europol 2.

50. Council Act of 3 November 1998 adopting rules applicable to Europol Analysis Files [1999] OJ C26/1, Art. 5.2.

51. In the Council Decision of 6 April 2009, this is formulated in the following lengthy paragraph (under Article 14.1): "The processing of personal data revealing racial or ethnic origin, political opinions, religious or philosophical beliefs or trade-union membership and the processing of data concerning health or sex life shall not be permitted unless strictly necessary for the purposes of the file concerned and unless such data supplement other personal data already input in that file. The selection of a particular group of persons solely on the basis of the above mentioned sensitive data, in breach of the aforementioned rules with regard to purpose, shall be prohibited". Perhaps a more guarded formulation, but still open-ended. What does "strictly necessary" mean, and who defines it?

With regard to contacts and associates, victims, possible victims, possible witnesses and informants, such intimate data could only be included after special grounds were given and upon explicit request from two or more Member States. In practice, these limitations were not particularly strict. For other categories of persons, no such limitations were given.

The implementation rules applicable to work files allowed the processing of around 70 (at minimum 68) types of "personal data, including associated administrative data", about persons registered in the central information system. The personal data are grouped in 12 categories, and they are:

> "personal details" (14 types of data); "physical description" (two types of data); "identification means" (five types of data; including forensic information such as fingerprints and DNA evaluation results, though "without information characterising personality"); "occupation and skills" (five types of data); "economic and financial information" (eight types of data); "behavioural data" (eight types of data; including "lifestyle, such as living above means, and routine", "danger rating", "criminal-related traits and profiles" and "drug abuse"); "contacts and associates" (sub-types not specified); "means of communication used" (a wide range of means given as illustrations); "means of transport used" (a wide range of means given as illustrations); "information relating to criminal activities" under Europol's competence (eight types of data); "references to other databases in which information on the person is stored" (six types specified, including "public bodies" and "private bodies"); "information on legal persons associated with the data referred to" under economic and financial information and information relating to criminal activities (ten types of data). (Europol 1999)

Obviously, registration constitutes a very serious challenge to the protection of privacy.

To reiterate, the above-mentioned types of data may not only be included about persons registered in the central information system, but also about possible witnesses, victims or persons whom there is reason to believe could be victims, contacts and associates and informants. People working in Europol have immunity within the EU, and though it is denied by Europol authorities, the Europol Police Force is said rapidly to approach the status of a European FBI.

The Europol Convention at the outset guarantees "[a]ny individual wishing to exercise his right of access to data relating to him which have been stored within Europol or to have such data checked" may make a request to "that effect free of charge" (Article 19.1). But such communication back shall be refused when such refusal is necessary to "1) enable Europol to fulfil its duties properly; 2) protect security and public order in the member States or to prevent crime; 3) protect the rights and freedoms of third parties". In effect, the guarantee amounts to almost nothing. Much of the same holds for the Schengen Information System, see above.[52]

Europol is planned with a view towards wide-ranging integration for example with the Schengen Information System. For example, Article 101A, paragraph 1, concerning some new functions of the Schengen Information System[53] reads as follows concerning access to the Schengen Information System by Europol:

> The European Police Office (Europol) shall within its mandate and at its own expense, have the right to have access to, and to search directly, data entered into the Schengen Information System in accordance with Articles 95, 99 and 100.

We recall that Article 95 concerns arrest and extradition, 99 concerns discreet surveillance and 100 concerns objects. After having said, in § 2 of Article 101A, that "Europol may only search data which it requires for the performance of its tasks" a rather obvious stipulation, Article 101A goes on to say, in § 3, that

> Where a search by Europol reveals the existence of an alert in the Schengen Information System, Europol shall inform, via the channels defined by the Europol Convention, the Member State which issued the alert thereof.

---

52. In the Council Decision of 6 April 2009, this is formulated as follows (Article 30.5): "The provision of information in response to a request under paragraph 1 shall be refused to the extent that such refusal is necessary to: (a) enable Europol to fulfill its tasks properly; (b) protect security and public order in the Member States or to prevent crime; (c) guarantee that any national investigation will not be jeopardised; (d) protect the rights and freedoms of third parties". The difference is negligible.
53. Council Decision 2005/211/JHA of 24 February 2005, *Official Journal* 15 March 2005.

The words "via the channels defined by the Europol Convention" strongly suggest that Europol has a clear communication network with other agencies, including the Schengen Information System. Among the "principal tasks" of Europol delineated by the Europol Convention in Article 3, the first is "to facilitate the exchange of information between the Member States". Words like "information", "intelligence", and "strategic intelligence" run through Article 3.0.

Authorities and agencies within the EU from which Europol may require information with a view towards national operations appear to be many. Other stipulations open-up the way for accessing information from international organizations. Adding to this, work has gone on for a long time regarding questions about compatibility between different systems, and Europol supports the principle of availability deriving from the Hague Programme, see below. It began early: In a lecture by the then liason officer in Interpol, Norwegian Iver Frigaard, an early attempt was made to review questions, problems and possible solutions in connection with the relationship between Europol, Schengen and Interpol (Frigaard, 1996). Frigaard discussed the relationship between the three systems on two levels—what he called the systems level and on the level dealing with concrete interchange of information. On the systems level he pointed to the fact that until 1996, the year he gave the lecture, "only" ten of the 45 States which participated in Interpol at the time were also connected with Schengen and Europol. He held the view that the number of States which participated in all three units should be increased. In connection with exchange of information in concrete cases, he pointed to the lack of harmonisation between the various data systems, and the great need for compatibility between them, as well as how this goal could be reached technically speaking.

Jumping ahead some years, as of 1 March 2009 Europol had by then agreements concerning access to information with 15 states, groups of States or other units. From 2000 until 2008 the general activity concerning information exchange (messages sent and received) grew from 35,366 to 283,377. The number of cases initiated grew from 1,919 to 8,377 over the same period. Illegal drug trafficking was the crime area with the largest number of initiatives taken (25%).[54] What "cases initiated" refers to is, however, not entirely clear. In Europol's yearly report from 2010[55] there is a concluding statement saying this (p. 65):

> Europol cooperates with a number of EU partners, and with third countries and organizations. The exchange of information with these partners takes place on the basis of cooperation agreements.
>
> Two types of agreement determine the nature of cooperation with third parties. Strategic agreements make it possible for the two parties involved to exchange all information with the exception of personal data, *while operational agreements also allow the exchange of personal data.*
>
> Europol cooperation is vital between EU and non-EU law enforcement authorities, and other partner EU agencies and institutions.
>
> Europol currently cooperates with 17 non-EU countries, 9 EU bodies and agencies and 3 other international organizations, including Interpol, which features in many aspects of Europol's operational work. [My emphasis]

The statement shows Europol's wide network of information exchange, inside and outside the EU, and the important tendency towards integration, with Europol as the main powerful figure, above and beyond the EU itself. We should also note that the Europol 2011 Report (mentioned earlier above) signals a significant external expansion of its networks. The report also lists the USA Government agencies from which it hosts officials.

In brief, from the point of view of this book, an important point is that Europol represents a great deal of vagueness concerning what kinds of persons are within its orbit (widely and diffusely defined categories way over and above convicted people and people under suspicion). In its work files it takes in a number of highly private pieces of information, and through its cooperation with other agencies it takes in information which is very broad. It runs counter to basic principles of protection of privacy and legal security.

---

54. *Europol Annual Report 2008* from 30 March 2009, pp. 34-35.
55. *Europol Annual Report 2010* from 20 May 2011, 10244/11 Enfopol 149.

Information Management Strategy

We may at this point refer to a text which is not a legally binding one and not specifically geared to Europol but more to the EU in general, on the "Information Management Strategy [which] will allow the relevant authorities to implement in an efficient and effective manner the future developments in information exchange policy".[56] The document is distinctly bureaucratic, as are most documents from the EU. But here the bureaucratic character is particularly important: it has to do with the information strategy of the EU, and by that token of Europol. I venture an accusation: Almost all central concepts in the particular document give the appearance of being precise, but are actually quite empty, void of concrete content and may therefore be interpreted in nearly whichever way you want. To be sure, it has led to a work programme being implemented, with practical action and data protection concerns,[57] but the document as such sets a tone or a way of thinking which legitimises vagueness and open interpretations. Some examples may be given:

On p. 1, the "Information Management Strategy" will allow the "relevant authorities" to "implement" in an "efficient" and "effective" manner the future "developments" in "exchange" policy. These are catch-all concepts where content may be taken for granted. What are "relevant authorities"? We may surmise that they are "law enforcement agencies" of some kind, but we don't know which agencies. What does "implement" for "future developments" mean? "Implement" means set out "in practice", "realise", but it also has other meanings, illegal or legal, unpeaceful or peaceful. What does "efficient" or "effective" mean?

On p. 2 it is stated that "The strategy is the top-level document and as such has a long term focus". Though a draft and not a legally binding text, we therefore expect a degree of precision. Instead of precision, the document goes on by saying that it "can be further developed and updated as the overarching vision develops or changes and should be reviewed by 2014 (what is the difference between "develops or changes"?). And so on, throughout much or most of the text. To be sure, in the present text you are reading right

---

56. From the Council of the European Union, General Secretariat to Coreper/Council 25 November 2009, "Draft Council Conclusions on an Information Management Strategy for EU Internal Security", 16637/09 JAI 873 CATS 121 ASIM 127.

57. For a summary, see http://www.statewatch.org/analyses/no-139-eu-ims.pdf

now, there are certainly imprecisions, catch-all phrases. But this is a top-level document in a large union of many States. To be sure, a top-level document in a large union of many States requires compromises which necessarily have to be broad and vague, encompassing much and many to get endorsed. This is the fate also of the various declarations of human rights which have been developed in Europe and the United Nations through the years. But this is hardly an excuse for such a remarkably high level of vagueness. "[T]he report of the Future Group of ministers for home affairs, recommending the implementation of a 'European Union Information Management Strategy' (EU IMS) to remedy the current situation of an 'uncoordinated and incoherent palette of information systems and instruments' which have 'incurred costs and delays detrimental to operational work…,'" also implies a high a level of vagueness.

In the case of Europol, vagueness on the level of principles, such as here, may be combined with a degree of precision on the operational level. The vagueness in terms of principles enables the Europol staff to stretch matters when they want to. They rely on low degrees of suspicion, even "mass suspicion" in general terms (see above under "The Europol Computer Systems"), while their operational implementation rules applicable to work files allow the processing of exactly 68 types of personal data, including associated administrative data, about persons registered in the central information system (again see above). The combination of vagueness and relative precision, and the ability to move in either direction depending on the circumstances, is a powerful tool on the part of a police agency such as Europol.

We will have more to say about Europol's communication inside as well as across the boundaries of the region later.

In 2011

In 2011 Europol used 777 people, of whom 92 are analysts and 145 liaison officers from Member States, non-EU countries and international organizations. Seven-hundred-and-seventy-seven people is a near doubling from 2007, when the agency employed 298 staff. In 2008, the agency's budget came to just over 60 million euros. In 2011 it was 84.8 million euros. The number of "objects" listed in Europol's main database (the Europol Information System, EIS) has also increased, with information on 41,193 persons now held—an increase of 5% over 2010. There are 183,240 "objects" listed in the system in total, and 111,110 searches were run through the system in 2011. In 2011 Interpol, Columbia and Switzerland were all provided with access to the Europol Secure Network, which connects Member States' law enforcement agencies, non-EU countries, and international organizations, and is described as the "backbone" of the agency's telecommunications infrastructure.

Europol also operates a system called the Secure Information Exchange Network Application (Siena)—which permits the exchange of "strategic crime-related information and intelligence". Note the wording—crime-*related*—a wide and diffuse category. 13,697 new cases were initiated via Siena in 2011, an increase of 17% on the previous year, with a monthly average of over 27, 000 messages sent via the network. There are now 287 authorities with access to the network. 103 were added in 2011.[58]

The future?

The Member States of the EU—and the world at large—are experiencing one of the worst economic crises since World War II. Unemployment is rocketing, also in the EU. Crucial steps are taken to save both banks and currency. Several EU countries, notably Greece and Spain, amongst others are threatening to leave the euro and go back to their respective national currencies.

One might expect this to influence the surveillance systems, notably Europol, which has not only one surveillance system but several, and which has expanded formidably during the past few years, now being a major police agency in the Western world alongside the FBI in the USA. Are there signs indicating that savings must be made?

Not a sign has reached me. There may be internal signs that do not reach the public sphere. But at least publicly the signs go in the opposite direction—more efficiency, more effectiveness.

This is more than noticeable in a Note from the Commission Services to the Standing Committee on Operational Cooperation on Internal Security (COSI) of 29 March 2012.[59] The matter had been discussed before. The overall goal, says the note, "is to improve Europol's operational efficiency

---

58. http://www.statewatch.org/news/2012/jun/03europol-powers.htm
59. 8261/12, JAI 205 COSI 13 ENFOPOL 86.

and effectiveness and at the same time its accountability". "Accountability" is included perhaps because of external criticism of unaccountability. The Note goes on to say that

> [n]o elements suggest its mandate should be broadened or reduced, but rather that an enhancement of its analytical and operational capabilities should be achieved. A number of objectives can serve to achieve this goal. In turn, several avenues could be pursued.

The Note lists a number of avenues (with a number of sub-points):

— Improving Europol's intelligence picture by enhancing the provision of information to Europol by [Member States], in quality and quantity

— Ensuring that Europol has more effective contacts with MSs: reviewing the role of ENUs in order to give more space to national competent authorities to liaise with Europol

— Facilitating access by Europol to private-sector held information

— Triggering investigative action at MS level: from Europol's analysis to national action: improving the follow-up given to Europol's findings

— More flexibility in information management for better effectiveness: redesigning Europol's data management concept

— Rationalising Europol's means to exchange information with 3rd partners. Combining the legal requirement to align the legal basis with the Lisbon Treaty with the possibility of obtaining and transmitting data according to operational needs

— Strengthening the external data protection supervisory authority.

The short sentence at the end about strengthening the data protection supervisory authority is the only point which does not have sub-points. The sentence seems to be a perfunctory exercise, included in order to ward off criticism from the outside. The main content of the note is that of strengthening Europol's access to private agencies and information from them, and increased information exchange (with Europol as the dominating partner) with the environment. There is new discussion on extending Europol's role.

EURODAC

A further information system is Eurodac — an automated fingerprint system under the Dublin Convention (1990).[60] The Dublin Convention establishes that only one European State is to be responsible for deciding on an application for asylum. Eurodac announced in 1991 an agreement which came into force in 1997, to be replaced by a regulation in 2002, and going online 15 January 2003. The regulation applies to all EU States, and to Iceland, Norway and Switzerland. Eurodac enables countries to identify asylum applicants and persons who have been apprehended in connection with "an irregular crossing" of an external border of the union. By comparing fingerprints EU countries can determine whether an asylum seeker or a foreign national found illegally within the union has previously claimed asylum in another EU country or whether an asylum seeker entered union territory unlawfully.

Eurodac consists of a Central Unit within the European Commission, one of the large number of units and agencies within the vast EU bureaucracy. The agreement concerns fingerprints which are to be taken of all asylum seekers over 14-years-of-age. Fingerprints are sent by EU countries to the central database via national access points. During the first year after going online (15 January 2003 to 15 January 2004) Member States transferred 246, 902 data entries of asylum seekers to Eurodac's central unit. Because Eurodac started as an empty database, this was considered a significant result by the European Commission.[61] During the second activity year (all of 2004),

---

60. The Dublin Convention of 15 June 1990. The so-called Common European Asylum System (CEAS) aims at a common asylum procedure and a uniform status for those granted international protection.
61. Source: Statewatch Analysis, 2007a, p. 3.

the central unit received 232,205 data entries.[62] Comparisons are made with already existing data. The data are stored for ten years.[63] There are only two exceptions to this — information about persons who have attained citizenship is to be immediately deleted, and information relating to foreign nationals apprehended in connection with an irregular crossing of an external border is kept only for two years (the information is erased before the end of the two years if the foreign national receives a residence permit, has left the EU or has obtained citizenship of an EU country). In the case of foreign nationals found illegally in an EU country, fingerprints are no longer stored after they have been transmitted for comparison purposes. Eurodac insists that security is high *inter alia* because only biometric data is kept and no names. But in addition to fingerprints, data sent by EU countries *inter alia* include the EU country of origin, the sex of the person, the place and date of the asylum application or the apprehension of the person, the reference number, the date on which the fingerprints were taken, and the date on which the data were transmitted to the central unit.

Eurodac's official goal is, *inter alia*, to avoid asylum seekers seeking asylum in more than one European country. In reality and potentially, it is a vast control system for whole categories of ethnic and immigrant groups. A recent proposal for police access of course only makes this more likely. A press statement from an EU observer (Nikolaj Nielsen) of 30 May 2012 says that

> The European Commission on Wednesday [30 May] proposed to allow law enforcement authorities access to Eurodac, a biometric database of asylum seekers… Police would only be allowed access in specific cases should they require information on a person suspected of terrorism or some other serious crime… Melita Sunjic, spokeswoman for the United Nations High Commissioner for Refugees (UNHCR) in Brussels told the EU observer that law enforcement access to the database would equate asylum seekers with criminality. [64]

The press statement also relates that

---

62. Same source.
63. Those who are apprehended for crossing borders illegally or residing in the EU without a permit are also compared, but supposedly not retained; see Statewatch Analysis, 2007 p. 3.
64. http://euobserver.com/22/116427

A similar proposal was already tabled by the Commission in 2009 but was quickly shot down by the European Data Protection Supervisor (EDPS) and the Meijers Committee, a group of experts on international immigration and criminal law.

So they try once more. Possibly as an attempt to placate opposition, the statement also says that

… a memo claims the provisions would prohibit authorities from sharing any information with "third countries, organisations or entities".

Meanwhile there are also demands to provide law enforcement access to the yet-to-be-constructed entry/exit system. A Statewatch memo states *inter alia* that

The day after the European Commission proposed giving police forces access to Eurodac… a meeting of the EU's Law Enforcement Working Party heard of the "need" for law enforcement authorities to have access to the proposed entry/exit system for third-country nationals… [I]t would be "an automatic system registering the time and place of entry and exit of Non-EU Member Country nationals admitted for short stays, both those who require a visa and those who do not".[65]

The sum is that access by police to Eurodac is likely to come in the not too distant future. Indeed, on 17 December 2012 the European Parliament agreed to the Council's proposal to give Europol and law enforcement authorities access to the Eurodac database.

The Data Retention Directive, and…

History
The storage of telecommunications data *is now made legal in the EU* by the so-called "Data Retention Directive".[66] Communications data concerns that for fixed and mobile telephones, e-mail and the Internet, place and time for

---

65. http://www.statewatch.org/news/2012/jun/05-access-to-migrant-database.html
66. EU directive 2006/24/EF, on the retention and storage of communications data. In force 15 September 2007.

the start of the communication, place and time for the end of the communication, who contacts whom, the time the communication has taken, and so on and so forth—all of this shall according to the directive be retained and stored for a long time, from six to 24 months. Content data is not to be stored. Retention and storing enable law enforcement agencies to monitor details about who you interact with for a long period of time.[67]

A major point is that communications data about *everyone* in society is to be retained and stored. However, everyone is of course not under surveillance at the same time. Data from the information which is stored is to be made known to the police when requested. The concrete procedure whereby data is made known to the police varies between Member States and associated states. In Norway it requires a court order before this can happen.

Actually, it is a long story. It all began as a collaborative effort between the EU and the FBI in the early 1990s. In 1993, a "seminar" was held in Quantico, Virginia, where the FBI academy is located. EU Member States and the FBI were represented (Norway, not an EU member, was also present). The meeting was convened by the FBI, who felt that support for the police monitoring people's telephones was low from the American community and political establishment. At the meeting there were, as far as I know, discussions of the storing of content as well as of communications data.

An outreach of the "seminar" was the so-called International Law Enforcement Telecommunications Seminar, ILETS. To cut a long story short, a memorandum on what the law enforcement agencies required was signed by the participating States (also Norway, the non-member of the EU, signed) in 1995.

As the years went by, the basic idea was discussed further, in a rather secret committee, in the so-called "*Enfopol papers*". The Enfopol papers were revealed in the Internet journal *Telepolis* and thus made public, creating quite a stir and debate. The documents in fact became considerably shorter and quite a bit less informative afterwards.

The discussion on mandatory data retention was shelved prior to September 2001. But at the special JHA Council on 25 September 2001 (right

---

67. Communications data *and* content are stored by service providers. The Data Retention Directive directly concerns communications data. *Access to the contents is covered by national law.* For example, the UK officially requires a warrant signed by the Home Secretary.

after 9/11) it was put straight back on the agenda. It was also in George W Bush's letter to the EU of 16 October 2001.[68]

A UK law on the matter was passed in 2001 in the Anti-Terrorism, Crime and Security Act of that year. The EU directive followed later. Below we are primarily concerned with the latter.

The London terrorist onslaught in July 2005 provided the opportunity for finalising the EU plan for retention and storing of communications data. In the panic following the onslaught, the idea got widespread support. The then Prime Minister, Tony Blair, quickly made a speech (at the G8 Summit in Scotland, which took place simultaneously) in which he proposed long-term storage of telecommunications data for all British citizens. Critics have pointed out that the enormous masses of data thus stored will not help, or only help marginally, in catching terrorists. [69] But they will certainly in a massive way threaten civil liberties. This, of course, is an important point, adding to it the more basic question of how far we can go in sacrificing fundamental principles of democracy and the Rule of Law in our struggle against terrorists. The final text of an EU directive was issued on 3 February 2006.[70] Under mandatory data retention a record would be kept of *everyone's phone calls, e-mails, mobile phone calls (including location) and Internet usage* (access to Internet usage actually also reveals the content of the pages accessed).

The process of decision-making has partly been carried out in secret. A week after the EU directive was adopted, USA officials raised the possibility of access to the information with the Council (in general, there is a great deal of contact between the EU and USA concerning information sharing and the like).

---

68. http://www.statewatch.org/news/2001/nov/06Ausalet.htm
69. The Belgian writer Joseph Henrotin has been one of the critics. His point has been that there is a rise in "small scale terrorist acts" which are damaging but extremely difficult to detect. In the light of this criticism it is interesting that according to Statewatch, in the UK out of the 91,568 stop and searches in order to prevent acts of terrorism, only 0.02 % — a minute minority–resulted in arrests connected with terrorism. 27 % of all stop and searches were carried out on Black and Asian people. Source: http://www.statewatch.org/news/2011/may/uk-police-powers-ho-11.pdf
70. Council doc. 3677/05, 3.2.06. Ref. http://www.statewatch.org/news/2006/feb/st03677-05.pdf

What important Articles say

On a general level, everyone in society is actually treated as a suspect. Some examples of important articles may be mentioned. Except for the content of communication by fixed telephone, mobile telephone and the internet — what is actually said or written — every aspect of communication between everyone in a society is retained for a long time.

Article 1 supplies subject matter and scope (Articles 1.1 and 1.2). Article 2.1, which provides definitions, is introductory. Article 2.2 provides concrete definitions:

(a) "data" means traffic data and location data and the related data necessary to identify the subscriber or user.

(b) "user" means any legal entity or natural person using a publicly available electronic communications service, for private or business purposes, without necessarily having subscribed to that service.

(c) "telephone service" means calls (including voice, voicemail and conference and data calls), supplementary services (including call forwarding and call transfer) and messaging and multi-media services (including short message services, enhanced media services and multi-media services),

(d) "user ID" means a unique identifier allocated to persons when they subscribe to or register with an Internet access service or Internet communications service.

(e) "cell ID" means the identity of the cell from which a mobile telephony call originated or in which it terminated.

(f) "unsuccessful call attempt" means a communication where a telephone call has been successfully connected but not answered or there has been a network management intervention.

The list continues. There is no end to the details. Furthermore, the obligation to retain data is secured in Article 3. Data retained are "provided only to the competent national authorities". They are provided in specific cases and in accordance with national law (Article 4). Who is provided with data is probably meant to be the police, but the stipulation is extremely vague. There is a long list of categories of data to be retained, with sub-types, which may be found in Article 5. The list is precise and probably exhaustive. Just to trace and identify the source of a communication, a large number of categories of data are to be retained; the data list is equally long to identify the destination of a communication; likewise the data necessary to identify the date, time and duration of a communication; data necessary to identify the type of communication; data necessary to identify the user's communication equipment or what purports to be their equipment, data necessary to identify the location of equipment. All aspects of communication except the content of the communication is to be registered, whether phone or sub-type of phone communication, phone or Internet communication, or a combination of these.

Retention shall take place for periods of not less than six months and not more than two years (Article 6).

Data protection and data security are covered by Article 7. The Article contains four brief subtitles, which are quite general and rather vague. Storage requirements are mentioned in Article 8 and are again quite general, focusing on transmission "upon request to the competent authorities without undue delay". A Supervisory Authority is to be established in Article 9 — "[t]hose authorities may be the same authorities as those referred to in Article 28 in directive 95/46/EC". The supervisory authorities get a double workload — and save time and effort?

The Data Retention Directive raises obvious and deep problems concerning privacy. As anyone can see, it intrudes heavily into the private zone. Whether the data which are retained are correct or not, is not exactly the main question. That question is whether the directive interferes too heavily with privacy and legal protection. In several countries there have been major protests on this basis. For example, in Germany the Constitutional Court has found the directive to be unconstitutional, and in Norway there was a vociferous public debate before the directive was finally accepted with a small majority (consisting of the governing Social Democrats and a majority of the Conservatives) in the Norwegian Parliament in the Spring of 2011. In Norway there will be a one year retention period.

Particularly interesting are the international protests which have taken place. On 26 September 2011, the President of European Digital Rights from Brussels and 39 co-signatories (NGOs), sent a long letter of protest to the EU Commission concerning in particular "the impact assessment on, and probable review of, the Data Retention Directive".[71] They argued that the impact assessment would have to be as credible and complete as possible, and that the impact assessment supporting the original directive "was exceptionally poor". The letter contains a series of critical questions — what is meant by "serious crime"; the huge time range, from six to 24 months; how citizens can have reasonable legal certainty regarding how their data is being processed; and so on.[72]

In the Article "EU: Mandatory Data Retention of Communication Data: Update and Developments", Chris Jones relates how opposition has mounted in Member States (Jones, 2011). "Perhaps the most well-known comment", Jones writes, "is that of the European Data Protection Supervisor, who referred to it as 'the most privacy invasive instrument ever adopted in the EU in terms of scale and the number of people it affects".[73] This statement reinforced the arguments made by numerous civil society organizations, individuals and politicians". Chris Jones went on by saying that

> … the directive was annulled or suspended by court decisions in several Member States. This happened in Bulgaria, the Czech Republic, Germany and Romania. Sweden has yet to implement the provisions, and its Government's recent decision to postpone implementation for another year puts the administration at risk of being fined up to 68 million euros by the European Commission. Austria also refused to implement the directive, but after facing the Commission at the Court of Justice in 2010 it has now done so. The Belgian transposition of the legislation is ongoing. A case brought by Digital Rights Ireland against the directive is

---

71. http://www.statewatch.org/news/2011/sep/eu-mand-ret-ngo-letter-to-com.pdf
72. Source: http://www.statewatch.org/news/2011/sep/eu-mand-ret-ngo-letter-to-com.pdf
73. European Data Protection Supervisor: "The 'Moment of Truth' for the Data Retention Directive: EDPS Demands Clear Evidence of Necessity", 3 December 2010.

waiting to be heard before the European Court of Justice... National controversy over the directive has arisen more recently in The Netherlands, where the Dutch Senate approved in July a shortening of the retention period to six months. At the same time, the Senate published its correspondence with the Dutch Minister of Security and Justice on the topic of April's evaluation report on the directive. The Senate considered the evaluation 'unsatisfying', 'unconvincing' and 'disappointing'... (Jones, 2011, p. 20).

It should be noted that Sweden has now voted to implement the directive, apparently after significant pressure from the police/law enforcement agencies.[74]

But it should in particular be noted that in the Austrian province of Kärnten 11,000 people (and one employee in a data company) have asked the Constitutional Court in Vienna to undertake a legal evaluation of the directive. The Constitutional Court has found that the directive may conflict with the Charter of Fundamental Rights of the European Union and the European Convention on Human Rights. If the European Court of Justice (the highest legal authority in the EU) concludes as the Constitutional Court in Austria does, the directive may fall in its present form.[75]

A revision of the Data Retention Directive has been in the making. Statewatch has revealed that the revision has, however, been put on hold "with no precise time table" by the European Commission. It is now seeking to establish a new data protection regime before revising the directive, at the same time as a conflicting piece of legislation, the e-Privacy Directive, is coming up. A letter to the European Commission signed by 34 non-governmental organizations (NGOs) (including Statewatch) has this to say:

> A comprehensive impact assessment is neither necessary for market harmonisation nor for the fight against serious crime and is, therefore, illegal.[76]

---

74. Information from Chris Jones, 15 July 2012.
75. http://m.itavisen.no/908469/naa-kan-datalagringsdirektivet-falle
76. http://www.statewatch.org/news/2012/aug/04eu-mand-ret.htm, http://www.statewatch.org/eu-data-retention.htm

Statewatch has revealed that the revision has, however, been put on hold by the European Commission "with no precise timetable". It is now seeking to establish a new data protection regime before revising the Directive, at the same time as a conflicting piece of legislation, the e-Privacy Directive, is coming up. A letter to the European Commission signed by 34 NGOs (including Statewatch) has this to say:

> A comprehensive impact assessment is neither necessary for market harmonisation nor for the fight against serious crime and is, therefore, illegal. [76]

A final note: We should not conclude that the Data Retention Directive is the only system in the world that caters to retention of communications data. The USA retains enormous quantities of communications data on its own vast territory as well as between its territory and other countries. On 4 June 2013, the *Guardian* reported: "NSA [National Security Agency] collecting phone records of millions of Verizon customers daily". An order, a copy of which has been obtained by that newspaper, "requires Verizon on an 'ongoing, daily basis' to give the NSA information on all telephone calls in its systems, both within the US and between the US and other countries". This is under the Obama administration. The *Guardian* goes on to say:

> Under the terms of the blanket order, the numbers of both parties on a call are handed over, as is location data, call duration, unique identifiers, and the time and duration of all calls. The contents of the conversation itself are not covered.

> … Under the Bush administration, officials in the security agencies had disclosed to reporters the large-scale collection of call records data by the NSA, but this is the first time significant and top secret documents have revealed the continuation of the practice on a massive scale under President Obama. The unlimited nature of the records being handed over to the NSA is extremely unusual…

The order compels Verizon to produce to the NSA electronic copies of "all call detail records or 'telephony metadata' created by Verizon for communications between the United States and abroad" or "wholly within the United States, including local telephone calls".

Privacy is vastly invaded, over most or all of the world.

But this is probably not all. There are indications that outside jurisdictions are used to circumvent UK national law (though denied in Parliament by British Foreign Secretary William Hague), further fuelling the Verizon debate.

Central is the so-called Prism programme in the NSA. Through this programme, USA security officials appear to have access to *at least nine large net giants*, including Facebook, Google, Microsoft, YouTube and Apple. The Obama administration confirmed on Thursday 6 June 2013 the existence of Prism, and up until then a top secret surveillance programme (source on Prism: Wikipedia).

On 8 June 2013, the *Guardian* revealed in large headlines, "Ministers to reveal British links to US spying data scandal". There are claims that "UK intelligence agencies have gained access to a vast reservoir of private data relating to people living in Britain—including emails and phone logs—collected by spies at the US National Security Agency". There are "growing calls for the government to reveal what it knows about the... scandal revealed by the Guardian ...". According to James Clapper, a top man in USA intelligence, the law only permits access to data on persons who are not USA citizens and who are not staying in the US. He says there are several inaccuracies in the newspaper articles, without saying more about what those inaccuracies are.

Facebook, reports that Mark Zuckerberg (the founder of Facebook), "has never been part of any programme to give the US and any other government direct access to our servers". But the *New York Times* reported on 8 June 2013 that key technology firms such as Google, Facebook and Microsoft have cooperated with NSA "at least a bit". Twitter is said to have declined to participate.

Henry Porter asks in the *Observer* of 8 June 2013, "Did GCHQ [the UK's Government Communications Headquarters] make use of NSA's Prism system to by-pass British law and spy on the public though covert access to Internet giants such as Google and Facebook?" There is a strong call on top politicians to say what they knew.

At any rate, we don't know. The Verizon case seems to be solid. It is almost a replica of the EU Data Retention Directive. The further Prism-ramifications, only related briefly here, are perhaps somewhat less clear. The Head of the Norwegian Data Inspectorate is somewhat uncertain, but says that if this is true, which it may be, it is extremely serious. I concur.

… the Passenger Name Record

In a study, the EU found that there is no need to introduce new instruments for cross-border information exchange. The study lists over 20 existing or proposed systems, databases, legal instruments or policy initiatives. Staff interviewed were not in favour of new systems: "Existing channels and existing IT communications networks should be used to their full extent before introducing new ones".[77]

However, before the study had been commissioned and published, Passenger Name Record (PNR) systems were actually in use,[78] and despite the study, the EU continues to push ahead for new systems.

What is PNR? Briefly stated: Data are provided by travellers to travel companies or carriers which is subsequently analysed and processed by law enforcement agencies, ostensibly for preventing, investigating and prosecuting serious crimes. The USA requires any flight entering its territory (and perhaps any flight near its territory) to supply PNR data to the Department of Homeland Security. An agreement between the USA and the EU was reached in May 2012. The EU also has agreements with Canada and Australia. The UK is very involved and is in favour of extending the system to sea and rail travel as well as that by air.

Sometimes pressure for new systems also comes from the outside. A good example is again the PNR. The pressure came from the USA.

In more detail: Just as with the Data Retention Directive, and along the same line of mass surveillance of (almost) everyone, goes the EU/USA bilateral relations and transfer of Passenger Name Records (PNRs). The only limitation as far as PNR goes, is that it so far concerns everyone who passes USA borders by air (it may be broadened later, see below). The agreement was signed on 28 June 2007 (and updated by an Agreement finalised later, in 2012[79]). Statewatch observes that EU negotiators agreed that PNR data will

---

77. http://www.statewatch.org/news/2012/apr/24eu-ix-study.html
78. Information from Chris Jones, 15 July 2012.
79. Information from Chris Jones, 15 July 2012.

be held for seven years, doubling the 3.5 years, and in addition agreeing that data can be accessed for a further eight years (the so-called "dormant" data).

Just after signing the agreement, the USA Government (30 July 2007) wrote to the European Council asking it to agree that all the documents regarding the negotiations leading to the agreement be kept secret for at least ten years. A draft reply (same source, EU doc. 12309/ 07) from the EU Council Presidency in August 2007 says that the EU "shares" this understanding regarding confidentiality.

The USA is planning to give exemptions from its Privacy Act for the Department of Home Security and for the "Arrival and Departure System" (ADIS), thus diminishing citizens' rights to find out what data is held on them and who it is held by.

We should be aware of the fact, however, that the events are not fully streamlined: For example in a note of 13 May 2011, the European Economic and Social Committee voices the opinion on EU PNR (we will return to EU PNR below) that "the often-cited choice between security and freedom or, in more practical terms, stepping up security at the expense of citizens' rights with regard to personal data, must under no circumstances run counter to the general principles underpinning fundamental personal rights".[80]

A late piece of news on PNR is the proposal for a Council decision regarding the conclusion of the agreement between the USA and the EU on the use and transfer of Passenger Name Records to the USA Department of Homeland Security.[81] The proposal for a Council decision in a positive vein says *inter alia*:

> PNR has proven to be a very important tool in the fight against terrorism and serious crime. The Agreement has secured several important safeguards for those whose data will be transferred and used. In particular, the purpose of the processing of PNR data is strictly limited to preventing, detecting, investigating and prosecuting terrorist offences and serious transnational crime. The retention period of the PNR data is limited and PNR will be used for a shorter period in the fight against serious transnational crime and a longer one for terrorism. In addition, the

---

80. Source: http://www.statewatch.org/news/2011/may/eu-pnr-esc-opinion.pdf
81. Source: European Commission Brussels, 23 November 2011 COM (2011) 807 final. http://www.statewatch.org/news/2011/nov/eu-com-council-decision-eu-usa-pnr-deal-com-807.pdf

data will be depersonalised after a period of six months. Individuals are provided with the right to access, correction, redress and information. The 'push' method of transfer is recognised as the standard mode of transfer, with which all carriers will need to comply within two years of the Agreement. Sensitive data is to be used in very exceptional cases and deleted after a very short timeframe. Compliance with these rules shall be subject to independent review and oversight by various Department Privacy Officers, as well as by the DHS Office of Inspector General, the Government Accountability Office and the US Congress.

And so onwards. Travellers protection of privacy is presumably well taken care of. Edward Hasbrouk replies as follows to this: "Revised EU-US agreement on PNR data still protects *only travel companies, not travellers* (my italics).[82] It follows that on

November 17, 2011, US and European Union officials signed a renegotiated proposed agreement… to authorise airlines to forward PNR data (travel reservations) to the US Department of Homeland Security (DHS). As an executive agreement, not a treaty, it doesn't require any further US approval, but it does require ratification by both the Council of the EU (national governments of EU members) and the European Parliament… *The latest version of the EU–US agreement on PNR transfers to the DHS fixes none of the fundamental problems we and the European Parliament have identified in previous drafts, as discussed in our previous articles, our FAQ about the previous version of the proposal, and our recent presentations to MPs.* [My emphasis].

In late December 2011, the fairly neutral agency EDPS, with Peter Hustinx as incumbent, issued an Opinion on the new EU-USA Passenger Name Record Agreement. The Opinion *inter alia* said that

Any legitimate agreement providing for the massive transfer of passengers' personal data to third countries must fulfill strict conditions. Unfortunately, many concerns expressed by the EDPS and the national data protection authorities of

---

82. http://papersplease.org/wp/2011/11/28/revised-eu-us-agreement-on-pnr-data-still-protects-only-travel-companies-not-travelers/ Information from Chris Jones, 15 July 2012.

the Member States have not been met. The same applies to the conditions required by the European Parliament to provide its consent.

On 26 April 2012 the Council adopted the new EU-USA agreement on PNR, which replaces the existing one provisionally applied since 2007. On 19 April 2012 the European Parliament gave its consent. MEPs agreed by a majority vote to let the USA Department of Homeland Security in the USA see data on the Passenger Name Record.[83] The EU currently has agreements on the transfer and use of passenger name records with Australia, Canada and the USA. Altogether, millions and millions of individuals are registered with sensitive data.

In passing we should also note that the G6 (comprising France, Germany, Spain, Italy, Poland and the UK, usually also attended by the USA Department of Homeland Security), working on justice and home affairs, at its meeting in Paris on 1 December 2011 *inter alia* discussed Schengen governance and, including the USA representatives, *inter alia* focused on *Transatlantic data sharing*. Will it never end?[84]

In a general review of data protection rules in Europe, which also includes PNR-data, the EDPS, significantly, goes on to say that EDPS welcomes a huge step forward for data protection in Europe, but also, significantly, regrets inadequate rules for the police and justice area. Peter Hustinx, the European Protection Supervisor, says in so many words about the police and justice area that

> The Commission has not lived up to its promises to ensure a robust system for police and justice. These are areas where the use of personal information inevitably has an enormous impact on the lives of private individuals. It is difficult to understand why the Commission has excluded this area from what it intended to do, namely proposing a comprehensive legislative framework.[85]

The EDPS regrets in particular that:

---

83. http://www.bbc.co.uk/news/world-europe-17764365?print=true
84. http://www.statewatch.org/news/2012/apr/eu-g6-dec-11.pdf
85. EDPS/02/12, Press Release, 25 January 2012.

— The Commission does not propose stricter rules for the transfer of personal data outside the EU;
— Data protection authorities are not given mandatory powers to effectively control the processing of personal data in this area;
— The possibilities for the police to access data processed in the private sector are not regulated.

Also, "… stricter rules for the transfer of personal data outside the EU" implies that the transfer of such data is *acceptable* between approximately 25 to 30 States—all of the EU containing different value-systems and different legal arrangements. Only *outside* these 25 to 30 States are such transfers more or less unacceptable. This point may not be so important for insiders in the EU, being engaged in a joint struggle to create common EU rules, as it is for this author—an outsider to the EU.

The Passenger Name Record Agreement is clearly envisioned as an important organizational advance in the struggle against terrorism and other serious crimes. That is a main message of a "Discussion Paper" under the headline "Financing PNR-systems", dated 26-27 January 2012. It is explicitly stated that the Commission is "called upon" "to present a proposal for the use of PNR data to prevent, detect, investigate and prosecute terrorism and serious crime". The paper tells us that in 2011, the Commission "presented a proposal for a Directive of the European Parliament and of the Council on the use of Passenger Name Record data for the prevention, detection, investigation and prosecution of terrorist offences and serious crime" (COM(2011)32). The proposed directive supplants a proposal on the same from 2007. One problem is financing such a concerted effort. Furthermore, there still are (despite the appearance of a Commission proposal for a directive) numerous disagreements between Member States as regards scope, retention periods, necessity, proportionality, etc.[86]

The effort was confirmed in a letter from the Council of the European Union of 10 February 2012.[87] On 26-27 April 2012 the Council again discussed the retention period, initially proposed by the Commission in 2010

---

86. Information from Chris Jones 15 July 2012. See http://www.statewatch.org/news/2012/apr/eu-council-eu-pnr-position-8448-12.pdf
87. 6351/12, JAI 80, Relex 018, Dataprotect 16.

to be five years. However, after 30 days the PNR data would have to be masked out, that is, the person-related elements of the PNR are no longer visible to the "front-desk" law enforcement officer, but can be seen only after specific authorisation. A number of Member States considered the initial storage period to be too short. The Council agreed to maintain the overall retention period of five years, but to *prolong* the first period during which the data are fully accessible to two years.[88]

The EU-USA PNR Agreement — and the proposed EU PNR System

At this point an important distinction must be made — between the EU-USA PNR agreement and the proposed EU-PNR System.

The proposed directive on an EU-PNR system would collect information on flights coming into the EU — just as the USA system seeks to record everyone entering and leaving the country. However, the proposed EU-PNR will go much further.

At a Council meeting on 11 April 2011, a discussion, initiated by the UK, was held on whether intra-EU flights should be included. In a Note from the Presidency to the Council of 23 April 2012 it is stated that Article 1a in the directive, which was drafted in line with indications given at the Council meeting on 11 April 2011, allows Member States to apply the directive to all or selected intra-EU flights. All Member States will in other words be allowed to collect PNR data from those intra-EU flights which it considers necessary.[89]

It has also been proposed that this be extended in the future to rail and sea travel as well — to cover travel by land and sea into and within the EU. This would mean that every type of collective transport would be under some form of automatic and human-directed surveillance, taking into account systems such as Automatic Number Plate Recognition (ANPR) in the UK, and the provisions of the Prüm Treaty allowing exchange of vehicle registration data. Cycling and walking obviously does not come into this, but you can be checked though CCTV no matter how you travel.

---

88. Press Release 3,162nd Council Meeting 26-27 April 2012; www.consilium.europa.eu/News-room. p. 8.
89. Note from Presidency to Council, 23 April 2012 8916/12 DGD D 2B GSnp.

Despite the intrusive and extensive nature of law enforcement use of PNR, no one seems to have any proof that it actually works according to purpose, beyond a few anecdotes.[90]

API — Advance Passenger Information[91]
Advance Passenger Information (API) is in many ways similar to Passenger Name Record (PNR) — it consists of information provided by travellers to travel companies which is subsequently passed on to law enforcement authorities for collection and analysis. It consists of the number and type of travel documents used, nationality, full name, date of birth, border crossing point of entry into the territory of the Member State(s), code of transport, departure and arrival time of the transportation, total number of passengers carried on that transport, and the initial point of embarkation. The relevant directive was enacted for rather vague counter-terrorism purposes. API data must also be handed to Canada, and may also be transferred to those countries with which the EU has agreements on PNR data (Jones, 2012, p. 23).

Why are so many States and institutions so keen on advancing these systems? There is no quantitative statistical evidence indicating that they are effective in finding terrorists or serious criminals (Jones *op. cit*, p. 24). The most likely reason is, as Chris Jones puts it, that

> Multinational IT and defence firms with an interest in the security industry — a number of which were invited to the most recent meeting of the Frontex Working Group — are seeking new markets, and there is no shortage of politicians anxious to demonstrate to the press and the public that they are 'doing something' to protect the populace from all manner of real or imagined threats... [It can at least in part] be explained by the confluence of corporate, political and bureaucratic interests...

The security-industrial complex sees significant opportunities in extending the collection and analysis of data initially collected for commercial purposes, in order to use it for law enforcement purposes. API data are easy to

---

90. See p. 10 of http://www.statewatch.org/analyses/no-169-eu-pnr-us-aus-comparison.pdf Information on the EU-PNR system from Chris Jones, 15 July 2012.
91. My *source* regarding API is Chris Jones, "Secretive Frontex Working Group Seeks to Increase Surveillance of Travellers", *Statewatch Bulletin*, Vol. 22 No 2/3 2012, pp. 23-27.

acquire, they originate from an airline's departure control systems that are routinely provided with information by travellers when they are preparing to cross an international border. The information is used for checking travellers against databases of known criminals and inadmissible persons. What these databases actually contain is, however, a very difficult question to answer.

API systems are plagued by two problems — timing and data quality: Passenger data are provided to Government after the aircraft is already en route, and data quality can also be a problem because passenger data is presented "as is", with spelling mistakes and all, and often in a format which is unintelligible to Governments. Attempts are made to resolve both problems with the development of an interactive API system — including internal data quality controls to ensure that only validated data are transmitted to governments in a format they can understand and use to carry out real-time checks. The area is fraught with problems.[92]

In 2004, the EU adopted the so-called "Spanish Directive" creating a legal framework for API collection in Europe. Chris Jones relates the following (Jones, 2012, p. 24) on API: Three conferences have been convened by Frontex (a major border-controlling agency in the EU, see below) during 2011/2012 under the name Working Groups on Advance Information Challenges, the first one in May 2011 at Frontex' headquarters in Warsaw, the last one a two-day meeting in 2012 in Brussels. At the first meeting, 18 EU Member States were present; at the last one 20 Member States were present along with two representatives from the Russian Mission to the EU and at least one representative of the USA Department of Homeland Security. Representatives of data protection authorities did not attend any of the meetings. Several interested corporations attended the last of the three meetings (Lufthansa; seven presentations were made by companies invited for their technological expertise and services — ARINC, IMB, SITA, Raytheon, CApGemini, Morpho, Indra). Major visions on the part of Frontex and many of the authorities of the Member States present were produced (for details see Jones, 2012, p. 24).

---

92. This paragraph is taken from Tom Marten's Briefing Sheet, SITA 2012. The brief is kindly provided by Chris Jones.

In General: How is the future fixed?

A final word on systems like the Data Retention Directive, PNR, PNR-EU, API: They represent the "tip of the iceberg" in terms of commercial information that could be provided to law enforcement authorities. Think of the amount of information people pass on to companies via phone bills, credit card usage, store "loyalty cards", use of cash machines, etc., etc. There are probably people within the law enforcement "community" who would love to get their hands on it if they could. And history shows that they can.

Alongside this, the development of mass surveillance systems covering "everyone" may be viewed as a final surveillance stage (but apparently only a beginning in terms technological refinements). The British criminologist Lucia Zedner asks, "How is the future fixed?" (Zedner, 2007/2009). Essentially, and without using exactly these words, she delineates three possibilities, going from prediction of *dangerousness* through the wider assessment of greater or lower *risk* of deviant behaviour, to a final possibility where even risk is abandoned, because risk predictions contain so many errors, in favour of *everyone* being potentially dangerous and therefore targets.[93]

The Data Retention Directive and the collection and analysis of API and PNR data by law enforcement authorities are very good examples. Others are coming up.

Finale: Echelon

A final information system in this enumeration is Echelon. This is at the outset on a somewhat different level, it began as a regular spy system involving the USA, Great Britain, Canada, New Zealand and Australia. Echelon appears to be able to take down vast amounts of telecommunications data from satellites, finding relevant information by means of a system of code words. It is uncertain how far the technology has come; what is certain is that Echelon exists and that the technology is developing rapidly. A report to the European Parliament by the journalist and researcher Steve Wright as early as 1998 may be quoted to indicate the activities of Echelon (Wright, 1998):

---

93. The argument was first presented by Zedner towards the end of the lecture (2007), perhaps more clearly than in the final printed version (2009).

A wide range of bugging and tapping devices has been evolved to record conversations and to intercept telecommunications traffic... However, planting illegal bugs... is yesterday's technology... [T]hese bugs pale into insignificance next to the national and international State run interception networks... Modern technology is virtually transparent to the advanced interceptions equipment which can be used to listen in... Within Europe, all email, telephone and fax communications are routinely intercepted by the United States National Security Agency, transferring all target information from the European mainland via the strategic hub of London then by satellite to Fort Meade in Maryland via the crucial hub in Menwith Hill in the North York Moors of the UK... The Echelon system works by indiscriminately intercepting very large quantities of communications and then siphoning out what is valuable using artificial intelligence aids like Memox to find key words. Five nations share the results... Each of the five centres supply "dictionaries" to the other four of key words. Phrases, people and places to "tag" and the tagged intercept is forwarded straight to the requesting country (Wright, 1998, pp. 18-19).

Wikipedia has *inter alia* the following to say about Echelon:[94] "Echelon is a name used in global media and popular culture to describe a signals intelligence (SIGINT) collection and analysis network operated on behalf of the five signatory states mentioned above. It was reportedly created to monitor the military and diplomatic communications of the Soviet Union and its allies during the Cold War, but after the Cold War it changed goals and is believed also to monitor terrorist plans, drug dealer's plans and political and diplomatic intelligence". In an article in *Wired*, James Bamford (2012) has the following to say (p. 2):

Under construction by contractors with top-secret clearances, the blandly named Utah Data Center is being built for the National Security Agency. A project of immense secrecy, it is the final piece in a complex puzzle assembled over the past decade. Its purpose: to intercept, decipher, analyse, and store vast swathes of the world's communications as they zap down from satellites and zip through the

---

94. http://en.wikipedia.org/wiki/ECHELON

underground and undersea cables of international, foreign, and domestic networks. The heavily fortified 2 billion center should be up and running in September 2013.

Bamford goes on to say:

> Flowing through its servers and routers and stored in near-bottomless databases will be all forms of communication, including the complete contents of private e-mails, cell phone calls, and Google searches, as well as all sorts of personal data trails—parking receipts, travel itineraries, bookstore purchases, and other digital "pocket litter". It is, in some measure, the realisation of the "total information awareness" program created during the first term of the Bush administration—an effort that was killed by Congress in 2003 after it caused an outcry over its potential for invading Americans' privacy. [95]

Echelon's capabilities and political implications were investigated by a committee of the European Parliament in 2000/2001 with the above-mentioned report by Steve Wright as a basis for this. A cloud of secrecy lies over Echelon, with rumours as well as facts — the facts being *inter alia* capability of interception of communication bearers including satellite transmission, police switched telephone networks (which in the past carried most Internet traffic) and microwave links.

The "Strategic Alliance Group" (SAG), or the "Five Country Conference", has begun cooperating, alongside Echelon, on the exchange of fingerprints as part of a migration programme; they have started a cyber-crime working group; and exchange information on anti-money laundering and terrorist financing initiatives.[96] The USA is believed to have an important role in Echelon through NSA — the National Security Agency — in the USA. NSA was established in 1952 by President Harry S Truman. It is a separately organized unit with the Ministry of Defence in the USA. NSA is a powerful agency which plans, coordinates, runs and executes intelligence involving signals while also having tasks concerning information security for defence and non-defence State activities. In this, it is probably the world's leading cryptological organization, which is relevant to Echelon's activities.

---

95. Bamford's article: http://www.wired.com/threatlevel/2012/03/ff_nsadatacenter/all/
96. Information from Chris Jones 16 July 2012.

A Plethora Indeed

The SIS, SIS II, Sirenes, TECS, Eurodac, VIS, the Agency for Large Scale IT Systems, the Data Retention Directive, PNR, PNR-EU, API, Echelon. These are only a few of the information systems or other kinds of arrangements which are operational, in the making or designed for the future. After 9/11, a large number of measures and regulations relevant to transnational, regional and global surveillance have been added. A central point has been the rapid development of a broad and diffuse definition of "terrorism" making it very clear — if it was not clear before — that the various systems were, or may be, used politically, far beyond any reasonable definition of terrorism (Mathiesen, 2002). In a *Statewatch* report (2005), Tony Bunyan, the editor, summarises the situation as of today well:

> The UK and the EU are facing a defining moment in their response to terrorism. Everyone understands placing suspected terrorists under surveillance and bringing them to court to face charges. But to create new offences [concerning] "preparatory" acts when no crime has been committed, and for apologia to employ surveillance techniques which could catch the innocent in the net, and to change the normal Rule of Law so that defendants will not know the evidence against them or its sources and to imprison or put them under house arrest on this basis, tips the balance in favour of security over rights. Where the rights and freedoms of the few are curtailed, so too are the rights and freedoms of us all.

> Since 11 September 2001 Governments, officials, ministers and officials at all levels of the EU have maintained that the swathe of new measures introduced have all been "balanced" as between the needs of security and respect for fundamental rights. Concerned civil society groups across Europe know differently as do refugees, those stopped and searched or detained, and the communities subject to surveillance.

> What has been seen as exceptional and draconian becomes the norm.

CHAPTER 4

THE COMMON FEATURES OF INFORMATION AND SURVEILLANCE SYSTEMS

Two features seem to be basic across the various information and surveillance systems which are developing: (i) the integration of systems; and (ii) the weakening of State ties.

Integration of Systems

The various information systems are established, as well as operated, by the same, or professionally very similar, organizations and agencies. During the early days before 1997, when Schengen was formally outside the EU, planning was organized so that essentially the same people could discuss Schengen issues in one meeting and EU issues in the next. Later, this differentiation of course disappeared completely. It is also possible to be more specific. I select Europol as an example.

A Revisit — Europol as an Example[1]

The system was clearly planned with a view towards far-reaching integration, *inter alia*, with the Schengen Information System (SIS). Let us re-visit Europol from this angle. We remember how the liaison officer in Interpol, Norwegian Iver Frigaard, back in 1996 fought for enhanced compatibility and communication between Interpol, SIS and Europol (see *Chapter 3*). This was 16 years ago. We have come further now. For one thing, Article 10.4. No. 1-3 in the Europol Convention established a whole range of authorities and bodies within the EU, from whom Europol could request information: the European Communities and bodies within them governed by public law; other bodies governed by public law established within the framework of

---

1. I rely more on the Europol Convention of 1995 than on the so-called Council Decision of 6 April 2009.

the EU and bodies based on an agreement between two or more Member States of the EU.

Notably, the Convention explicitly mentioned, in Article 10.4 No. 4, that information could also be requested from "third States" — that is, States outside the union. Also, Article 10.4. No. 5-7 established that information could be requested from international organizations and subordinate bodies governed by public law, other bodies governed by public law based on an agreement between two or more States, and Interpol. Clearly, this opened the way for integration with the SIS and other surveillance systems. As a matter of fact, as early as on 9 April 1997, before Europol was operational, the "High Level Group on Organized Crime" explicitly recommended that Europol should be given access to the information stored in the SIS.[2] This and other recommendations were on the agenda of the Justice and Home Affairs' Council (JHAC)[3] at the meeting on 3-4 December 1998 in connection with the action plan on establishing a so-called area of freedom, security and justice, and the recommendations were also discussed in a report of 26 February 1999. Thus, concrete work directed towards facilitating and easing compatibility between Europol, Schengen and other systems has been going on continuously for a long time. It may be added that at its meeting on 19 March 1998, the JHAC agreed, without debate and as an "A" point, on rules allowing Europol to request and accept information from non-EU sources (pursuant to Article 10.4. No. 4 of the Europol Convention, see above). The report covered the receipt of data from "third States and third bodies" (a relevant country was Turkey), and included only the most minimal safeguards on data protection. The plans were to be supplemented by a series of "memorandums of understanding" between Europol and the central services of each of the non-EU states with which data were to be exchanged.

The above-mentioned statement shows that the story of efforts towards integration goes far back into the history of Europol. More recently, and beyond Europol, numerous integrating ties are in the making on the national level as well as between systems such as the ones we have discussed.

---

2. See document 7421/97 JAI 14.
3. We remember that this comprises Justice and Home Affairs (JHA) Ministers of the EU Member States.

The Hague Programme

The crucially important Hague Programme, adopted on 5 November 2004, introduced the so-called "principle of availability", meaning that *in principle all data/intelligence held by a law enforcement agency in one state should be available to every other agency in the EU.* At this point we may go beyond the relatively brief statements about the Hague Programme made earlier.

The Hague Programme contains a supranational plan to make relevant intelligence data available, in principle, to all members of the European Union—easy to access and use across borders in the Union. The principle of availability is precisely that, a *principle* to be followed wherever and whenever possible within the union. The principle of availability is defined as follows in the Hague Programme:

> With effect from 1 January 2008 the exchange of such information should be governed by the principle of availability, which means that, throughout the Union, a law enforcer in one member State who needs information in order to perform his duties can obtain this from another Member State and that the law enforcement agency in the other Member State which holds this information will make it available for the stated purpose, taking into account the requirement of ongoing investigation in that State.[4]

This is plain speaking, to say the least. The memo goes on to press the point in the following words:

> The methods of exchange of information should make full use of new technology and must be adapted to each type of information, where appropriate through mutual access [meaning reciprocal access, my interpretation] or the interconnection of national databases based on their interoperability or direct (on-line) access, including for Europol, to existing central EU databases such as the SIS. The creation of new centralised databases should be based on studies that have shown their added value.[5]

---

4. 13302/1/04 REV 1 GdK/Kve p. 17. DG H.
5. *Op. cit.*

The principle of availability is contextualised within three major topics in the memo, strengthening *Freedom*, *Security* and *Justice* in the European Union. The terms are also used earlier in EU's history but now stand out in bold relief.

In a short while it will be clear why we discuss the three concepts in a different order—rather than in the order of freedom, security and justice, we first discuss freedom, then justice, and *finally security.*

Freedom, Justice and Security

Freedom and *Justice* have in common that they are phrased in ideological terms:

- the first topic, Freedom, contains the central right of citizenship of the union (implying free movement and residence in the territory of the union, codified law of the union bringing clarity and simplicity);
- it further contains the *asylum and migration* policy of the Union (a common policy "should be based on solidarity and burden sharing and include closer practical co-operation between Member States,…");
- furthermore, a common European Asylum System ("…a common procedure and a uniform status for those who are granted asylum or subsidiary protection"—my comment: in other words, supposedly a very considerate system);
- furthermore, legal migration and the fight against illegal employment (my comment: presumably a timely and correct approach);
- integration of third country nationals (my comment: nice words are used—integration "is a continuous two-way process", integration includes "anti-discrimination policy", integration implies "respect for basic values", integration requires "basic skills for participation in society", integration "relies on frequent interaction and dialogue between all members of society", integration "extends to a variety of policy areas");
- but there is also an external dimension to asylum and migration—there "must be partnership with third countries", partnership "with countries and regions of origin", partnership "with countries and regions of transit", and several other sub-topics;

- words like "co-operation and humanitarian assistance", "intensifying co-operation and dialogue with neighbouring countries", "persons to be returned in safety and dignity", and so on abound. As Statewatch has observed in another context: "When the Commission talks about 'dialogue and partnership' you know it is really about 'security and migration'".[6]

This is not a complete review of the first of the three topics—the topic of freedom—in the memo, but is intended to show the ideology and tone in addressing questions.

The ideology and tone is similar throughout the third topic, that of *Justice*—with an emphasis on the European Court of Justice, confidence building and mutual trust, judicial co-operation in criminal matters, mutual recognition, approximation of law[7] (probably meaning ensuring that everyone has the same minimum standards, the lowest common denominator), and Eurojust in cooperation with Europol (concentrating on serious and complex cases).

Zooming in on "security"

It is in the second part of the document, the part between "freedom" and "justice", concentrating on the topic of "strengthening security", that the essence of the document lies. It is in other words, contextualised by the far less dangerous topics of "freedom" and "justice".

The package of freedom, security and justice sounds like just the right balance, and these words are used together over and over again in the years which follow.

When you unwrap the package, and view each of the parts in it separately, you get an understanding of what the middle part—security—implies. Tony Bunyan comments as follows, indicating that he has fully understood:

> For a long time bilateral and multilateral agreements have been in place for law enforcement agencies in one EU Member State to make requests to those in

---

6. http://www.statewatch.org/news/2011/may/eu-com-med-memo.pdf
7. Probably meaning to reach the lowest common denominator, such as the common minimum standards which nations with different laws can agree on.

another EU State on specific cases .... The "problem" for the law enforcement agencies is that this procedure takes time, involves a formal request and sometimes judicial authorisation (Bunyan 2006a, p. 1).

The Hague Programme simplifies matters and alleviates this.[8]

The European Commission followed up the Hague memo on "strengthening security" with *"Communication from the Commission to the Council and the European Parliament on improved effectiveness, enhanced interoperability[9] and synergies among European databases in the area of Justice and Home Affairs"*, COM (2005) 597 final (24 November 2005).[10] The Communication of the Commission is committed to the so-called "interoperability", "connectivity", "synergy" and "principle of availability" of IT systems, focusing specifically on the second generation of SIS (SIS II, see the description in *Chapter 3*), the VIS, which is to "share a technical platform" with SIS II, and the European Asylum System (Eurodac). The language is unnecessarily technical and bureaucratic.[11]

Only a few months before this (on 17 March 2005), the Presidency stated in a Note to the Police Cooperation Working Party entitled "Approach for Enhancing the Effective and Efficient Information Exchange among EU law enforcement agencies" (7416/05 ENFOPOL 29), i.e. in principle

---

8.   The European Data Protection Authorities have produced a declaration, a common position and a checklist on the "principle of availability", covering the collection and use of, and access to, personal data for the purpose of law enforcement. The question is how helpful this will be in the context of massive data exchange between States.

9.   "Interoperability" between databases simply means integration of the databases — reciprocal access to them.

10. The Note has kindly been provided by Simen Wiig before taking a new job in the Norwegian Sirene office.

11. The Communication has kindly been provided by Ben Hayes, Statewatch. The comments are from Chris Jones. I understand to "share a technical platform", or to speak of a "common technical platform" to be a deliberately convoluted way of describing a single computer system. This despite the Council's maintaining that "the VIS and the SIS II will be two different systems with separated data and access." "Interoperability" is institutional speak for the integration of databases — either the data sets, or access to them. The Council has already agreed that there will be a broad law enforcement access to VIS (including access for security and intelligence services), providing, in conjunction with SIS II, an EU-wide fingerprint database of wanted persons, suspects and all VIS entrants.

the JHA's [Justice and Home Affairs Council's] IT-systems should be widely accessible to the law enforcement authorities in order to combat terrorism and organized crime;…[L]aw enforcement authorities [should] have access to the national law enforcement data of all Member States, in particular to identification, DNA and fingerprint data, on a hit/no hit basis. [L]aw enforcement authorities [should] have a direct access to national administrative systems of all Member States (e.g. registers on persons, including legal persons, vehicles, firearms, identity documents and drivers licences, as well as aviation and maritime registers).

The European Commission in the longer term proposes a "European Criminal Automated Fingerprints Identification System [AFIS] … combining all fingerprint data currently only available in national criminal AFIS systems". This will begin with an index for convicted third-country nationals who have no EU "home" State to take responsibility for their criminal record. Thus, the EU will benevolently take on that role and, in the interest of equal treatment, subsequently extend an EU-wide criminal fingerprint database to all those convicted within the EU.

Statewatch Observatory has followed up in less complex language as follows:[12]

1. *The European Criminal Records Information System — ECRIS.* Ecris is intended to permit the exchange of information extracted from criminal records between Member States' judicial authorities. The primary intention is to ensure that individual's prior convictions can be taken into account if they face new criminal proceedings in a different Member State. However, the desire for a swift and systematic exchange of information has led to the development of a highly problematic system. It is marked by serious gaps in data protection, a reliance on potentially untrustworthy automated translation, and a significant lack of oversight.

2. *The European Police Records Index System — EPRIS.* The legislation to establish Epris is currently being developed by Council Working Parties and Europol. It is intended to provide national police forces with the

---

12. Press Release: Implementing the "principle of availability", 31 August 2011.

ability to search each others' databases, to find out if and where information and "intelligence" ("hard" and "soft") on individuals can be found. The insistence of the Commission and a small groups of Member States for its development has already been questioned, partly due to concerns for the potential establishment of an EU-wide police database. Greater scrutiny of this measure is urgent.

In many ways the idea behind these two systems is similar to the Prüm Accord (see later in this chapter for details) — the interlinking of national databases, rather than the construction of a centralised EU database with national access points. A distinction could be drawn between centralised large scale IT systems and decentralised information exchange networks.[13]

3. *The Information Exchange Platform for Law Enforcement Authorities — IXP.* The IXP is the most recent of the three developments, and proposes to centralise access to all the EU law enforcement information exchange instruments. Its development is still in the early stages, but a suggestion to extend access to the European Union's bureaucracies — including a number of Directorate-Generals of the European Commission, and the General Secretariat of the Council — would breach the "separation of powers" between the law makers and the law enforcement agencies (whose job is to implement the law). As with Epris, greater knowledge and scrutiny of the proposed system is vital to anyone concerned with civil rights.

Statewatch researcher, Chris Jones, has said:

All three systems demonstrate that attempts to permit law enforcement agencies to function inside the borderless EU frequently take place at the expense of the individual rights that the European Union is supposedly founded on.

The latest news on "the principle of availability" is a Statewatch Memo, by way of introduction saying that "Widespread implementation of the

---

13. Chris Jones has kindly furnished me with this point.

'principle of availability' further eases information exchange amongst European police forces". It goes on to say *inter alia* that

> The vast majority of EU and Schengen states have now transposed the Swedish Framework Decision, a 2006 piece of legislation aimed at implementing the "principle of availability". This idea was introduced by the EU in the 2004 Hague Programme to ensure that the cross-border exchange of information held by law enforcement authorities is not "hampered by formal procedures, administrative structures and legal obstacles".

It goes on to state *inter alia* that

> 31 states—the 27 EU Member States as well as Iceland, Liechtenstein, Norway and Switzerland, who participate in provisions of the Schengen Agreement—are supposed to have implemented the Decision, although only 24 of the 29 who provided information to the Council on implementation have done so.

It also says that

> The Decision obliges States to respond "within at most eight hours to urgent requests for information and intelligence regarding offences referred to in Article 2(2) of [the European Arrest Warrant], when the requested information or intelligence is held in a database directly accessible by a law enforcement authority".

When it is necessary to apply to a judicial authority, however, responses to the questionnaire forming the basis of the report indicate that time limits frequently cannot be met. Nevertheless, as a whole the report gives the impression that the application of the "principle of availability" with reciprocal information exchange between police forces is moving stridently ahead. In spite of this,

> the report makes no references to data protection or privacy, and there is very little mention of the internal checks and balances which, while fairly minimal, are permitted by Article 10 of the Framework Decision—authorities can refuse to supply information if it would "harm essential national security interests",

"jeopardise the success of current investigation or a criminal intelligence operation of the safety of individuals…".

In short, a vast system of interchange of information is under way. For further details, see the added reference.[14]

How to reach "security" — The Prüm Treaty and beyond

The interlinking of national DNA-data systems and other national databases containing fingerprints and information on vehicle registers is particularly interesting. Questions about direct access to such databases in other EU States have arisen. The so-called Prüm Treaty (named after a city not far from the town of Schengen, but on the German side of the border, where an agreement between seven EU states was originally signed on 27 May 2005), provides the states concerned with such access, thus stepping up cross-border cooperation.

The Prüm Treaty is the full-born child of the principle of availability. The EU is, at the time of writing, in the process of implementing the provisions on information exchange of the "Prüm Decisions". This allows for automated access by Member States to other States' data on DNA, fingerprints and vehicle registration.

The main purpose of the Prüm Treaty is to improve greatly the exchange of information between the Contracting States, *particularly by giving reciprocal access* to national databases containing DNA profiles, fingerprints and vehicle registration data. The Council of the EU has agreed to incorporate this into the mainstream EU *acquis*. This, for example, would allow unregulated searching on a 'hit/no-hit' basis, followed by the automatic handing over of the file if there is a "hit". As Tony Bunyan has commented: "'Hit/no-hit' access would allow 'fishing expeditions' to be carried out without any checks at all" (Bunyan 2006a).

Chris Jones, researcher at Statewatch, has shown that there certainly are problems attached to the Prüm Accord (Jones 2012). Jones tells us that "26 August 2012 marked the date by which every EU Member State should have finished the legal and technical changes required by the Prüm Decisions.

---

14. http://www.statewatch.org/news/2012/oct/12eu-swedish-framework.htm

It is clear that the majority has failed to do so, for a variety of reasons" (p. 15). There have been lengthy mutual legal assistance bureaucratic procedures, and there has been uneven implementation. Romania, for example, has shown almost no progress, Ireland does not yet have a fully operational database, and Italy is still waiting for the installation of the so-called Combined DNA Index System (CODIS), a system produced and sold by USA's Federal Bureau of Investigation (FBI) that "blends forensic science and computer technology into an effective tool for solving crime" (quotation from FBI, Jones 2012, p. 16[15]), and so on. Yet, some progress has been made, and more is likely to come.

Eric Töpfer, Senior Researcher at the Centre for Technology and Society in Berlin, has given a useful account of the Prüm Treaty as of 2008 in an extensive article (Töpfer 2008). He has *inter alia* this to say:

> Having "abandoned" proposals for an EU DNA-database, the Member States are instead linking their national databases to achieve the same objective. Three years after the signing of the Prüm Treaty, the automated comparison of police cross-border networked DNA databases is in operation in six European countries. Core elements of Prüm were transferred into the legal framework by Council Decision 2008/615/JHA on 23 June 2008, and the other 21 EU countries will log in within the next few years.

Property crimes

Töpfer has more to say. Making DNA files available to other States at request, was according to the plan going to be used against "serious crimes" — murders, rapes and violent crimes where DNA files would be particularly useful. Instead Töpfer maintains that the DNA is used more or less *en masse,* more or less beyond the limits of serious crime and extending to relatively simple property crimes and unidentified stains. No wonder, then, that

> … the number of stored DNA profiles is growing. More than 5.5 million people are registered in the EU Member States' databases, 13 years after the United

---

15. FBI, "CODIS Brochure"; http://www.fbi.gov/about-us/lab/codis/codis_brochure

Kingdom established the first national database in Europe, which accounts for 70 per cent of total entries.

Töpfer expands on this extremely important point as follows in another part of the same article:

> An interim report on DNA data matching with Austria, Spain and Luxemburg, published on 1 June 2007, shows that around 85 per cent (1,257 hits) of the then 1,508 hits were related to property crime, such as theft or fraud.[16] Moreover, a more detailed account of the results of German-Austrian DNA data matching published in March 2007 reveals that nearly one half of the German hits are only related to anonymous crime scene stains from Austria.[17] Thus, European data exchange has not changed the balance of the national databases: the quantitative criminalistic value lies in the domain of property crime.

The fact that ordinary property crimes are included, does not only make the effort expensive, but of course increases the clearance rate. This does not remain unnoticed by politicians. Töpfer goes on to say that it

> was reported that for Germany, the comparison produced almost 600 hits in the Dutch database with more than 1,000 Dutch hits on the German side. These will be assessed and, if necessary, cleared. However, Schäuble was satisfied: "The benefits of data exchange are already obvious." He stressed the "enormous time-saving effects and the significant increase in efficiency" for cross-border cooperation (Bundesinnenministerium, 2008).

The Prüm Treaty is also known as Schengen III, and does not only govern the automated searching and comparison of police DNA-databases for the purpose of criminal investigation, but also the automated searching of fingerprint data and national vehicle registration data for preventive purposes. In the case of vehicle data, it even tracks administrative offences. The treaty apparently also sets out the framework for information exchange to

---

16. *Bundesministerium des Inneren Ergebnisse auf Seiten Deutschlands im Rahmen des DNA-Datenaustausches mit Österreich, Spanien und Luxemburg nach dem Vertrag von Prüm*, 3 July 2008.
17. *Bundesministerium des Inneren, Vertrag von Prüm*, 3 July 2008.

prevent "terrorist crime" and cross-border police operations such as joint patrols and administrative assistance in case of major events or natural disasters. Likewise, it mandates the establishment of national contact points for the exchange of information on terrorism/public order issues in the case of major events—political summits, football/sports tournaments, etc.[18]

Largest pan-European network
Furthermore, Töpfer informs us that

> on the initiative of the German Presidency, the Council of the European Union decided to transfer core elements of the treaty into the legal framework of the EU on 12/13 June 2007. The Council Decision on "stepping up cross-border cooperation" of 23 June 2008 completed the transfer of Prüm eventually and, thus, established the legal basis for the creation of the largest pan-European network of police databases. Moreover, it is planned to authorise the police to access the Visa Information System (VIS), and the European fingerprint database EURO-DAC, which is currently only allowed for asylum proceedings. A joint European backbone for SIS II, VIS, EURODAC, Europol, Prüm, etc. came into existence with the start of the "Secured Trans European Services for Telematics between Administrations" (STESTA) communications infrastructure in 2007.

The development moves fast. As an example, it may be noted that (21 December 2012) a Note from the Presidency to JHAC councillors explained matters by emphasising "the need for Europol to be able to request the comparison with Eurodac data for the purposes of preventing, detecting and investigating terrorist offences and other serious criminal offences." Two main reasons were detailed—Europol as the EU information hub, and Europol's role in protecting victims of labour and sexual exploitation. Power is increasingly centred in Europol.[19] Peter Hustinx, the European Data Protection Supervisor, called forthcoming EU-wide information sharing a "nightmare".

At least at the moment, it seems that the full realisation of Prüm is hindered by problems of interoperability and lack of standardisation. No surprise

---

18. I owe the latter point to Chris Jones.
19. Sources: http://www.statewatch.org/news/2012/sep/eu-council-europol-eurodac-access-14081-12.pdf

then, that the "Future Group" proposed a "convergence principle" as an "underlying thread to a coordinated management of European… security issues…"[20]

So much for Töpfer anno 2008. But further important errors may be noted.

A note on error — slowness

The Prüm Treaty is not without its problems. Eric Töpfer has also gone into some of these. In another article, called "Network with Error" (Töpfer, 2009), EU member states are said originally to have had 16 August 2011 as the final date for implementation. This deadline could not be met by all Member States. By October 2010 only ten of them were exchanging DNA data profiles, seven were exchanging register data and five had made their databases available for cross-border searches.

This, however, is not a "poor" result, even if slower than expected. There have been many causes for the relative slowness — difficulties in mobilising parliamentary majorities for the necessary legal adjustments, power struggles between agencies, scarcity in personal and financial resources and so on. A more serious problem has been the regulation of the technical details and an understanding of genes and chromosomes in the implementation of the Prüm Treaty (Töpfer, 2009, p. 3).

A note on error — adventitious matches

The rise of the Prüm network, with more Member States coming in, increases the risk of, so-called, "adventitious matches", easier understood as "false matches" or "false positives". A leading Dutch forensic expert, Kees van der Beek (whom Töpfer refers to) has estimated that on the basis of a bio-statistical calculation in a sample of 1,600 hits, there would be 190 "false matches". This is actually a serious problem, because it involves 190 false matches for a crime which the person is likely not to have committed. This is glossed over in the wealth of information from the pro-Prüm criminal justice system.

---

20. Informal High Level Advisory Group on the Future of European Home Affairs Policy June 2008. Statewatch.

A note on error — three options

In a more recent paper (2011) van der Beek outlines *three options* for understanding DNA results, based on Dutch data. The first option is this (Option 1):

> The total number of Dutch Prüm results — 10,138 on 1 July 2011 — are compared with the number of results actually reported to the prosecution office and the police. The latter number is much lower — 2,175. "[I]t can be seen", van der Beek argues, "that most of the obtained results apparently are not [deemed] *relevant* to the public prosecution office and the police" (p. 1). [21]

What politicians would like to know, is the number of investigations actually *aided* by Prüm-results. But they do not get information on this, because they only know the number of *reported* Prüm results, not how many of the reported Prüm-results are actually used by the prosecution office and the police. This leaves us with the two remaining options.

Option 2 is to present the results that *could* aid an investigation. These are the results which the Dutch prosecution office and the police have indicated may be relevant, and that they want to receive in order to decide whether to act on them or not. This, however, in turn, requires a National Contact Point which is able and allowed to filter the initial results into relevant and irrelevant results, and it is not known to the Dutch delegation whether such filtering can be implemented in all EU countries.

This leaves us with a last option (Option 3), which is to present all obtained results with a detailed explanation of what they mean.

A number of points are raised in connection with one or both of the two last options — the relationship between outgoing and incoming requests, the fact that many matches are obtained more than once, match quality, false positives, matches considered irrelevant. The choice is: "Do we choose to present unfiltered statistics with an explanation how these should be

---

21. Van der Beek does not tell us what "results" stand for, and why most of the results "apparently are not relevant" to the prosecution office and the police in view of the great difference between total and reported results. Who decides what results to report? However, we leave these questions aside for the moment.

interpreted (Option 3) or do we choose to filter the statistics to make them more meaningful (Option 2)?" (p. 4).

An additional problem is that authorities in smaller States apparently have had to (or may have to) limit national agencies' access, because the bigger States "crash" the police data bases in smaller States. This problem also seems to be glossed over.[22]

A note on error — limited efficiency in Great Britain

The British Home Office has reported an astonishingly high success rate when using DNA data. The Norwegian criminologists Johanne Yttri Dahl and Heidi Mork Lomell have taken a close look at the material (Dahl and Lomell, 2008). Their criticism is based on a critique of data from the Home Office by Green Watch.[23]

In 2004/05 there were registered 5.6 million reported crimes in Great Britain. In 16.2% of these crimes, 913,717 crimes, the police conducted a crime scene investigation. At 109,051 of these crimes DNA was gathered. The DNA gathering resulted in 49,723 DNA profiles. They were placed in the DNA-database (the others were impossible to use, *inter alia* because their quality was low or because of errors made by the police). The DNA profiles which were placed in the DNA-database were, in other words, only 0.88 per cent of all registered crimes.

Among these 0.88 per cent of all crimes, the police reported a 40 per cent clearance rate (this was the same as saying that DNA registration contributed to a 0.35 per cent clearance of all crimes in Great Britain).

On the political level in Norway, however, it was mistakenly (or wilfully?) argued that the 40 per cent clearance rate concerned *all crimes*, not *the 0.88 per cent of all crimes*. A correct understanding of the figures in other words lowers the clearance rate drastically.

A note on error — limited efficiency in Norway

Biological material from all so-called "assault-rapes" in Oslo (regularly taking place outdoors), totalled 46 cases between 1 January and approximately

---

22. http://database.statewatch.org/article.asp?aid=29304
23. http://www.genewatch.org/uploads/f03c6d66a9b354535738483c1c3d49e4/DNAexpansion_brief_final.pdf

1 October 2011. They were sent to the Forensic Institute for analysis to see if DNA could be secured. [24] Only in a few cases was it possible to secure DNA. None of the 46 arrested were identified on the basis of DNA-proofs. Out of the 46, 39 remained unknown. Only seven rapists had been arrested.

The Oslo Police District has gone through the cases which have been cleared up. In none of the seven cases had the arrests taken place on the basis of DNA-findings. Being asked how they were able to identify and arrest the seven, the chief inspector replied:

> Good, old-fashioned police investigation. Thorough questioning of the offended and of witnesses. Description of the suspect, the scene of crime and travel route, combined with securing and going through video films. DNA for clearance of rapes is very much exaggerated.

Norway has recently said yes to an invitation to join the Prüm Treaty.

· · · · · · · · · · · · · · · · · ·

Problems abound. Despite problems not yet solved, or maybe unsolvable, Prüm advances rapidly forward. In addition, Prüm is advancing in the shade of lack of transparency and lack of democratic practice. Listen to what Elspeth Guild and Florian Geyer have to say about the way Prüm was initially handled in Germany (Guild and Geyer undated, to be published in the 3rd issue of the *Journal of European Criminal Law*):[25]

> Furthermore political reality has shown that national parliaments are not able to guarantee democratic control over purely intergovernmental agreements. Germany provides a telling example: after signing the Prüm Treaty in May 2005, it was not until April 2006, only a short time ahead of the FIFA World Cup, which was seen as a potential major security threat, that the Government tabled a ratifying draft. With less than two months left, the draft was declared "urgent" leaving the *Bundestag* only some weeks for parliamentary scrutiny—including committee work—and merely thirty minutes for discussion and vote in the plenary. In the

24. Source: *Dagsavisen* (daily), 8 October 2011.
25. http://aei.pitt.edu/11629/1/1411.pdf

debate of 19 May 2006, coalition MPs did not even bother to speak but instead submitted their statements in writing. Consequently only three MPs from the opposition gave a short speech, concentrating less on the content of the Prüm Treaty but criticising—with justification—the entire procedure.

This has mostly been on DNA. As I have said, there are also fingerprints and vehicle registers. "European register(s) for travel documents and identity cards"—*de facto* EU population registers—are also planned along with the "creation of an entry-exit system … to ensure that people arriving and departing are examined and to gather information on their immigration and residence status" (information from Ben Hayes, Statewatch). For a critique of the Commission's Communication, see European Data Protection Supervisor (EDPS), "Comments of the Communication of the Commission on Interoperability of European Databases", Brussels, 10 March 2006.

The importance of the Hague Programme embodied in the Prüm Treaty can hardly be overestimated. In the end, the Hague Programme in practice means a more or less free flow of information across the borders of Europe, with cross border access to national databases as well as crosswise access to the major European bases discussed in this chapter. An entirely new situation is in the making. Its importance, for example for protection of privacy, will be great, to say the least. Generally, the planners of the various information systems are careful to point out that the information controlled by the systems is only to be used in relation to the particular goals of the systems. As indicated earlier, the goals in question are often vague and diffuse in the first place. As Simen Wiig (2007) has pointed out, now comes the added important fact that information in systems designed for one set of goals, will be open for scrutiny and use by other systems with other goals.

And the integration of systems is taking leaps forward. The story of the Prüm Treaty gives us a brief glimpse of those leaps. Five of the seven parties to Prüm were the five parties to the 1985 Schengen Agreement and the 1990 Schengen Convention. In both cases, a minority of (powerful) States agreed on a treaty which was open to all, with little or no possibility of change. The European Data Protection Supervisor (EDPS), who was partly critical, commented in the press release (EDPS/07/3, 11 April 2007):

15 Member States propose to extend the application of the Treaty of Prüm, *concluded between seven of them, to the whole EU without allowing for any major revision* [My emphasis].

Therefore, the EDPS went on to say, laconically:

The EDPS' suggestions mainly serve to improve the text without modifying the system of information exchange itself.

We recall that essentially the same procedure was followed when Schengen itself was established in the 1990s. The example of Prüm is important in showing how attempts, even by established and responsible agencies, to modify basic structures of information and surveillance systems may be curtailed by swift and general political decisions finalising matters. A safe prediction is that the examples from Schengen in the 1990s and Prüm in the early 2000s will follow us. A vision of an increasingly integrated information and surveillance system is near at hand. With all its dangers to privacy and civil rights, even a small political change will, in view of the surveillance monster that lies ahead, threaten democracy as we know it.

Weakening of State Ties

The second feature that information systems have in common is the weakening of ties between ordinary nation-State agencies and the increasingly integrated surveillance systems themselves. There is a development toward a generalised political sphere, above the reach of the ordinary nation-State agencies, responsible for the surveillance systems.

National Parliament members do not have the time or energy to dig deeply into the heap of documents pertaining to decisions about Schengen, Europol, Prüm or what have you. Parliamentary debates become superficial and short, accepting the premises of ministries and even police agencies. In Norway the decisions of Parliament clearly follow the proposals of the Government, and the Government, in turn, seems to follow the signals and proposals which are central to police culture and thinking. The mass media, supposedly the controllers of it all, are not interested in going into the detail necessary for efficient control. The media, to a large extent a part of the entertainment industry, backs off: the dreary details and complexities of the surveillance systems are not in tune with the news criteria of the entertainment industry. A concrete example of the weakening of State ties in the *context* of the Hague Programme is given by Tony Bunyan:

> From the first draft of the Hague Programme (11 October 2004) the "principle of availability" was set in stone. At the European Council (Summit) on 5 November 2004 the Hague Programme was simply nodded through without debate — all Prime Ministers had other more important matters to discuss. Statewatch had put the first draft online on 18 October but there was little or no time for parliaments or civil society to comment or intervene.

> It was a programme drawn up by officials and agencies, endorsed by Ministers and then Prime Ministers in secret meetings without any real democratic input. Thus was the justice and home affairs programme of the Council Presidencies and the European Commission for the next five years adopted (Bunyan 2006a p. 3).

Availability — But also Force

The Hague Programme, with the principle of availability and its embodiment in the Prüm Treaty, to a considerable extent belongs to the future in terms of surveillance. The next five year plan, 2009-2014, is the so-called Stockholm Programme. It is a new five year plan in the area of migration and asylum politics. The two seem to fit together — the Hague principle of availability is an important principle for the Stockholm quest to gain a harmonised migration and asylum policy for the EU States. Thus, there is a logic to the series of programmes. The relatively recently established *European Asylum Support Office,* EASO, will support the European countries in their practical work with asylum applications. But there are also other issues involved. During the period 2010-2012, the various EU institutions issued 60 decisions, communications, reports etc. on four areas in all, "Ensuring protection of fundamental rights", "Strengthening confidence in the European judicial area", "Ensuring the security of Europe (Drugs policy)", and "Others (future financing)".[26]

---

26. Source: http://www.statewatch.org/news/2012/sep/eu-com-justice-stockholm.pdf

But a harmonised migration and asylum policy over the coming four-five years needs not only "soft" surveillance principles like reciprocal availability. It also needs *force*; it has to oscillate between the soft measures of availability and measures of force. Something, towards the end, about the side of force.

There is force in *Frontex,*[27] a border police unit briefly mentioned earlier and established in 2005. This is the EU's organization for security at the external borders, with its office in Warsaw. Frontex defines its vision as follows: "Frontex is the cornerstone in the European concept of integrated border control, by... the highest level of professionalism, interoperativity, integrity and reciprocal respect with the interests which are involved." [28] Frontex further defines itself as follows (Article 1.2 in the Frontex Regulation with revisions as of 2011): "...the Agency... shall facilitate and render more effective the application of existing and future European Union measures relating to the management of external borders, in particular the Schengen Borders Code. It shall do so by ensuring the coordination of Member States' actions in the implementation of those measures, thereby contributing to an efficient, high and uniform level of control on persons and surveillance of the external borders of the Member States".

Statewatch's general description is quite different, emphasising *inter alia* the many surveillance systems (SIS, SIS II, VIS) which will be utilised. Statewatch also emphasises other measures, and views Frontex as a quasi-military border police in rapid development patrolling *inter alia* the Mediterranean.[29] They seem right in doing so: In Frontex' Work Programme for 2012 it is for example, efficiently and "militaristically" stated, under "Technological factors": "A number of Member States are currently upgrading or building

---

27. From the *French—Frontières extérieures,* in English *European Agency for the Management of Operational Cooperation at the External Borders of the Member States of the European Union,* for short called *The Agency.*
28. Council Regulation (EC) No. 2007/2004 of 26 October 2004. See also Peers, 2011 for revisions agreed on "in principle" between the European Parliament and the EU Council.
29. *Request to Comment on ECLN Call on the Stockholm Programme,* 9 March 2009, p. 2. In his great biography on Julius Caesar, Adrian Goldsworthy (Norwegian ed. 2007) has given a fascinating account of Roman control of the Mediterranean at the time of Caesar, relating for example about Caesar being taken prisoner by pirates, and general Pompeius' successful campaign, with his advanced naval fleet, in eventually crushing them. In an extensive report for Statewatch, Ben Hayes has analysed the military industry's role in a surveillance society, *Arming the Big Brother—The EU's Security Research Programme,* Amsterdam, 2009.

new earth-based surveillance systems with the aim of acquiring or deploying modern 'integrated' systems… Face-recognition technology is increasingly being used in automated border-crossing systems… "[D]evelopments [in biometric technology] will drive the further progress of the 'smart borders package' with the Entry/Exit System (EES) and the Registered Travellers Programme (RTP) at its core. The systems will further call for synergising VIS and SIS II" (p.15).[30]

The important point is that Frontex is not only having an *integrating role*, with consequences for the various surveillance systems, by having personnel recruited or mixed from various nation states. It is also *weakening its ties* to the individual nation State by being built as a unit over and above the State and under a control emanating from the EU.

It is truly quasi-military — and the equipment and installations of Frontex has a distinctly military and highly technical flavour (not to mention that numerous staff, including the Head of the Agency, are drawn from the ranks of the Member States' military forces). The headquarters of Frontex are located in a 192 metres high, 40-storied skyscraper in Warsaw. The agency occupies floors 22 and 23. In 2009 it had a complement of 226 employees in its administration, increasing to 281 in 2010. In 2010 it had a budget of 87.9 million euros. It coordinates operational border security, carries out risk analyses, takes part in so-called joint return operations, assists in training border guards, follows border security research and development, assists in circumstances requiring increased technical and operational assistance, deploys rapid intervention teams to Member States, and provides the Commission and the Member States with technical assistance and expertise. It has 35 border guard training schools throughout Europe. It has a Common Core Curriculum (CCC) in all languages and it has mid-level courses organized in seminars for four weeks for 15 persons in the training centres of the Border Guard School in Vilnius, the Police Academy of Bratislava, the Bundespolizei Academy in Lübeck and the ILEA Academy of Budapest. It has created "Rapid Border Intervention Teams" (RABITs) because of a proposal of the Hague Programme to act collectively against the influx of migrants. The Rabits are fast reaction teams constituted by experts able to supply a

---

30. http://www.statewatch.org/news/2012/jan/eu-frontex-2012-wp.pdf

speedy and short-term technical and operational support to the national border guards in periods of migrant influxes from outside the borders of Europe. The experts enter the service of the host state, and during operations they wear their own national uniform and the blue armband of Frontex.

Frontex has at its disposal 25 helicopters, 21 airplanes, 113 vessels in addition to mobile radars, thermal cameras, infra-red cameras and heartbeat detectors. Pictures show that those who train students are armed (probably with semi-automatic guns).[31] As far as is known, they are so far not yet using drones, although they certainly have a strong interest in them.[32] These are only aspects of their advanced technical equipment. A new provision will now allow the agency the option of acquiring equipment directly, and this could turn it from a talking participant to a customer. The new Regulation No: 2010/0039 confirms the mitralization of border surveillance and migration control.[33]A plan showing the Integrated Border Management System of Frontex has ties to or communicates with the Schengen Treaty, the Schengen Information System (SIS), SIS II, European Finger Print Data (Eurodac), BORSEC Study (Biometrics and e-documents), BORTEC Study (the Building of European System for Border Surveillance), and more.[34] See also the 2012 Frontex Work Programme which states (p. 15): "Those developments [in biometric technology— *inter alia* face recognition used at automated border controls, mostly for EU nationals (same place)] will drive the further progress of the 'Smart borders package' with the Entry/Exit System (EES) and the Registered Travellers Programme (RTP) at its core. They both envisage the creation of a centralised European database, which potentially includes

---

31. Frontex has a "Code of Conduct for All Persons Participating in Frontex Activities". Generally, it speaks of Frontex as having the highest possible ethical standards. Articles 19 and 20 set out the strictest possible rules for the "Use of force" (19) and the "Use of weapons" (20). For example, while performing their task the Frontex people "may only use weapons *with the consent of the home Member State and the host Member State, in the presence of border guards of the host Member State and in accordance with the national law of the host Member State*" (from Article 20.1. on the Use of weapons). It is hard indeed to see how quick action as a reply to unpredictable situations (which inevitably arises in semi-military situations such as this) is at all possible if all of these four conditions have to be met.
32. See, for something from late 2010: http://www.ipsnews.net/2010/11/europe-drones-may-track-migrants/
33. See preceding note.
34. All information is taken from Frontex: "Presentation of the Current Role and to Come from the Agency", 2010. Illustrated.

highly sensitive biometric data such as fingerprints and facial images (Hayes and Vermeulen, 2012 p. 40). The systems will further call for synergising VIS and SIS II".[35] The exact details of the smart borders initiative are not yet known (Hayes and Vermeulen 2012, p. 40).

Criticism

There has been plenty of criticism of Frontex. An example: In the autumn of 2011, the Green Party in the European Parliament issued a press release with the headline "Half-hearted improvements on human rights protection fall short". The Green spokesperson on migration and home affairs said inter alia:

> The measures adopted today to improve the guarantee of human rights on Frontex missions are half-hearted and unconvincing. At least 1,500 people have already died this year on Europe's borders and, against this background, it is not acceptable that human rights protection should be an afterthought for the EU's border agency. Unfortunately, EU Governments were unwilling to include sufficient, binding measures to ensure the guarantee of basic rights as part of this legislative revision.

Human Rights Watch has published an extensive and highly critical report on Frontex' involvement in ill-treatment of migrant detainees in Greece. [36] The report goes into great detail through the various semi-military atrocities Frontex has been involved in. Human Rights Watch carefully notes how migrant detention in Greece varies but according to the European Court of Human Rights generally constitutes "inhuman and degrading treatment", and then goes on to say that

> Frontex provided Greece with both manpower and material support, made available by participating states, which facilitated the detention of those migrants in sub-human conditions in Greece's overcrowded detention centres… Although the ECtHR categorically ruled the transfer of migrants to detention in Greece

---

35. http://www.statewatch.org/news/2012/jan/eu-frontex-2012-wp.pdf
36. *EU's Dirty Hands. Frontex Involvement in Ill-Treatment of Migrant Detainees in Greece* , September 2011 58 p. See http://www.hrw.org/sites/default/files/reports/greece0911webwcover_0.pdf

would expose them to prohibited abuse, an executive agency of the EU and the border guards from EU member states knowingly facilitate such transfers. (p. 1).

Human Rights Watch goes on to say that

Frontex describes its mission as one of coordination, research and surveillance. But Frontex sent equipment such as vans, buses, patrol cars and a helicopter, provided by participating states, and covered the expenses incurred by the Rabit operation. Frontex also operated in close proximity to the four detention centres where human rights violations have consistently been recorded. During the Rabit operation, guest officers[37] from participating states who went out on patrols with at least one Greek officer were authorised to apprehend migrants and then transfer them to Greek counterparts who ran the facilities (p. 1).

Also, Frontex "facilitated the transfer of migrants to centres of detention within Greece where Human Rights Watch documented the same inhuman and degrading conditions as those condemned by ECtHR [European Court of Human Rights]". In a January 2011 review the ECtHR concluded *inter alia*:

All the centres visited by bodies and organisations that produced the report... describe a similar situation to varying degrees of gravity: overcrowding, dirt, lack of ventilation, little or no possibility of taking a walk, no place to relax, insufficient mattresses, no free access to toilets, inadequate sanitary facilities, no privacy, limited access to care. Many of the people interviewed also complained of insults, particularly racist insults, proffered by staff and the use of physical violence by guards. (p. 2).

The Mediterranean has been a major headache for the EU and thereby Frontex. Flows of migrants have tried to cross the ocean from the African side, often in vain. Major attacks for transgression of human rights have

---

37. "Guest officers" are, according to the report, chosen from a pool provided by participating EU Member States and other non-EU States" In this case, RABIT deployed 175 border guards contributed by "Norway and EU-member states to the Greek government's effort to manage the influx of migrants..."

been launched against Frontex for standing in people's way. *Fortress Europe,* a blog run by Gabriele del Grande, has hard facts. She has estimated 1,674 deaths in the Sicilian Channel. That is 84% of the 1,931 who have died in the Mediterranean Sea during the first seven months in 2011. This figure is the highest ever recorded for the Mediterranean. It outstrips the worst year ever for the Mediterranean, which in 2008 was 1,274 deaths for the whole year. The results indicate one death for every 130 arrivals from Tunisia. From Libya there were 1,486 recorded deaths, which amounted to one death for every 17 arrivals. Gabriele del Grande has recorded 13 cases of boats and exact dates carrying approximately 1,669 people who died en route.[38]

A report from Statewatch[39] tells us that the criticism of Frontex is mounting. Unworthy vessels sinking on their way to Europe is not new, but the publication of new figures by UNHCR, an independent observer, estimates that about 1,500 people died in the Mediterranean in 2011 — followed by a series of events which prompted the European States' reaction to what appeared to be a failure to uphold international search and rescue standards. A series of examples is given. The figures on deaths is a little lower than one of the estimates of Gabriele del Grande, but still extremely high and, as I said, made by an independent observer.

Finally, Frontex has been engaged in land-based deportations. On 20 April 2012, it was noted that for the third time in 2012 a group flight of deportees had left Düsseldorf headed for Belgrade in Serbia. Germany, with the assistance of Frontex, has been carrying out a policy of systematic expulsion against the Roma community, at a pace of one or two flights each month, in the direction of Serbia or Kosovo. Since 2006, Frontex has been coordinating the organization of so-called "conjoints", joint return flights, between different Member States of the EU, which serve to deport irregular migrants.[40]

Global Control Without a State?

We are nearing a first general conclusion. Setting aside the very earthly quasi-military unit Frontex, are we then developing an over-arching, far-reaching

---

38. Source: *Statewatch Bulletin* Vol. 21, No. 3, 2011, pp. 12-13.
39. http://www.statewatch.org/analyses/200-frontex-search-rescue.pdf
40. http://www.migreurop.org/article2113.html?lang=fr

integrated global control system existing in and of itself, essentially without a State?

In 1997, Gunther Teubner edited *Global Law Without a State* (Teubner, 1997). Among the interesting contributions to the volume is Teubner's own introductory piece "Global Bukowina: Legal Pluralism in the World Society" (Teubner 1997, pp. 3-28). Teubner's main concern is the development of *Lex Mercatoria*, the transnational law of economic transactions, mostly transactional contract law, which he views as "the most successful example of global law without a state" (*ibid.*, p. 3). Global law, according to Teubner, has some characteristics which are "significantly different from our experience of the law of the nation-state" (*ibid.* p. 7).

— The boundaries of global law are not formed by maintaining a core territory and possibly expanding from this, but rather by invisible social networks, invisible professional communities and invisible markets which transcend territorial boundaries.

— General legislative bodies are less important — global law is produced in self-organized processes of what Teubner calls "structural coupling" of law with ongoing globalised processes which are very specialised and technical.

— Global law exists in diffuse but close dependence not on the institutional arrangements of nation-States (such as Parliaments), but on their respective specialised social fields — in the case of *Lex Mercatoria*, the whole development of the expanding and global economy.

— For nation building in the past, unity of law was a main political asset. A worldwide unity of law would become a threat to legal culture. It would be important to make sure that a sufficient variety of legal sources exists in a globally unified law.

In my own words, ideal-typically about *Lex Mercatoria*: transnational economic law is developed not by committees and councils established by ministries in nation-States and subsequently given sanction by Parliaments, but through the work of the large and expanding lawyers' firms, the jet-set lawyers operating on the transnational or global level, tying vast capital interests together in complex agreements furthering the capital interests. As *Lex Mercatoria* develops, it is not given subsequent primary sanction by national Parliaments but is self-referential and self-validating, finding suitable "landing points" in quasi-legislative institutions (Teubner, 1997, p. 17) such as international chambers of commerce, international law and all sorts of international business associations. It develops as a system of customary law in a diffuse zone around valid formal law or at least valid legal interpretation. It develops continuously, one step building on the other, in the end validating a law or a set of legal interpretations far from the law of the nation-States.

The independence of law and legal development is the crux of the matter. There is a great deal of debate going on concerning the independence of *Lex Mercatoria* — Teubner calls it a 20 years' war. I will not enter that war here, but simply ask the question: Do we, in developments in the late 20th or early-21st century, see signs of a developing independent global control system, a kind of frightening *Lex Vigilatoria* of political and social control? Global control without a State?

Lex Vigilatoria?

The question is complex. There are certainly ties between nation-states and say Schengen, the Sirene exchange, Eurodac, communication control through retention and eventual tapping of telecommunications traffic data, the spy system Echelon, and so on. For one thing, some of the systems are established or proposed on the national level first. The above-mentioned story about how the EU directive on mandatory retention of telecommunications traffic data came about is an example. Secondly, some of the systems are established through various joint national efforts — some of them complex (meetings and memos over ten years concerning communications control; the lengthy negotiations over Schengen), some simpler (framework decisions involving agreements of Ministers from the nation-States) and some very simple (quick common positions cleared by Governments). Thirdly, agreements such as partnerships in Schengen, Europol and Eurodac have to be sanctioned by national Parliaments.

At the same time, there are signs suggesting that systems, such as the ones I have discussed, are not only increasingly becoming integrated or "interlocked", but also increasingly untied or "de-coupled" from the nation states. For one thing, as I have alluded to already, the parliamentary nation-State sanctioning of arrangements such as Schengen, Europol and Eurodac largely takes place without in-depth debates in public space, and, significantly, without parties and members of parliaments really knowing, to any degree of detail, the systems they are sanctioning. Parties and members must necessarily trust the work being done by various sub-committees and so on deep inside the EU structure, over and above agencies of the nation-States. There is neither time nor motive for anything else. An example is the scrutiny of the various *acquis,* enormous heaps of documents drastically reducing transparency for an ordinary Parliament member (or even a researcher).

Furthermore, once the various interlocking systems are up and running, they interlock further through informal agreements and arrangements, rapidly expanding their practices — a kind of customary law, again in the diffuse zone of valid formal law. And the systems expand by internal sociological forces and logic, far from the control of nation-State institutions. In other words, the systems are increasingly integrated "horizontally". There seems to be an important relationship between the "horizontal" integration or interlocking aspects of the various systems, and the "vertical" weakening of ties or de-coupling aspects to nation state agencies. The more integrated or interlocked the systems become ("horizontal" integration), the more independent of or de-coupled from national state institutions they will be ("vertical" weakening of ties), when the agendas for future developments and operations are set. Integration, interlocking, links the systems together in functional terms. Given moves are therefore simply regarded as "necessary" or imperative, irrespective of the thinking which might be valid on the nation-State level. Interlocking at the system level also makes particular developments seem imperative from the point of view of the nation-State level. For example, the "package" consisting of the SIS, Europol and Eurodac, in which all three systems are increasingly intertwined in terms of cooperation and goals, has made it increasingly "obvious" and "necessary" for Norway to participate in all three of them—if not without debate, at least with a minimum of debate. The question of Norwegian participation in the first of these, the SIS, created some critical debate. Norwegian participation in Europol and Eurodac hardly reached the newspapers or TV at all.

Eventually, the interlockings and de-couplings are taken as *fait accomplis,* simply to be reckoned with. System functionaries—and there are thousands of them taking pride and finding legitimacy in such developments—become part and parcel of their system, defining their system as something they should foster, feeling great satisfaction when they manage to make the system function still better. These are entirely commonplace processes; this is how we all become more or less enveloped by the systems we are working in (Mathiesen, 2004b).

A small example: in a discussion with Norwegian Schengen personnel some years ago. I ventured to guess that their workings were not all that rational after all—they probably took great pride and satisfaction in the computerised technical and complex activities they were involved in and were continuously developing. The response was instant—fumbling with papers, some blushing and some openly agreeing. To be sure, the various interlocking systems have their "landing points", but, much like *Lex Mercatoria,* not in responsible parliamentary settings, but in quasi-legislative institutions—in this case especially, branches of the law enforcement agencies with their strongly vested interests.

Does *Lex Vigilatoria* Catch Terrorists?

A cautious conclusion for the time being: the various interlocking systems do not develop quite of their own accord, but with what I would call increasingly *diluted* ties to the institutions of the nation-States. While not global law fully without a State, a dilution of connections with the institutions of the nation-State is taking place. Most significantly, the institution of parliamentary sanction and control has become, at least in quite a few European States, a perfunctory exercise with a silent public as a context. *Lex Vigilatoria* grows, having not two but many eyes, scanning Europe without the various sanctions and controls from the past standing in the way.

This conclusion leads to a further question: If the connections with the nation-State are diluted, is this a development which is productive as far as catching terrorists goes? The question is decisive. If we could be reasonably certain that terrorists actually were caught through a globalised surveillance technology with eyes scanning the whole region or even the whole globe, doubts about a development towards *Lex Vigilatoria* would placated. The argument would be that the nation-State, which through various actions and mechanisms has many stop orders — parliamentary and other committees where doubts and even votes can go against surveillance, movements and protest organizations which also can go against, referendums and so on, in addition to national law in general — would have its stop orders weakened and thus have its road towards a surveillant society if not as easy as falling off a log, at least less rough and rocky.

Where do we find data on the success or failure of a developing *Lex Vigilatoria* in finding terrorists all over the place through its many and varied eyes? Let us be a bit more precise: Where do we find data on success or failure in finding terrorists *before the act*? This is the core question.

But first, let us take a look at terrorists found *after* the act, *after* they have carried out their intention of terror?

Terrorists Found After the Act
We have good examples of terrorists, or at least groups of terrorists, found (or at least first identified) after the act. Below I list eight major examples of terrorists during the first 12 years of the 21 century who were found or first identified *after* the act of terror had been committed (the list contains examples and is hardly exhaustive):

1. **2001**: An attack by flying four passenger planes towards major buildings in the US, two of them hitting the Twin Towers in New York and one of them hitting the Pentagon, both on 11 September. The terrorists were identified after the acts as al-Qaeda members or sympathisers.

2. **2002**: Forty to 50 Chechens took about 900 hostages in the Dobvoka Theatre in Moscow. After close to three days the theatre was gassed and stormed by Russian forces. At least 129 hostages and 39 terrorists were killed. The terrorists were identified after the act as Ingush and Chechen Islamists.

3. **2004**: Terrorists, probably inspired by al-Qaeda, detonated a number of bombs on a train in Madrid, Spain. 191 people were killed during a series of explosions.

4. **2004**: Ingurian and Chechen Islamists and separatists took over 1,000 people as hostages at a school in Beslan, Russia. Most of them were children. During and after the attack the Russians stormed the school, killing 334 hostages.

5. **2005**: Four Islamist suicide bombers attacked a subway and a bus in London during the morning rush hours. Fifty-two people were killed, in addition to the suicide bombers.

6. **2008**: Islamist terrorists attacked a number of goals in Mumbai. The attacks seemed to be geared towards Western citizens in India. A total of 172 people were killed, many of them foreigners.

7. **2011**: A bomb killing seven people in the Government buildings and 69 young people (and wounding many) on 22 July, the latter participating in a political (social democratic) summer camp on an island outside Oslo, Norway. As I have said before, the terrorist was a right-wing extremist Norwegian citizen.

8. **2012**: A suicide bomber made a bomb go off at the airport Burgas in Bulgaria on 18 July 2012, killing himself and six others. Five were Israeli tourists, the sixth person was the driver. They had just boarded the bus which was to take them to their hotel.

One of the eight attacks, then, was performed by a right-wing extremist. Four of the eight were performed in Europe (Madrid 2001, London 2005, Oslo 2011, Bulgaria 2012). I have not listed school massacres which were probably without a political motive. Nevertheless a mixed bag. However, they all had in common that the authorities were reasonably or fully correct in pointing out who were the attackers, at least as groups — *after* the act.

But *before* the act? A core issue in the present book is that this is much more difficult, especially when links to the nation-States are diluted and a *Lex Vigilatoria* is developing, and stop orders at "ground level" are weakened.

Terrorists Found Before the Act.

Though rare, it is of course possible to find terrorists before the act. Let us first make that point clear. An example:

> On 14 November 2011 Norwegian *Dagsavisen's* readers could read that three people were in fact indicted for terror plans in Norway. Though the plans had originally been broader, including the blowing-up of the Chinese Embassy in Oslo, the State Attorney had limited the indictment to plans to blow-up the Danish newspaper *Jyllandsposten*, which originally had published caricatures of Muhammad, and of killing Kurt Westergaard who had drawn the cartoons.

There are also other examples, including bomb plots in Great Britain, such as the presumed plot at Birmingham. A trio of "central figures" were arrested when fears of a bomb attack were imminent, and found guilty of 12 counts of preparing for acts of terrorism between December 2010 and their arrest in September the following year. Four men were sent to Pakistan to receive training, and pleaded guilty for preparing acts of terrorism. Other Birmingham men also pleaded guilty. Nine men in all were convicted as a result of the investigation.

But there are uncertainties in the Birmingham case. The jury heard that the security services had the men under close surveillance and they were recorded laughing and joking about their plans, and how they did not have to worry about their car's MOT, because as suicide bombers they would be dead by the time it expired. The police and the jury were convinced, while one of the three major participants said he had pretended to be a terrorist because he wanted to end rumours in his local community, the second denied wanting to be a terrorist, and the third did not give evidence in his defence.[41]

No precise targets were discussed by the three men. It is also unclear when the attack was planned, although the group made references to "five

---

41. Source: BBC News, 21 Febuary 2013.

months, a year, two years", said senior investigating officer Adam Gough. On the other hand he said the men were "the real deal" and, if successful in detonating their devices they would have perpetrated "another 9/11 or another 7/7 in the UK".[42] The reports I have read (on Google.no) interestingly only take the arguments of the prosecution and police into account, not those of the defence.

The case indicates some of the problems involved in taking into account peoples *thoughts and plans* as targets of surveillance and punishment. The issue will be discussed in further detail in *Chapter 5*. At any rate, to find terrorists before the act is difficult. What makes it so difficult?

Lone wolves

So-called "lone wolves", terrorists who operate alone, and who don't have any known network of co-planners with whom to communicate. When they act alone, and do not communicate with anyone, they are extremely hard to detect beforehand. They leave few or no traces. They are increasing in numbers, and Europol acknowledges this. Member States report to Europol that a diverse spectrum of actors poses a risk

> **from organized terrorist groups** to **radicalised individuals**, inspired by extremist ideologies. These latter individuals are often hard to identify, as they **act alone** and their activities can be unpredictable and difficult to prevent (TE-SAT 2011 for 2010 p. 15, bold relief in original).

In the same report for 2010, Europol goes on to say on p.6 that

> [C]ommand and control from outside the EU is decreasing and more **lone actors** with EU citizenship are involved in terrorist activities (bold relief in original).

In TE-SAT report 2012 for 2011 p.9 Europol continues to emphasise and stress even more lone actors:

---

42. Source: Yahoo! News, 21 February 2013.

Serious threats emanate not only from established terrorist organizations but increasingly from lone actors and small groups in EU Member States, whose radicalisation takes place largely undetected. This development is facilitated by the Internet, and — in the religiously inspired strand — is also incited by al-Qaeda core and affiliates to compensate for diminished capabilities to direct operations. The practice of "individual jihad" was advocated by al-Qaeda in the Arab Peninsula (AQAP) through its online magazine, Inspire, and in a video inspired by the organization in June 2011. However, the incidents in Norway in July 2011 prove that attacks performed by individually-operating actors are not a practice limited to al-Qaeda inspired terrorism.

The major blowing-up of Government buildings and the subsequent massacre outside Oslo on 22 July 2011 referred to by Europol is a concrete example of what may happen when a lone actor or lone wolf attacks. We will come back to this dramatic event in detail in *Chapter 5*, here only this. When asked why they didn't have a trace/tail on this man before, the answer on TV from the then head of the Norwegian Secret Service went as follows: This man had been totally law-abiding for many years, his various anti-Islamist statements on the Internet had not been worse than those by many others, the only thing the police had "registered" him for was a transaction with a person in Poland worth 121 krona concerning some chemicals which were legal. He had gone "under the radar". The head of Secret Service went on to say: If people like him were registered, Norway would be full of registered people, and we would essentially have a police state which we don't want for other reasons. Even STASI during the Communist Regime in East Germany would not have registered a man like this. While she later apologised for the reference to STASI, she vehemently maintained her core argument. Her statement was clearly corroborated by witnesses from the police much later, during the trial against the 22 July perpetrator which followed in the early summer of 2012. During the careful and lengthy investigation taking place before the trial, the police had not been able to unravel all of the various contacts of the perpetrator on the Internet. Still, the police were unequivocal in their view. *Aftenposten's* commentator sitting in on the trial noted, 31 May 2012:

...the conclusion of the police is, however, on one point crystal clear: the defendant was alone in planning and carrying out the 22 July tragedy. There is no trace of the two silent cells which the defendant right after the arrest maintained were ready for further actions... There is neither a trace of the European knights' order the "Knights Templar" which the mass killer in a rather detailed manner described in his manifest.

The events illustrate how poor our thinking will be if we believe that a build-up of the surveillance systems will help us in looking for lone wolves. We may be a little better at looking into the past to see what *has* happened, but even this is difficult, and looking *into the future* as far as lone terrorists goes is nearly a hopeless or at least extremely difficult task.[43]

Several scholarly books have appeared on lone wolves. One of them is *Lone Wolf Terror and the Rise of Leaderless Resistance*, by George Michael (2012). As he demonstrates, the most notable examples are not isolated cases. They represent the new way of warfare which will be conducted in the 21st century. Another is *Lone Wolf Terrorism: Understanding the Growing Threat*, by Jeffrey D Simon (2013). Lone wolves have demonstrated that they can be as dangerous as organized terrorist groups.

Small scale attacks

Terrorist attacks do not have to be large scale. Because large scale attacks are costly, require extensive organization and are easier to detect, small scale attacks are on the rise. The Belgian expert on terrorism, Joseph Henrotin, *inter alia* the editor the French journal *Défense et Sécurité Internationale* and a frequently used expert commentator in the Belgian and French media, has pointed out that increased cooperation and surveillance during the last few years has led al-Qaeda to change tactics. As large scale terrorist attacks are becoming more vulnerable to detection in advance, tactics are changing to smaller scale attacks. "These smaller scale attacks are almost impossible to reveal in advance," says Henrotin. He refers to vigilance among ordinary people as the best way to control terrorism. Correct information and

---

43. Later on, the sequence of events in Oslo during the summer and autumn of 2011 indicated that though it would have been most difficult to find such a "lone wolf" ahead of time, it would, in this particular case, perhaps not have been impossible.

preparedness among people that terrorism may take place, will boost the morality among people and weaken the surprise effect of terror, he claims. "You cannot attain security with surveillance cameras. They are not intelligent. The only intelligent controllers are people".[44]

Information overload

Many of the large surveillance system described earlier are not easy to use, or close to unusable, when it comes to finding terrorists in advance, whether lone wolves or groups. This goes for Eurodac, the Data Retention Directive, the various PNRs, the API, the Prüm Treaty, and perhaps also for the Schengen Information System. These five or more systems face a common threat, namely what we may call *information overload*. There is far too much information — in all of the systems, which makes the picking out of terrorists on an individual or group basis in advance extremely difficult. The Data Retention Directive, the various PNRs and the Prüm Treaty are perhaps particularly vulnerable to this.

Take the Data Retention Directive. It collects all information concerning communication (except content) on all citizens in a given State. The information has to be retained for a long period of time — up to two years. Simple arithmetic tells us that the information which has to be, and is, retained, becomes colossal. Let us say that a particular State is small, and has roughly five million inhabitants (Norway is a small country, and had 4,920,300 inhabitants on 1 January 2011; we will soon have 5 million).[45] Most inhabitants have telephones, often several mobile telephones, as well as access to the Internet and other communication technologies. Say that communication technology equals the number of inhabitants, five million for one year. This is clearly an underestimation, but roughly the average retention period — Norway has in fact a retention period of one year. If the given State has decided on mandatory retention for two years — which is the limit — the database contains not five, but ten million technologies. However, the technology contains a large number of data entries. If the given State has decided on mandatory

---

44. Source: Information and quotes from the Norwegian daily, *Aftenposten*, 3 July 2007.
45. Most studies of population size are much more detailed, counting or not counting children say under 15, and so on. We do not go in detail, and count everyone. Children, incidentally, are way into communication technology.

retention on all communication — who owns the communication technology which is used, who uses the communication technology in question, at what time does the communication begin, at what time does it end, from where is the call is taken and from where is it received, whether the caller or the called or both are moving around during the communication, to where they have moved, all of this and a number of other data entries for one year brings the database to an enormous number of millions of data entries per year. After one year the data which is stored has to be deleted. But it never ends, because a similar number of data entries are stored for each individual and for all of the five million inhabitants for another year, and another year and another year….. Add to this that not only the inhabitants of this particular State are in the system, but so are all of the inhabitants of all the States of Europe (and outside States, like Norway). You end up with a fabulous number of data entries which turns the famous finding of the needle in the haystack into a reality — to say the least. For States deciding on two years of mandatory retention — the limit — the number of data entries will be doubled — even more fabulous. Many of the EU States are much larger than Norway — Great Britain had 61 million inhabitants in 2009. There are 27 large and small States in the EU. You stop counting.

Similar counting experiments may be made for the other large surveillance systems — the Passenger Name Record with all air passengers crossing the American border and other borders external and internal to the EU, each one of them with a series of data entries, remaining in the database for a given period of time; Eurodac with fingerprints and other information on all refugees and a proportion of irregular migrants in the EU down to the age of 15; the Prüm Treaty with an increasing number of EU States as members which gives the signatories access to each other's national databases containing DNA profiles, fingerprints and vehicle registration data.

A European Directive limits the retention of DNA-data to that of people convicted of an offence (with possible exceptions). Originally and Scotland apart, the UK (which has the biggest DNA-database in Europe: see also the end of *Chapter 1*) disregarded this and retained DNA following arrest, even when the entirely innocent suspect was released. This led to *S and Marper v. UK* [2008] ECHR 158 in which the ECtHR — noting that the UK was "the only Member State expressly to permit the systematic and indefinite retention of DNA samples of persons who have been acquitted" — ruled that blanket retention of the DNA of innocent people is indiscriminate, unlawful and a disproportionate interference with Article 8 ECHR (right to private and family life). Four years later, the UK, having not implemented an earlier correcting provision of 2010, passed the Protection of Freedoms Act 2012, under which indefinite retention is only lawful following conviction (or for a limited time in relation to serious "qualifying offences", juveniles and national security as permitted, so it seems, by the Directive). Implementation of the 2012 Act is being promised for October 2013 (along with comparable provisions for fingerprints: for a briefing note to MPs indicative of the less than prompt progress, see www.parliament.uk/briefing-papers/SN04049).

But this does raise questions about how DNA-profiling is actually practiced — and if Britain could be so dilatory concerning Prüm-related or European obligations, she could do something similar again. Other countries involved could do the same. Law is partly a matter of culture.

We have seen that the Prüm decision says it covers combating terrorism and cross-border crime, concepts which are open and evasive, and that masses of relatively simple property crimes are also included in Prüm. You have to add that DNA may be manipulated in various ways. The DNA may be substituted, or corrupted. And a common database may eventually come, so that you may succumb to information overload (see Töpfer's account summarised above).

After the terrorist act and with some information about possible terrorists already in hand, the Data Retention Directive, the PNR, Eurodac or Prüm may to some extent be useful, *but before the act, and without any additional and important information already in hand, they will be (close to) useless.*

I add here that the Norwegian daily, *Aftenposten* had an interesting account of information overload on 8 November 2012 (after the above text was first written). Mind you, *Aftenposten* is a liberal/conservative newspaper which is regarded as very solid, and which has large resources for research at its disposal. Under the major headline "A Tidal Wave of Data", the paper covered what I have called "information overload" *inter alia* as follows (my translation):

Our society drowns in enormous quantities of web-based, unstructured data. Ninety per cent of all data in the world is created during the past two years. Eighty per cent of all the data are unstructured, and contain all the GPS data and pictures for videos and sound. And this is only the beginning. In addition, the use of social media such as Twitter, Facebook, YouTube and a string of other social networks lead to incomprehensible information quantities being available... When we in addition apply smart phones, the data quantity explodes further. Next year the estimate is that half of the internet use occurs from places other than a computer. There are seven billion people on this globe. Four billion people have cell phones. Two-and-a-half billion have smart phones.

Aftenposten relates part of the story of the 22 July terror attack (more about this in *Chapter 5*), and goes on to inform the readers about what went wrong:

The police did not have the ability—or the will—to look at the data which were right in front of them on their own computers... The errors which came up front on 22 July are strikingly similar to the errors made in the US on 9/11 [emphasised by major-general and earlier intelligence director John M Custer elsewhere in the write up]. The police did not manage to put the pieces together, whether they were small traces from [the perpetrator's] chemical purchases or a tip about the car he used. The police had an old data and communication structure, and lacked the possibility of sending dynamic information, GPS data or other vital information, straight out to police cars. This is clearly a key to understanding what happened, says Custer. In the commercial market "big data" has released both panic and dreams of success.... [A]bility to collect, store, analyse and understand the enormous quantities of data which modern consumers leave behind, means the difference between success and failure.

The paper ends its write-up by referring to the successful use of data in Barack Obama's presidential campaign in 2012. The write-up perhaps to some extent blurs the distinction between ability/inability to control and use the enormous quantity of information that exists and increases, and the information overload as such. But this is realistic, because information overload increases by leaps and bounds so that agents and agencies—in our case the police — never permanently catch up and all the time become losers in a competitive race.

John Custer, mentioned above, has become adviser to the Norwegian police on how to handle large quantities of data — "big data", as it is called (see *Chapter 1*). A new fully automatic search engine now sifts through millions of pages of open sources on Facebook, Twitter, LinkedIn, blogs, pages containing debates and other open sources in the hope of finding traces. *The most difficult task, however, is to analyse everything which is found on the police's net search.*[46]

And, we might add, to do so when an unpredictable crisis is occurring. One thing is to sift, analyse, put together and find a pattern in large masses of data under normal and everyday occurrences. Quite another is doing it when a crisis is suddenly happening, or likely to happen.

Court Trials

We will end this section with some limited data that do not differentiate between terrorists after and before the terrorist act. We will ask: what do court trials tell us? Though the data do not tell us whether the terrorists stand trial for acts in the past or planned acts in the future (or both), what are the rates of convictions and acquittals?

Information on predicting terrorism is scant. This is partly due to the secretiveness of the secret police in various States. They tend to keep their mouths shut, especially if wrong predictions are many. Another way of putting this is to say that the *false positives* are many — many of those predicted to be terrorists, and who consequently stand trial therefore, are acquitted and by this criterion turn out not to be terrorists.

A rough indication of numbers predicted to be terrorists who turn out *not* to be terrorists may be found in the first Table on p. 39 in TE-SAT 2011 for 2010. It shows that in ten EU States, the overall conviction rate is 72.6%. The acquittal rate in the same States is consequently 27.4%, a minority, but a very substantial one. It shows that *close to 30% of those predicted to be terrorists with such certainty that they are brought to court for it, are in fact acquitted.* This would not have held water in any prediction table on dangerousness.

---

46. Source: *Aftenposten,* 11 November 2012.

TE-SAT 2012 for 2011 shows a similar picture. The table on p. 40 in TE-SAT 2012 for 2011 is clear. In 12 EU States, the overall conviction rate is 69.1%. The acquittal rate in the same States is consequently 30.1%, even slightly higher than for 2010. It is still a minority, but a very substantial one. *30% of those predicted to be terrorists with such certainly that they are brought to court for it, are in fact acquitted.*

The State in 2010 with the highest acquittal rate is Spain, with 38% acquittals (76 out of 198). The second highest is Italy with 27% (six out of 22), followed by the UK with 26% (five out of 19) and the Republic of Ireland with 17% (three out of 18). Spain contributes considerably to the high total acquittal rate in 2010, but if we subtract Spain with its unusually high rate, we end up with an overall acquittal rate of 11.2% (15 out of 134), which still is quite high (especially in view of the fact that five States — Denmark, France, Germany, Sweden and The Netherlands — had no acquittals).

With some variations we find the same picture for 2011: Spain has 42% acquittals (98 out of 235 verdicts); Italy, however, has no acquittals (and this year only four verdicts); but with the UK we are back to order with 33% acquittals (four out of 12 verdicts) and the Republic of Ireland with 11% acquittals (one out of nine, figures actually too small for percentages). If we once more subtract Spain with its unusually high acquittal rate, we end up with an overall acquittal rate for the remaining eleven States of 8.2% (nine out of 111), which still is high especially in view of the fact that Belgium, Germany, Demark, Italy and The Netherlands had no acquittals. The concentration of acquittals outside of Spain is to be found in Sweden (100 %, two cases), Greece (33%, one case out of three), the UK (33%, four cases out of 12), Ireland (11%, one case out of nine), and France (2%, one case out of 46), altogether 12.8%.

The proportion of acquittals gives at least a rough estimate of how correct predictions of terrorism are in the various EU States. The overall picture is that predictions measured this way are fairly incorrect.

Civil Liberties and the Rule of Law

But the various surveillance systems may be "good" at one thing: While close to being unable, through the growth of surveillance and the *Lex Vigilatoria*, to find terrorists before the act, the systems are able to threaten civil liberties and the Rule of Law for many.

We return once again to TE-SAT 2011 for 2010. The percentages of what I have called *false positives*—the number of people who are predicted to be terrorists but who in fact are not—is high, though some countries have no acquittals and thus contribute to lowering the total figure. Close to 30% acquittals when Spain is included is an extremely high acquittal rate also from the point of view of the Rule of Law. With an overall of 11-12% acquittals when Spain is excluded is also high. A similar picture emanates from TE-SAT 2012 for 2011. If they had not been charged and consequently acquitted, the acquitted would have gone through their lives with the stigma "terrorist" added to their record. This would in turn have barred their access to many rights upheld in civil society and to many of the standard norms and rules which we, altogether, call "the Rule of Law". This is like those prisoners in Guantánamo Bay, who have gone through long years of imprisonment without a regular trial, and which, if trials had been held, might have been acquitted and thus have obliterated or at least weakened the stigma of "terrorist" on their foreheads.

At the same time, we know that many people are in fact convicted without being guilty or without being no more than partly guilty or probably guilty. We know this on the basis of the evidence established by the surveillance systems, which we cannot trust as definite, but which in many instances is based on possibilities or probabilities. DNA proofs may be corrupted, the contents of the Data Retention Directive may be doubtful—was it inside or outside the particular location of the murder? And so on.

What Should be Done?

A final question. Where does this lead our thinking as to methods which should be used against terrorists? Firstly, at least in the Western world there are few terrorists, and terrorism is a relatively small threat, as compared with say reckless drivers causing damage and lost lives. Relatively hard data are presented on such comparisons elsewhere (Hammerlin 2009).

Secondly, what we should do to protect ourselves against the relatively few terrorists, is definitely not to develop further the *Lex Vigilatoria* of European countries (or for that matter the USA)—an increasingly integrated surveillance system with diluted ties to the nation state, a world of its own "above" the State. Such a surveillance system inevitably loses its grip on knowledge of the practical and the concrete, it loses its touch with the happenings of the real world. The only practical thing to do is to stay *in* the world, engaging in concrete police investigation and police work.

This does not mean that we should develop a "police state". But it does mean that we should have equipment ready to act fast and with precision when needs be to the sites that are necessary, and equipment that equals the equipment that we know terrorists normally have available. Ordinary, painstaking police work—see the Norwegian experience related earlier—is what may give results.

Above all, however, we should defend ourselves by relying on *the basic values of our society*. Although the USA did so after 9/11, we should *not* build on revenge, harsh retaliations and weapons in the struggle against terrorism. We should defend ourselves with solidarity, democracy and compassion—and constant vigilance concerning debate on these values.

We should enter debates wherever we can—among those who work in kindergartens, among those who are students in our schools, colleges, universities, Facebook, Twitter, our numerous civil organizations and in similar public arenas. We should constantly meet extremism with discussion. The State and the various municipalities in our countries should plan for such discussion by giving moral support to it and by allotting money to it—despite present-day economic problems. This concerns thinking about and plans regarding extremism. Actual attacks have of course to be met by legal measures. But the legal measures should always be guided by humanism and proportionality. In our despair and sorrow we should not rush to harder sanctions, longer sentences, death penalties. To remain within standards of humanism and proportionality are also basic values in Western societies, even if they are sometimes disregarded. To show that they are held high even in times of crisis is a value in itself, and is, I believe, a strong antidote to extremism when coupled with determination and relied on in the context of other liberal values, or as part and parcel of these liberal values.

These are values which the terrorists want to break down. Our best defence is to build these values stronger, not weaker. We do this by discussion. If we manage that, we have won.

In this section I have talked about methods with which to stop terrorism. I have sometimes used the word extremism. A final word: Is extremism an increasing phenomenon in Western societies?

It seems that it is. Critical economic conditions characterise several large and small European countries—like Greece, Hungary, Spain and others. It also characterises the USA. The OECD provides figures for Europe indicating increased differences between people, generations and regions of Europe. Every fourth Spaniard and every fifth Greek is out of work, and in a long string of European countries the unemployment rate is between ten and 20 per cent. Probably as a consequence of these and related conditions, hateful and intolerant expressions and attitudes are becoming common *inter alia* on social media. It reminds a little of the conditions in the 1930s. Torgeir Larsen, Secretary of State in the Norwegian Foreign Department (next in political command, below the Minister), has this to say about right-wing extremism:

> The combination of a short democratic history, social crisis and increasing differences provides fertile soil for anti-democratic forces. The pressure on minorities increases, the chase for scapegoats is stepped up and Europe's right-wing extremist movements is strengthened.

At the time of writing, Muslim extremism is also portrayed in Norwegian newspapers. The emphasis is on very small groups, but groups which may get a broader sounding board if integration remains a problem. These are signs showing the vital importance of such discussions of central democratic values.

More about this in the final chapter, which is an "Epilogue" written after a draft of this book was finished.

CHAPTER 5

EPILOGUE: THE BOMB AND THE MASSACRE

Methodological note: This chapter on the Norwegian case of terrorism is not primarily based on primary sources, but mostly on secondary sources—especially newspapers. Papers widely considered reputable, informative and with a national coverage are mainly chosen as sources. The reason why I have based myself primarily on secondary sources such as newspapers, and largely have not waited for the primary sources to become public, is that I have wanted to give a reasonably correct presentation of the events right after or on the days when they occurred—a kind of diary as life goes on. Relying on primary sources would take vastly more time; so much time that a reasonably correct presentation of the events right after or on the days they occurred, would have been impossible. That, I think, would have been a loss.

But I have in some places used primary sources, partly to corroborate statements based on secondary sources. In particular, the so-called "22 July Commission", NOU 2012: 14 (which was appointed by the Government on 12 August 2011 and delivered its report on 13 August 2012) has been important, and called upon in some places. I should perhaps mention specifically that our Prime Minister, who became popular during the first days of the events for his speeches, values and political perspectives, and who made a deep impression on large segments of the population, was a year afterwards, together with his Cabinet, severely criticised by the 22 July Commission Report, and asked by some newspapers to leave office. The criticism was based on the many errors made by high and low ranking civil servants, for which the Prime Minister is ultimately responsible, in addition to being ultimately responsible for the police.

But I should also mention that his initial popularity survived, at least during the early phase of the aftermath: During the days immediately following the publication of the 22 July Commission Report, 61 per cent of a nationwide sample had an increased or unchanged confidence in him, whereas only 32 per cent had a lowered confidence (the rest, seven per cent, did not know). Sixty-nine per cent thought he should remain in office, whereas only 19 per cent thought he should leave office (12 per cent did not know). Other opinion polls had similar results. But the police received wide-ranging and devastating criticism.

It should perhaps also be mentioned that as I write these words, in December 2012 and one-and-a-half-years after the terrorist onslaught, the Prime Minister, so popular after the event, has lost political confidence partly due to several mishaps unrelated to the terrorist event. Gallup polls suggest that he may lose the national elections in the autumn of 2013.

It was 15.05 pm Norwegian time. I left my office to run out on a quick errand two blocks away. Having done my errand in the store, I walked back towards the university building where my office is located. But instead of walking into the office, I went into a coffee shop to get a quick cup of coffee on the way. It must have been 15.25 pm, and it was Friday 22 July 2011.

As I was waiting in line for the coffee, at 15.26 pm, I heard an enormous blast. It struck me that the windows in the coffee shop could break. But they didn't. I thought, as I heard the blast, that it must have been a big accident. At the same time I said to someone else in the line, as a kind of a joke, that I was old enough to have experienced World War II. Strange that I *thought* it was an accident, but *said* to someone else that I had experienced the war.

I got the coffee. A young man sitting besides me was looking at a particular picture on a laptop which he had just opened. It was a still picture of the main Government building, 17 stories high, very close by. There was litter, broken glass, blood and, it seemed to me, wounded or dead people all around. It struck me that this was serious. Then I heard sirens, from police cars and ambulances. A serious accident?

The Bomb

I hurried away from the coffee shop and into my university building. There was nobody there, except two or three people on the top floor. They later told me that the building had swayed. I heard more sirens, and decided to leave my office to run for a tram or a taxi. But I stopped when the phone rang.

It was my stepson, a journalist. He was wondering whether I was alive. He was very excited. Later I understood why. The newspaper building where he worked had been hit. Windows had been smashed. When he called, he had just come back to town from Utøya, a small island on a lake outside of town where young Social Democrats were holding their traditional summer camp.

Every summer for years young Social Democrats from the Labour Party had held their political summer camp there. Several different parties regularly organized summer camps, but this camp was especially well known. He had been on the island to cover a speech by a quite well-known senior Social Democrat, an elderly woman, the "mother" of the Labour Party. A man had arrived on the island, probably with the intention of meeting up with the woman—but something had postponed his arrival, we don't know what (the traffic?) and she and my stepson had both left the camp when he arrived. I later understood that this had probably saved their lives.

There were no trams, no taxis. The streets were quite empty. By now I understood that a bomb had been detonated outside the central Government building and those around, and caused great damage and death. The police had had no inkling of the perpetrator beforehand, except for pictures provided by film strips from the local video surveillance alongside the Government complex, taken seconds before the explosion.

I had to walk home. I got there, which was not far, I called my family to see if they were all right, and reached the bus to Gardermoen, the main airport, to meet up with my son and grandson who were coming to Oslo from the West Coast.

The airport buses were in other words operating, but no trains, no trams (later it appeared that trams were running, but there must have been few). On the bus I heard the news. An enormous bomb had been detonated near the main Government building, and also other buildings, tearing buildings to pieces and killing many people. It turned out to be eight, in addition to many wounded. This was serious.

If I hadn't gone into the coffee shop, but for example to a bank which I often use and that was located in a building nearby, I might have been killed. Part of the building where the bank was located was hit by the blast.

Coming back from the airport on the bus with my son and grandson, I heard from a lady sitting next to me that a man, dressed as a policeman, had begun shooting young people at *Utøya*, the island where many young people had their summer camp. Ten youngsters, the lady said, had so far been shot at *Utøya*. She had heard it on the radio. The youngsters on the island, some of them down to 15-years-of-age, had used their mobile phones and in despair called their parents. Several had been shot while doing so.

As I have said, this was where the yearly traditional summer camp for Social Democratic youth — members of the Labour Party's youth organization — was being held. It turned out that it was done by the same man who had detonated the bomb down town. It was well-planned, he had set the time for the detonation in town in advance, and driven a second car to the island.

In the early evening the Prime Minister appeared on television. He did so together with the Minister of Justice. The Minister of Justice informed us that the terrorist was *a Norwegian*. "It has been confirmed that he is a Norwegian", were his words. Later he also gave the man's name, a distinctly Norwegian name, 32-years-old, born and raised in Oslo. I felt a strange sense of relief. He was not a Muslim. Later several people told me that they had felt the same kind of relief. Was it better to be killed by a Norwegian?[1]

The Prime Minister's talk was short, but it struck me that it was extremely important. It struck me then, and it would be reinforced during the following days, that it was very different from USA president George W Bush's first words after the terrorist attack on 9/11. Bush's first words gave a clear impression of hate, and of revenge as something he and the USA intensely wanted. A short while afterwards the bombing of Afghanistan began, and that war is not over yet. Norwegian Prime Minister, Jens Stoltenberg's talk on the evening of 22 July 2011 contained words and had a tone of voice which indicated grief, but also solidarity and democracy. Of course, he said that "we are all shaken by what hit us so brutally and suddenly". He expressed mourning the dead with their relatives. But only four lines into his talk he said: "I have a message to the one who attacked us, and to those who are

---

1. Muslims are still considered the main threat for Norway. In her yearly speech on the threat level for 2012, at 20 January 2012, the then head of the Norwegian Secret Service maintained that the major threat for the country comes from extreme Islamism. On the day of the talk the Norwegian Secret Service started investigating the placement of a threat-video, threatening Norwegian top politicians, on YouTube. A demonstration, permitted by the police, also took place on 20 January 2012. According to an estimation there are few extremist Muslims — about 100 persons — in Norway (see also the Te-Sat report from Europol).

behind this. The message is from all of Norway: You will not manage to ruin us, our democracy. We are a small but proud nation. No one will be able to bomb us to silence, no one will shoot us to silence." A bit later he continued: "… The reply to violence is more democracy, more openness, but not naïveté. We owe that to the victims".

The words "more democracy, more openness" were key words in this first talk on the very evening of the attack. The Prime Minister repeated them forcefully several time that summer. They summarised the values he wanted to convey; he wanted more democracy, not less, more openness, not less. By acting so quickly in emphasising this line of thinking, and not the opposite as a basis of defence, he made a deep impression on large segments of the population.

The Massacre

The next morning we were up early, and heard that around 85 youths had been killed on the island. This was later toned down to 68. The killer had left the city in one of two hired cars, and had been walking all over the island, shooting everyone he saw, in tents, outside tents, in buildings, on cliffs, in the forests. There were few places to hide. He had been dressed in a police uniform, which in the beginning had created confusion. The opening of the massacre is of some interest. It shows how it takes both coolness and ability to plan and to act convincingly on the spur of the moment, if you are to get away with it. *Aftenposten*, Norway's largest daily newspaper, reports a witness during the trial which followed much later (the skipper on the ferry to the island, *Aftenposten*, 4 May 2012):

> "It was a rainy day, I sat in the main house watching the news about the bomb in Oslo. I received a telephone call from a sailor with the message that we had to go over to the land side to fetch a policeman…" The skipper then tells his partner YY, called "Mother Utøya", to come along to the land side. She says hello to NN [the terrorist], and neither she nor the skipper become suspicious. [The terrorist was dressed as a policeman and had identified himself]. NN [the terrorist] fetches a big box which he says contains bomb-seeking material. The box was carried on board. "I didn't get any special impression of him, he was calm and determined. One of us asked him to cover up the weapons, he fetched a plastic bag without

protesting. He was tense and had a somewhat stiff expression, and was drinking all the time from a drinking bag he had along. On the way from the land side to Utøya he and YY were standing talking with each other, it was for the most part a one-way dialogue. YY talked. He nodded…"

The 48-year-old skipper manoeuvres the ferry into the harbour and gets the heavy box up to the main house in a car. In the meanwhile ZZ comes along. ZZ, YY and the perpetrator walk to the main house. "As I was rounding the corner of the house. I saw or heard shots. I don't know whether he shot ZZ or YY first. I thought it was an exercise, but then I would have known about it…" After a while he got a report to the effect that his daughter was safe on the island. [but his partner, YY, was killed]. After the perpetrator had been detained, the skipper took part in the extensive rescue-action, all the time until four in the morning.

People on the island, youngsters down to 15-years-old and older people, were shocked, dismayed and scared for their lives. They had reason to be. Some performed heroic acts, such as trying to stop the man and help younger friends. Some tried to hide in the bushes, others in cliffs in mountainous terrain near the shore and still others tried to swim away in the water (which was icy cold, though it was July). Some drowned. Some people vacationing on shore had boats and resolutely went out to rescue youngsters, some filled their boats to the brim until they apparently had to leave people behind in order to prevent their boats from sinking. All the while the man was shooting incessantly. He had plenty of ammunition. Several times the man called the police, allegedly wanting to surrender (during the later trial, the police argued that there had been fewer calls). He was not able to, the lines were busy. In any case, he continued shooting.

On TV, the Minister of Justice told us the same man had been observed in the centre of Oslo. The two attacks, the explosion and the massacre, were likely to have been committed by the same man. This turned out to be the case. It also transpired that he was an extreme right-wing person, who had left a 1,500 page manifesto which he had written and placed on the Internet for everyone to read. Later on it was translated by others into several languages for further distribution. He wanted to clean Europe of Muslims, which would finally occur in 2083, and which made a revolution necessary.

The killing of as many young Social Democrats as possible was necessary as a first step towards this.

This is not the place for a detailed account of what happened as time went on. That belongs to another book. In brief: To repeat, the bomb in town went off at 15.25 pm, at 17.26 the local police registered for the first time shooting on the island, the killer was subsequently arrested on the island (without resistance) at between 18.32 and 18.34. At least 20 people were reportedly killed between 18.15 hours and that arrest. At 18.08, well before the arrest, the head man in the helicopter unit had received the message that for the time being there was no need for a helicopter.[2] The perpetrator was kept on the island during the night for interrogation (the police at that time thought there might be other terrorists on the island, but there were none—the perpetrator was alone); he was subsequently brought before a remand court, he was detained and isolated in a top security prison just outside Oslo. By 15 August 2011, he had been interrogated for a total of 50-60 hours by the police (by mid-October around 100 hours, by the middle of March 2012 over 200 hours). Apparently he was calm during interrogation and eager to give detailed information. He has wanted to express his views to the world.

Continued Emphasis on Values

But above all, late-July and early-August were characterised by a continued emphasis on what I would call deep-seated Norwegian values, already formulated, as I have said, by the Prime Minister on the very evening of the attack. Norwegian public opinion received the shocking news with sorrow and mourning. Not only the Prime Minister, but also other ministers, the Crown Prince, the Mayor of the capital city Oslo and many others very

---

2. The 22 July Commission wrote (p. 295): "At 18.08 hours the Head of the Helicopter Service called from his vacation abroad the Operation Center in Oslo to ask whether the police helicopter should be mobilised. *He received the information that this was not necessary, because a helicopter from the Defence was on its way*. He later informed the employees in the Helicopter Service by SMS at 19.06 hours that they were not mobilised, and that the Defence assisted…" The 22 July Commission summarised as follows (p. 296): "The commission is of the opinion that the police helicopter without doubt would have been a very relevant tool for the police on 22 July, and that it would have been natural to try to mobilise it immediately for observation and security." The police have one helicopter. Helicopters from other agencies were involved. p. 298: "Helicopter from the Defence was never mobilised in time to be relevant to early security of Oslo or as a part of a general increase in preparedness".

quickly made speeches stressing the need for solidarity, openness, democracy and compassion, even love. *The emphasis during the three first weeks or so was definitely not on revenge and tougher punishments, but on the values listed here.*

A particularly important point in time was a rally outside the Oslo City Hall on Monday 25 July (the attack had taken place on the afternoon of the preceding Friday; other rallies were held in other cities and towns). Nearly 200,000 people were estimated to be present, showing their sympathy and respect for those in grief and sorrow. Everywhere fresh roses could be seen, especially outside Oslo Cathedral and in the streets nearby. The Prime Minister, a Social Democrat in a Coalition Government with two other parties, had shown extraordinary leadership from the first minute in emphasising these and related values. In front of Oslo City Hall he repeated several times some of his key words from the evening of 22 July (the Prime Minister made some 50 speeches after the terror occurred[3]):

> Thousands and thousands of Norwegians, in Oslo and all over the country, are doing the same thing this evening. Conquer the streets, the market places — public space with the same stubborn message: We are broken-hearted, but we don't give up. With torches and roses we give the world this message: We do not let fear break us down. And we do not let the fear silence us. The ocean of people I see in front of me today, and the warmth I feel from people all over the country, makes me certain. Norway passes the test. Evil can kill a person, but never conquer a people. This evening the Norwegian people write history. With the strongest of all the world's weapons, the free word and democracy, we line up the direction for Norway after 22 July 2011…More openness, more democracy, determination and strength. This is us. That is Norway. We will take safety back…Show compassion…Out of all the evil we paradoxically sense the dawning of something valuable. What we see tonight may be the biggest and the most important march which the Norwegian people have started out on since World War II. A march for democracy, solidarity and tolerance…Every one of us can do the weaving of democracy a little stronger. We see that here…To the young people I have this to

---

3. Source: Language researcher Sylvest Lomheim, earlier head of the Norwegian Language Council, in *Aftenposten,* 28 September 2011. Lomheim also made the interesting point that the Prime Minister did not just send out a speech electronically. Why? "The answer is that this is not good enough. Physical presence was necessary".

say…Engage yourself. Bother. Enter an organization. Participate in debates. Use the right to vote. Free elections are the jewel in democracy's crown. By participating you say a resounding *yes* to democracy.

Revenge was not mentioned or alluded to, not one word. Tougher prison sentences were not mentioned, not one word. War was not mentioned, not one word. Just the words I have mentioned. The King, the Crown Prince and many others used similar words. The Crown Prince turned out to be an excellent speaker. He even added the word "love":

This evening the streets are filled with love. We have chosen to answer evil with nearness. We have chosen to meet hatred with solidarity. We have chosen to show what we stand for. Norway is a country in grief…We will meet every day, armed to struggle for the free and open society we are so fond of…This evening the streets are filled with love…We want a Norway where we live together united and with freedom to think and express ourselves, where we see differences as possibilities, where freedom is stronger than fear. Tonight the streets are filled with love…

The Mayor of Oslo, a Conservative, closed his speech with the following words:

…After the tragedy we have in fact become the warm, generous society we have dreamt about. This warmth and the generosity will, in respect for the victims, bring with us far into the future.

(Applause)

Together we will punish the murderer. Our punishment will be more generosity, more tolerance, more democracy.

(Applause)

The various authorities and the crowds of people did not simply pay lip-service to these symbolic sentences and words.

How did it come about?

The largest rally in Norway' capital city since the end of World War II? Wollebæk *et al* (2011) give us an explanation. The traditional media were important. Voluntary organizations and simply the word-of-mouth were important. But 200,000 in two days? Above all, Facebook was important. "Social media", in so far as they are in fact "social" and not just targets for commerce by capital, are inexpensive and accessible, they are wide-ranging, they are based on networks, and the networks are combined with other networks. In the study, Facebook, Twitter and blogs were compared. The study showed that Facebook was the most important compared with Twitter and blogs when seen in relation to various activities (p. 33). Facebook was especially important among the very large number of Facebookers who used it when it came to finding information about arrangements and events and expressing support to victims and relatives (26%). This is directly relevant for their ability to mobilise for such activities. Twitter is used far less in Norway — only 15% of the sample of Internet users replied that they used Twitter more than once a week. But Twitter was important when it came to obtaining and bringing about news about what was happening. Thirty per cent of the relatively few who used Twitter, used it for obtaining or bringing about news. Among those who used blogs, few used them for such activities — the highest was 4% who used blogs for obtaining or bringing about information about the events.

Notably, the use of social media, especially Facebook, does not come automatically. It presupposes receptivity for the particular message in the population. Facebook was easy to use and met a highly receptive audience. A message containing the news that a Muslim had detonated a bomb in Oslo and killed 69 young people on an island would have been quite a different message, eliciting quite different connotations and probably fewer or even far fewer people (as well as different talks and symbols used by politicians).

During the following weeks, a few individuals published articles emphasising that the punishment level would have to be raised, or at least debated, not for the present terrorist, because new punishments could not be used after the act, but for future terrorists.

But those who voiced such views were very few, and though there may have been more hateful opinions hidden from the public eye, there was, notably, no "moral panic", at least up to this point. Tendencies in this direction drowned, in a sense, in roses at market places and corners all over the city. And in other cities.[4]

A colleague said to me, "Today I am proud to be a Norwegian". Several authority figures asked for forgiveness for having thought that the person in question had to have been a Muslim before it was announced that he was in fact a regular Norwegian. Imagine that—asking for forgiveness not for acts, just for *thoughts*. Memorial meetings were held in churches, several in the main Muslim church where the Norwegian authorities were also present. In one Muslim church, where the first burial of a victim from the island took place, the sermon inside the church was held by a Norwegian bishop, and the burial outside was performed by a Muslim imam. The two left the church together, a fact which strongly symbolised the togetherness and solidarity which other authorities had talked about beforehand. Senior Norwegian politicians attended Muslim masses which brought the same message out to the world.

With the strong emphasis of the national leaders on basic values as a defence, and a population which was receptive to this emphasis, Norway up to this point actually emphasised an important alternative to surveillance and tougher sentences as responses to terrorist acts. The terrorist had wanted us to become less open, less democratic—more in fear. Norway's leading politicians and others had emphasised, entirely to the contrary, more openness, more democracy. A "22 July Commission" had been appointed in 2011 which finalised its report in a year (in August 2012). Relatives of victims, and especially their lawyers, were critical because they wanted answers earlier. Nonetheless, the new way of thinking was very important.

The longer it goes on, the better the prognosis is for a civilised reaction even to terror and mass murder, and by that token a continuation of a civilised criminal policy. The values implied that *a man like this, and a threat like this, should be met by maintaining values*, not by weakening or changing

---

4. As also mentioned in another footnote, a life sentence today has a maximum of 21 years, a crime against humanity has 30 years, and preventive detention has 21 years but may be prolonged. In addition, the perpetrator may be found insane at the time of the crime or at the time of observation, and subject to impunity and compulsory psychiatric care. At a much later point in the terrorist case, this suddenly became a very relevant option.

values. Fear would imply that the man had achieved his goal and won. An insistence on upholding our most central values would imply that we, and our society, had won.

An Interlude on Confidence

The results from a Norwegian public opinion poll carried out towards the end of August 2011 — a little over a month after 22 July — may be seen as following the line of the Prime Minister's important speeches on the 22 and the 25 of July. Three questions were asked. The same questions were asked in 2006, after the terrorist attacks in London and Madrid. The proportion who thought the authorities should have had the right to listen in on people's telephone conversations had gone *down* with 18 per cent; the proportion who thought the authorities may stop and search people by chance on the street had gone *down* with 14 per cent; the proportion who thought the authorities should have had the right to keep people in preventive detention (remand) for as long as they wanted without their being brought to court, had gone down by three per cent. Remember that the Prime Minister's words were "the reply to violence is more democracy, more openness…" Later we shall see that other important authority figures used exactly the same or similar words.[5]

---

5. Source: *Aftenposten*, 22 September 2011. The study was carried out on behalf of four researchers at the Department of Administration and Organization Theory at the University of Bergen, Norway. Admittedly, there are several possible interpretations of the data. For example, to hold people on remand without a court order is unacceptable and illegal in Norway. On this basis Professor Tore Bjørgo at the Police College in Oslo thinks it is surprising that about half of the sample thought it would be all right to place a person on remand without a court order (even if the proportion holding this opinion had gone down slightly). Bjørgo believes that the data indicate Norwegians' willingness to drop plenty of legal security to avoid a terrorist act. On the other hand Magnus Ranstorp, researcher at the Swedish Defence College "and one of leading terrorist experts in the Nordic countries", supports the interpretation given by the Norwegian researchers. He thinks that the Norwegian people quickly managed to place terrorism in a societal context. "I see these figures as a reply to Stoltenberg's request for more openness and more democracy", he says.. "That this tone of voice was placed so quickly on the agenda is absolutely decisive for what the population focused on as a nation…". Though the Norwegian terrorist was a white Norwegian man, it is of some interest to note that 25% of the Norwegian population thinks there are too many Muslims in Norway, and that Islam is a threat to Norwegian culture (information from a national public opinion poll performed by Norstat for the Norwegian Broadcasting Company). In a TV interview the Prime Minister turned this around and said that three out of four, 75%, do not think there are too many Muslims. Confronted by the fact that 2/3rds of these did not think there were too many Muslims

Interestingly another study, on *confidence* in central social institutions and in foreigners, showed related and similar trends (Wollebæk *et al*, 2011). Two representative population samples (1,000 people, Internet users aged 16-79) were compared, one sample in March/April 2011 and the other a short time after the terrorist attack, in August 2011. In addition a panel study was carried out on people who used social media twice a week or more (a sample was asked questions in March/April, and again in August 2011). A number of studies have shown that the level of confidence between people is higher in Norway and the other Nordic countries than elsewhere in Europe. It may have to do with the degree of cultural and economic equality, the cultural heritage from Protestantism and a gradual democratisation based on peaceful mass mobilisation which has created a strong civil society. At any rate, during the last 15-20 years the development has been more varied in Western Europe, somewhat negative in Southern and Eastern Europe and quite negative in the USA (Wollebæk *et al*, 2011, p. 9). In their study comparing the degree of confidence in Norway before and after 22 July 2011, Wollebæk *et al* found a *much higher degree* of "generalised confidence" after the terrorist event than before. The increase has been clearest among grown-ups and middle-aged people, weaker among the eldest. There is the greatest confidence in people close to you — family and so on — the more abstract forms of confidence are somewhat weaker. But Wollebæk *et al* summarise as follows (p. 14-15):

> Anyway there are, comparatively speaking, very high values also on questions concerning whether one trusts other Norwegians, people of a different religion or nationality, or people one meets for the first time…Alongside increased confidence in other Norwegians, we find the strongest increase in the most demanding types of confidence, that is, confidence in people who are unlike ourselves even as far as central criteria goes, meaning nationality and religion.

> …In Norway confidence in other people is closely related to confidence in institutions…The first period after the terror attacks was characterised by a great degree of collectivism round the upper echelons of the political leadership, which has received much praise for the handling of a collective behaviour during the

and 1/3rd did not know, the Prime Minister answered that the latter group, the 1/3rd who did not know, at least did not mention that there were too many (TV1, 26 October 2011).

crisis. This has probably been very important for the positive findings concerning confidence between people which are reported above.

Those were the initial reactions, less than a month after the event. We will return to long-term trends later, towards the end of this chapter.[6]

Increasing Criticism

But it must be admitted that as time went on, and probably as an addition to the emphasis on openness and democracy (see what happened at the trial almost a year later which will be described in due course), increasing criticism of the police for lack of preparedness and slowness of action began. Formally, the Minister of Justice is responsible for the actions of the police and related agencies. He was fiercely criticised by other politicians, by the media and by so-called "assistance lawyers", lawyers who in a general way provide assistance and support to relatives of victims and others. The Minister of Justice defended himself: The State budget for 2012 was made official on 6 October 2011. The headlines of the first press release on the budget were "Over 2 billion more to safety and preparedness". The press release said that

---

6. The 22 July Commission criticised severely that a particular street, called *Grubbegata*, was open for traffic on 22 July, so that the perpetrator could drive his car with the bomb all the way to the main entrance of the Government Building. If the particular street had been closed, the bomb attack would easily have been avoided. There had been a discussion for years, *inter alia* between the municipality and the State, on whether or not to close the street in question. Security reasons counted for, the principle of an open society and traffic considerations counted against. The 22 July Commission said on p. 433-424: "To close a street permanently presupposes a regulation of the area. The individual municipality has the authority of regulation. However, where societal considerations say so, the State can decide on a regulation plan…There is lack of tradition for using a State regulation plan, and the State chose — apparently without discussing the question — to close the street through a municipal plan". This was under continual discussion, but never happened. On p. 443 the 22 July Commission noted: "By way of summary it is the Commission's view that a lack of understanding of vulnerability and risk, an exaggerated secrecy, and an increasing pulverisation of responsibility with exaggerated respect for constitutional responsibility were causes behind the scenes [*bakenforliggende årsaker*] for making it possible to park a car with a bomb outside the Government Building on 22 July." During the public debate after the 22 July Commission had published its report, it was maintained that if the street had been closed, the perpetrator could have taken his bomb, e.g. to the Parliament Building, which was very accessible and with many people, or the Palace.

The Government continues its work to create more safety and less crime and proposes to increase the budget to the Police and the Prosecution with 696 million crowns in 2012. "At the same time we will increase the appropriations to a [digital] emergency Net with 1.5 billion crowns. It will be one of the greatest backings of societal security ever in Norway", says Minister of Justice Knut Storberget.

Some argued that the terrorist had his supporters on the Internet, and that the perpetrator was certainly not alone in terms of values or points of view, though this of course did not meet the argument that he had *acted* as a loner. Though the man had emphasised connections with several terrorist cells, the police became increasingly certain that he had been (capable of) acting alone—as a lone wolf. This was reiterated and expanded on under banner headlines in early January 2012,[7] and during the trial in May/June of the same year.

In the end, and following a significant speech to Parliament on the criticism, the Minister of Justice in fact had to (chose to?) go.

Despite the terrorist apparently acting alone, rather wild rumours circulated as early as right after the explosion down town, 22 July. The Oslo Police log shows that during the first 20 minutes, the police received warnings of eleven false bombs in town. Four of the eleven warnings came from the police patrols themselves. Also during the first half hour false messages continued to stream in. Twelve suspicious messages concerning suitcases and cars were checked for bombs during the evening. At 20.36 (according to the 22 July Commission, the time was 21.20 hours) even the church spire of the Cathedral was reported as possibly containing bombs.[8] One very important message, from a reliable witness, drowned in the confusion. The witness had seen a man at 15.35, ten minutes after the explosion, run away from the scene of the crime in a uniform and a helmet with a gun in his hand. The

---

7. Source: *Aftenposten* 2 January 2012. Based on statements by the police, the psychiatric experts and the defence lawyer.
8. The 22 July Commission wrote, on p. 295: "Once he became aware of the fact that the police helicopter was not mobilised, the Head of the special section ordered the fastest possible manning of the police helicopter, despite the vacation. This took place at 19.09 hours...The helicopter took off from Gardermoen [airport] at 21.06 hours, and was in the air over Oslo at 21.18 hours... *The first task was to help investigate a suspicious object in the spire of Oslo Cathedral, at 21.20 hours*" (My italics).

witness became so suspicious that he jotted down the number of the runaway car, which turned out to be the car which the man used for driving to the summer camp on the island. The police did not have its tips log ready before almost half an hour at passed. At that time the witness was called again. At 16.09, three-quarters-of-an-hour after the explosion, this important information was brought on to other police districts. At 16.43, about an-hour-and-a-quarter after the explosion, the car was searched for nationwide. At this time the man they were looking for was already on the island.[9]

Many Other Questions

The questions were many, and increasingly debated publicly. Why did the police arrive so late, and by a detour to the island? Why didn't the police use a helicopter to get more speedily to the island? Several somewhat confusing answers to the latter question were given — among other things the police helicopter was located on a military airport rather far away, and it would take time to make it ready. And why did heavily armed policemen finally take off in a small rubber police boat (and had to have help from

---

9.   Source: *Aftenposten*, 2 February 2012. The 22 July Commission corroborated this on p.86: "At 15.35 hours [ten minutes after the blast] a witness reported to have seen a person in a police uniform with helmet and pistol, who had driven along in a car with registration number ****. The police did not manage to make use of these pieces of information." The Commission continued by referring to more detailed information on pp. 98-104: "…Among these [messages] was the observation of a uniformed and armed person who shortly before the explosion had driven away from the area in a car marked ****. "The message was phoned to the emergency telephone of the police at 15.35 hours and was received by a telephonist at the switchboard of the Police District. The observed person turned out to be [the perpetrator] on his way away from the area after having parked the bomb car in the government block. From the place where the witness' observation was made, [the perpetrator] drove without interference via Sandvika to the mainland side of [the island], where he arrived at about 16.26 hours…". The Commission continued: "To ensure that the information was promptly delivered, the telephonist wrote a short message on a piece of paper and left it on the desk of the Operation Head…She saw that the Operation Head was busy, but established eye contact and said to her that she thought the piece of paper was important…at 15.56 hours an operator called back…The operator had by coincidence become aware of the piece of pape…and understood the content to be very important…". After a detailed description of various delays (it was among other things impossible to come through on the communication net) the following is made explicit in the 22 July Commission's report (p. 102): "Not before over two hours after the information had been telephoned and shooting on [the island] had started, the Operation Centre in Oslo reported the description of a possible perpetrator to all units. It was about 17.47 hours"—two hours and 20 minutes after the bomb had exploded.

larger and faster private boats on the way)? In a photo with a large vessel behind as a contrast to the tiny red police boat made of rubber, the police certainly looked helpless.[10]

No Knowledge Beforehand?

And above all, why did the Secret Police have no knowledge of this man beforehand? This question goes to the heart of the matter, and to the core of this book. The question probably became the most hotly debated point in the early and late autumn of 2011.

Remember how Europol points to lone terrorists or "lone wolves" as extremely hard to catch before the act (*Chapter 3* of this book). Remember what the Head of the Norwegian Secret Police had said on television and in the newspapers right after the Norwegian event (see earlier): This man had been totally law abiding for many years, his various anti-Islamist statements on the Internet had not been worse than statements made by many others, the only thing the police had "registered" him for was a transaction with a person in Poland worth 121 krona concerning some chemicals which were legal. He had gone "under the radar".

---

10. Source: *Aftenposten,* 4 January 2012. Several factors where behind the late arrival of the police boat on the island. The 22 July Commission corroborates the story described in the text in the following words (pp. 138-140): "When the boat was to be reversed out from the [place where people and equipment was loaded] there were eleven men with their equipment, two shields and a pile driver on board…The boatman quickly understood that the boat was too heavily loaded. He again turned around toward the quay to let some people off, but was given the message to continue the advance. The boat was, however, only 17 feet long, registered for five people…leading to the advance of the police at 18.21 hours being slow. The engine did not respond as normal [Eventually it stopped]. A short while afterwards the officers discovered another civilian boat with a course towards Storøya [another island]. Four officers went into this boat with their equipment, and the advance continued with two boats. The last mentioned boat was fastest and landed on the island at 18.27 hours. Boat number two — which later performed the arrest — arrived at the island one minute later". Under a photo on p. 138 the 22 July Commission said: "The boat left Storøya [another island] at about 18.15 hours. The boat was overloaded. The boat stopped at 18.19 hours. Boat H came to its rescue. At 18.21 hours the advance continued with slow speed in this boat. After a short while also Boat C came, and the action increased after four men transferred to it. All the points in time are the estimate of the Commission." *I add*: Boats H and C were civilian boats. The original police boat was, as I have said in the text, made of rubber. A needle would have made it sink and all (originally eleven men) would most probably have drowned due to the heavy equipment.

Theoretically it had probably been possible to single out the man before-hand, but it would have been extremely difficult. He had left behind very few traces. Two traces of him are perhaps important.

Firstly, the international anti-terror operation Global Shield, which was in operation for a while, was co-operating internationally on anti-terror at the time of the events. Global Shield was supposed to detect people who dealt in bomb-material. The Norwegian authorities received lists of currency transactions from Global Shield. The Norwegian terrorist's name was on one of the lists, for a small currency transaction. For a period of up to four months the Norwegian Secret Service has legal authority keep the information in order to evaluate whether it may be relevant to the service.[11] The list was apparently sent to the Norwegian Customs Authority. They reacted by sending it over to the Secret Police Section for counter-terrorism and organized crime. According to the head of the Secret Service, it was apparently received by a man who went on leave a few days later. He was gone until after 22 July. The head acknowledged that they had received a list containing names "in connection with a currency check from an international customs project". The list was apparently[12] not checked against registers of weapons.[13]

The list would never have come to the attention of the Norwegian Secret Police had not the Golden Shield anti-terror operation started.[14]

---

11. Instruction for the Police Secret Service § 15.
12. Instruction for the Police Secret Service § 15.
13. This above gives a very condensed description of the Golden Shield programme, and may contain errors. The 22 July Commission spent some 20 pages on it, and summarised as follows: "The Commission is of the opinion that the Secret Service should have undertaken a serious evaluation of the tips from December [2010] and made a decision as to whether it should be followed up. By using another work method and a wider focus the Service could have found considerably more information about the perpetrator. Whether the Service then also would have revealed his plans, is impossible to say. This would have demanded considerable aggressiveness, and to some extent challenged rules concerning professional secrecy of the Customs Directorate. In addition it would have presupposed that the Secret Service had given the case high priority, also relative to work with cases where the image of threat and the information already in hand says that the threat was concrete and pressing. *The Commission can, because of this, not ascertain that the Secret Service could or ought to have found the perpetrator*" (My italics). But the Commission described, over several pages, improvements which would lead to learning. *Aftenposten* maintained that the terrorist act could have been avoided if the police and the customs department had co-operated more closely.
14. The Secret Service Report, made known in *Aftenposten*, 15 March 2012.

Secondly, there were indications from which the police with great imagination and daring speculation could have surmised that something was possibly going to happen in the future. In March 2011, someone called the switchboard of the Government buildings — a switchboard which every day receives an extremely large number of calls, many normal and some over to degrees of threats directed to a broad range of people. The person talked about a manifesto and about shooting a person/shooting members of the Social Democratic youth organization. The caller also scolded the Government.[15] It led to no action, among all of the other calls that day. If the Data Retention Directive (see *Chapter 3*) had been operative, it would hardly have led to any further action.

But after the act? The terrorist's defence lawyer said on TV after 22 July 2011 that the call to the switchboard was important, because it could have been the terrorist himself or someone who knew the perpetrator's plans. The police had planned to interrogate the perpetrator about the information on 11 January 2012, well after the fact. However, the perpetrator by that time refused all interrogation because the police on their side refused him access to a laptop and printer. The police denied the promise, and the man's defence lawyer had acted as a go-between.[16] On 28 January interrogation opened up again. *Aftenposten* reported the defence lawyer to have said that the defendant had admitted the call, but could not remember the contents of it. The telephonist said she had received a call, probably on 11 March 2011, containing a threat as described, and had informed her superior, but the case had not been taken further. The defence lawyer criticised the police for leaving the case with the Ministry rather than taking it on themselves.[17]

You might refer to these two occurrences as "hints" that something out of the ordinary would happen some time in the future. The "hints" were

---

15. Source: The Norwegian Broadcasting Company (NRK) cited in *Aftenposten*, 7 January 2012.
16. Source: *Aftenposten*, 24 January 2012.
17. One other telephone call was just possibly of importance but extremely difficult to follow up. Over a year before the terrorist attacked the ministerial buildings and the Social Democratic youths at their summer camp, someone called the Ministry of Renewal, Administration and Church Affairs asking about membership registers in youth party organizations and funds going to such organizations. The person who had the call transferred, thought it was a journalist. The Ministry in question had no such information, and that was apparently the end of the conversation (Source: *Aftenposten*, 7 January 2012).

understandably not followed up and brought to action. We do not live in a police state.

Crime or Illness?

The Case for Insanity

Then, on 29 November 2011, came the news. Two experienced psychiatrists, appointed by the court, had gone through the case in detail. They had carefully written a 243 page report. They were in total agreement with each other. Their conclusion? At the time of writing, the report is classified information, but the conclusion is clear through the media: The man was suffering from *paranoid schizophrenia*. In plain Norwegian: He was insane, at the time of his criminal acts and during the observation. His insanity had developed over a long period — through his grandiose delusions, he had over time developed the illness. His insanity made him unaccountable for his criminal acts, and therefore subject to impunity.

It was made clear that a paranoid schizophrenic could well think logically, and plan intelligently, as this man had done. His rationality would, however, according to the psychiatrists, be within his framework of thinking, which presumably was entirely different from almost anyone else's framework in our society. For a long time he had lived in his own universe. He counted on becoming sovereign ruler (regent) of Norway. He viewed himself as a coming leader of Europe. He was the most perfect knight after World War II. According to him, the organization Knights Templar would take over power in Europe. The terrorist decided over life and death (he referred to the "executions" on the island). He wanted to establish a separate breeding centre (or separate centres; "*avlsprogram*") for Norwegians.

The reaction to the insanity conclusion was public shock. Apparently, few people had expected this, rational as this man had appeared to be. Notably within his universe of discourse.

During the days which followed, a number of different views were voiced, in the media and between people. If this conclusion later was upheld by the court, the man would be transferred to a hospital with a secure section. The general view was in the beginning a fear that he would be released again and walk the streets. Some relatives of victims said they trusted the system, and that their security would be upheld. Though I have not been able to make a count, it seems that many others were in doubt — should someone who had committed such terrible acts be sent to a hospital, and not to prison? Still others — journalists and academics — also had a variety of views. There was a great deal of bewilderment, after a while there was a strong public emphasis on the view that this man should be punished, and that even a long stay in a secure mental hospital ward was not "enough". The many words, about more democracy, more openness, compassion, seemed to be forgotten by many.

The Commission on Forensic Medicine, Section on Forensic Psychiatry, studied the report. The court makes the final decision about the report, and whether it will be followed, at the end of a trial. The experts do not serve as witnesses for the prosecution or the defence. They are appointed by the court, and are presumably only "objective" advisers to it. In reality they are important decision-makers, making decisions concerning the future fate of an offender. If the court turns the report down, which very rarely happens, a new committee of forensic psychiatric experts will be appointed. The Commission may also raise minor points which warrant additions to the report.

In this case, the report was upheld: The Section on Forensic Psychiatry took the stand that there was no error in the relationship between premises and conclusions. The section did not, as I understand it, take a stand on whether the premises as such were correct. The Commission on Forensic Medicine had no serious (*vesentlige*) complaints regarding the report. A massive debate immediately followed. It was pointed out that the Commission had in fact been in disagreement, but had finally landed on the common point of view mentioned here. Was it an agreement to defend the profession? We will probably never know. The bystanders in television — and newspaper debates were split in two:

Two views

On the one hand, you had those who wanted a *new experts' report,* so the court would have two reports — the first and the second report — to choose between. Presumably, this would give the court a broader basis for decision-making. Major newspapers, vocal assistance lawyers and others strongly advocated this. If the first report had concluded with accountability rather than *un*accountability, I do not think an argument for a broader basis of decision-making would have been launched.

On the other hand, it was argued that if a new report led to a different conclusion, that of accountability, it would not bring anything new, but only add doubt to the first conclusion, and "the benefit of the doubt" would be given to the perpetrator, which would mean that the conclusion of unaccountability would remain standing. This view seemed to be based on the old-fashioned notion that being unaccountable and sent to a mental hospital is a more humane conclusion than downright prison. A saying goes like this: It is better to place a sane man in a hospital than to place a sick man in prison. I don't think it necessarily holds for Norway today or in our recent past.[18] Somewhat later the Attorney-General, who had held this view, changed it in a public talk.[19]

Two committees

By mid-February 2012, there were 176 lawyers who operated as assistance lawyers for about 800 clients. Very vocal assistance lawyers wanted a new report, while the perpetrator and consequently his lawyers did not want to cooperate with a new team of experts. The Attorney-General as well as many others also wanted to have only the first report. It turned out that the two-report conclusion was in the minority among victims (the wounded) and afflicted relatives. The vocal assistance lawyers had admitted this, but not emphasised it, in my mind creating a wrong impression.

The court decides on such a question (which rarely is brought to the fore) and makes the choice between one report and an added second report. Beforehand representatives of the assistance lawyers and the prosecution and others negotiated and in this case found it difficult to come up with new experts who were unbiased, the reason being the incessant and bewildering debate. The two parties finally agreed on *three psychiatrists* whom they thought would be sufficiently unbiased. Beforehand Norwegian psychiatrists in general had been in total disagreement on the conclusion, but on

---

18. See Mathiesen 1965 for an analysis in the early-1960s of inmates' preferences between a medium security institution with several psychiatrists, social workers and so on, and a regular prison.
19. Source: *Aftenposten,* 10 February 2012.

balance they had mostly sided with sanity. In this bewildering situation the court decided on *two of the particular three psychiatrists* making up a new, second committee.

This way we see that the Attorney-General and even more so the court were most likely heavily influenced by pressure and public opinion in one of the greatest terrorist case in Europe or in the world to date. The Attorney-General, the defence lawyers and the assistance-of-victims-lawyers eagerly debated with each other, in public and long before the trial, matters which essentially belong to the realm of the court.

I have never experienced a case where the court has been so clearly in the "hands" of public opinion and influenced by that opinion in a major decision before the start of the trial.

Two appeals

As I have said, at first the defendant did not want to cooperate with any second committee. Since, traditionally, the psychiatrists' interviews with defendants are based on hand-written notes and not on videotapes, the second committee was unable to base itself on the first committee's interviews. This was important in as much as the defendant had maintained that 80% of the contents of the first interviews were false.[20]

On 18 January 2012 the defendant and his lawyers lodged an appeal to the Court of Appeals against the decision to establish a second committee, partly — as I understand it — on the grounds of an error in the mode of treatment of the case. The error was that the warden in the prison where the perpetrator was located had hired an experienced forensic psychiatrist as adviser. The forensic psychiatrist had written several reports to the warden concluding that the perpetrator was not psychotic or schizophrenic and consequently not unaccountable. She had sent copies of the reports on to the State's lawyers who in turn had sent them on to the court. The court had used the documents, which included privileged health information, as grounds for establishing the second committee.

The use of privileged health information presumably constituted an error in case processing. A few days later the defence lawyers sent an expanded

---

20. Source: *Dagsavisen*, 8 February 2012.

appeal to the Court of Appeals in order to prevent the appointment of the second committee.[21] The court could presumably not appoint a new committee unless the prosecution or the defence had asked for it. In turn, a major law firm in Oslo, which employed several lawyers acting as assistance lawyers for victims, sent a counter-appeal defending the appointment of a second committee. Again a purely legal question had gone public rather than remain within the realm of the court. The media themselves were probably to a considerable extent responsible for this, fishing, enlarging and popularising the conflict ("eminent lawyers against eminent lawyers"). But the lawyers themselves may also have been partly responsible. It goes to show how the case vacillated between sensational news and refined law—and perhaps back again.[22]

On 2 February the Court of Appeals turned down the defendant's appeal. "It is understandable that the Court in the light of the public debate…found it necessary to appoint new expert observers", the Court of Appeals stated. On 9 February the defence team resolutely appealed to the Supreme Court, but on 15 February that court also turned the new appeal down. The court handling the case had beforehand decided to have the defendant psychiatrically observed coercively (!) for several weeks, until the end of March. The plan was to confine the defendant to a psychiatric hospital with a secure unit, so that they could observe the man's interactions with others continuously. The final decision was to move the whole hospital unit with its health personnel to the top security prison where the defendant was staying. This had never been done before in Norwegian legal-psychiatric history.

For a time it was maintained that the trial would have to be postponed,[23] another clear example of how public pressure (through intervention of assistance lawyers) in a decisive fashion would have changed a decision (the timing) of the court. All of the decisions mentioned above were immediately made public in the newspapers and on TV.

The appeal to the Supreme Court having been turned down, the perpetrator changed tactics and decided after all to cooperate with the new committee and to talk with them, on the condition that the talks would

---

21. Source; *Aftenposten*, 21 January 2012.
22. The rest of the source material on this point somewhat unclear—*Aftenposten*, 21 January 2012.
23. Source: *Aftenposten*, 11 and 15 February 2012.

be taped,[24] so that a record might be documented and kept. His lawyers, after internal discussions and doubts, followed suit. The main reason for the turn-around on the part of the perpetrator was probably that as a sane person, which the new committee might perhaps conclude, the perpetrator would gain legitimacy in the wider community. But the decision to transfer a whole unit from a psychiatric hospital to the prison was upheld.[25] Observations in the unit began in late February/early March, and would not last longer than four weeks.

The upshot of it all, then, was that the perpetrator with his team of lawyers, and the assistance lawyers for the victims, *both* sided for a second committee. A second committee would increase the chances of a sanity conclusion. A sanity conclusion would imply just responsibility in the eyes of some or many of the victims (we do not really know how many) and political legitimacy in the eyes of the perpetrator.

On the other hand the Attorney-General with the prosecution sided for an insanity conclusion, but with the view that the prosecution might change its stand during the trial, depending on the information which would be brought forward then.

The sharing of views by perpetrator and victims (however different their premises were) and the Attorney-General's pleading for treatment rather than punishment (however hesitant that pleading was), are, to say the least, most unusual. They are diametrically opposed standard roles.

A Noisy Affair

Several others things happened which created new noise with regard to an already very noisy affair. The 22 July Commission met with central politicians, asking the latter questions about what happened that day in July. The Commission members found the answers unsatisfactory. The head of the Secret Service suddenly left office sensationally and without warning, on the grounds of an allegation of a breach of professional secrecy (she had reported to the 22 July Commission about Norwegian Secret Service activities in Pakistan). The police were admonished for not asking the military for help earlier during the crisis hours on 22 July. The police were also thinly

---

24. Same source.
25. Source: *Aftenposten*, 11 February 2012.

manned in the centre of town during the crisis hours, why was this? Someone had claimed they were threatened (by superiors) not to report on criticisms of people on stand-by duty during the crisis hours—was this documented? Apparently not. And so on. Maybe as a reply to the many questions from the Commission, and to improve the image of the Government's ability to react to crises, the newly appointed Minister of Justice said a little later[26] that she wanted to establish an around-the-clock "civilian situation centre" in the Ministry of Justice (the centre was opened in July 2012), furthermore *inter alia* improve security by having the Ministry take over the responsibility for the National Security Authorities (Norwegian abbreviation NSM; in English NSA).[27]

Criticism of the Police

Above we saw that strong criticism was launched against the police for their handling of the terror onslaught. Some assistance lawyers were particularly vehement. Not once during the first eight months did the police apologise for anything having gone wrong. But suddenly, on 15 March 2012, a major internal police report had a different tone. Perhaps there was a prediction involved to the effect that the independent 22 July Commission report, which would come in August (see the methodological note at the start of this chapter), would be quite critical. If so, the authors were right. It was a report from and on the general police, and had been held secret for three months. The police director at last apologised in a general way for what had happened. Although the apology was a bit vague, the self-criticism was clear. Several politicians were satisfied. "Wise", was one comment. The police force listed 54 points of improvement, and behind this list was a still longer list of concrete errors explaining why it took 74 minutes before the perpetrator was arrested on the island. One of several major causes why the police came so late to the island was, as I have said, that their small rubber boat became too heavy and was severely damaged on the way. There were also a number of other accidents and errors.[28]

---

26. On the 100th day of her appointment as Minister of Justice, *Aftenposten*, 11 February 2012.
27. Same source.
28. Source: *Afftenposten*, 15 March 2012.

A few days later the general police report was followed up by a report from a major national newspaper telling its readers that over 200 million police krona were not used, but saved by the police in 2011. For example, the Oslo police helicopter was not used in order to save money during the summer vacation. This was explained in various ways, partly as a consequence of paying for equipment in 2011 with cash as of 2012. The answers were not found satisfactory by politicians. "I can hardly believe this", said a central right-winger in Parliament. "This is something we are not happy with", said a high-ranking politician in the Ministry of Justice.[29]

The day after the official police report (16 March 2012) came a second official police report—the Secret Service Report. Also the head of the Secret Service apologised for what had happened on 22 July, and for the service being unable to protect the population against this case of terrorism. But this apology was more of a ritual than a reality, because according to the head nothing was done wrongly in the Secret Service. Neither was there much criticism to be heard from the journalists present.

In the close to 40 page paper it was also referred, more in passing, to sparse resources and "a culture of caution" in the Secret Service, due to earlier criticism.

Not one question from the staff or the many journalists present was spent on the strange telephone calls to the Government buildings before 22 July 2011. The Golden Shield programme, however, was scrutinised. We have looked at it before: Some 70 countries had participated in the programme. On a particular day an e-mail had been received from outside and had immediately been checked. It turned out not to be the perpetrator. His name had, however, been found on one of the other lists received, composed of 41 people including the perpetrator. He had dealt with explosives from Poland worth 121 Norwegian krona (about 20 USA dollars). All of the economic deals had been entirely legal. Various scenarios were discussed in the report. Even if registration had been intensified, the Secret Service maintained, it would not have been possible to find the man beforehand. For that the Secret Service would have needed concrete tips, which the service did not get.

The following statement was made towards the end of the written report:

---

29. Source: *Aftenposten,* 29 March 2012.

> On the basis of an ordinary mode of treatment of the case, there is nothing to go
> on ("*ingen holdepunkter for*") for the Secret Service, in view of the project Global
> Shield and the list which the Secret Service received from TAD[30] 3 December
> 2010, to have uncovered NN and thereby prevented the case of terror on the 22
> July. Neither is there anything realistic to go on for a substantial prioritisation
> of the mode of treatment in Global Shield to have uncovered NN and thereby
> prevented the case of terror on the 22 of July. [31]

Towards the end of the press conference the head made an important oral statement which again goes to the core of this book: After having emphasised that the perpetrator was an anti-Islamic "solo terrorist" (leaving few or no traces), he went on to say:

> We are unable to find [the perpetrator] through surveillance ("*overvåke oss selv til*
> *NN*"). I don't think surveillance is a road to walk for the future.[32]

The sensation this time was not the Secret Police, but the many flaws and serious mistakes made by the regular police force.

Politics or Illness?

The relationship between crime and illness has a long history in Norwegian criminology and the sociology of law (Aubert 1960; Christie 1962; Mathiesen 1965 and more). Here, the question is more the relationship between politics and illness. Why is this important? Because through history the notion of illness has so often been used to neutralise political opposition. The radical opposition advanced by many of us, advocating a liberal but changed democratic society, is an example. For this reason, it is important not to succumb to convenience when we choose between a political standpoint or a standpoint based on illness. It is important to have a principled outlook. Let us do so briefly.

---

30. *Toll-og Avgiftsdirektoratet*, or in English: Directorate of Customs and Excise.
31. For more information about Golden Shield, see earlier footnote and the 22 July Commission.
32. Source: The Secret Service press conference, 16 March 2012.

The Contextual View

Whether world views such as those of our Norwegian man are understood as symptoms of insanity or as examples of political opinion, depends on the context. In the case of the 9/11 terrorists, there were people in their surroundings who adhered to the same extreme beliefs, and certainly many people around who took a less extreme view of things but relied on the same general values. In the case of our Norwegian man we may say much of the same. There are certainly adherents of extreme right-wing views in the environment, on the Internet and elsewhere, though few would perhaps go so far as this particular man. If you view political beliefs, however extreme, as a rationalising sign of sanity, a sign of a choice of means to reach given ends, you end with the conclusion that the 9/11 terrorists *as well as* our Norwegian man are sane and accountable for their acts (even if the political beliefs in the two cases would be utterly reprehensible to us).

There are right-wing extremist Norwegians around. Though alone in the sense of committing his acts alone, the existence of similar views around has been testified to through searches on the Internet and other sources (Bjørgo, 2011). The documentation seems solid. It is also documented by *Aftenposten* which has had access to a part of the first psychiatric report, that the two psychiatrists who first evaluated the Norwegian man's mental state *viewed his political viewpoint as lying outside their mandate. Aftenposten* stated on its front page of 1 December 2011 under the headline "Disregarded politics and ideology":

> NN says that many of his acts are motivated by a political standpoint. The experts behind the psychiatric report judged this to lie outside their mandate. Problematic, think researchers,

referring to a well-known philosophy professor and others.

Yes, it is problematic. The point is further emphasised on *Aftenposten's* page 4. Again the headline, now over five columns, stated: "Have disregarded NN's political message and standpoint". In the article itself it was emphasised, as a starting point: "Nor his so-called manifesto have the two experts given much weight in their evaluation of the mental health of the man charged with terrorism". And they go on, *inter alia* (apparently verbatim from the report), "This of course belongs outside the experts' mandate". The two experts have, according to the report, only "to a small extent" (again apparently verbatim from the report) taken his compendium as a point of departure in their review ("*gjennomgang*") of NN's political views, and his use of concepts related to this. Without a political/ideological rationale, NN's acts and statements become weird, totally meaningless, utterly sense-less reading. They are then clear signs of insanity, paranoid schizophrenia. No wonder the experts found him, when stripped of a political/ideological background, legally unaccountable. But when interpreted within context, notably the context of extremist right-wing political views which also are catered to by others, his actions may be interpreted differently.

Nazi Torturers

Top Norwegian (and German) Nazis during the occupation of Norway in World War II could reasonably have been found unaccountable for their acts of torture etc. if they had been stripped of their political beliefs as a background for committing these and other acts. If Vidkun Quisling (1887-1945, executed), Henry Rinnan (1915-1947, executed) and others had been stripped of political background in this way, their various acts could or would be judged as weird, impossible cruelties, and most likely or at least possibly they would have been found unaccountable for their acts and confined in a mental hospital for the rest of their lives (they might still have been executed, but that would have been as revenge).

But they certainly had a political background and an ideology which they tried to realise. A part of the Norwegian population were on their side politically during World War II, even if they did not agree with the extrem-ist actions and views (as far as they knew about them), and a few agreed with them even. The media under Nazi control, or even without too much Nazi control, was one important feature. It was impossible, in view of the political context, to find them unaccountable. A case in point is the Nor-wegians' co-responsibility for the Holocaust, the 70 years' commemoration of the transport vessel "*Donau*" taking 532 deported Jews from Norway to be exterminated in Nazi gas chambers. To be sure, German Nazism stood behind. "But it was Norwegians who carried out the arrests. And they were Norwegians who drove the cars".[33] Among others, 100 taxi drivers.[34]

The stripping of NN's actions, sayings and deeds of political/ideological background makes the psychiatrists' conclusion of insanity possible. NN is then exempt of punishment, and is to be confined in a secure mental hospital. On the other hand, taking political/ideological background into account as (part of) his motivation, makes sanity—and punishability—a possible conclusion, irrespective of our moral view of this background.

· · · · · · · · · · · · · · · · · ·

To repeat, the terrorist was found to be suffering from paranoid schizophrenia. Despite some internal disagreements in the Commission, the report's conclusion was, as I have said, followed by the Commission on Forensic Medicine's section of Forensic Psychiatry. Not only the two psychiatrists responsible for the report, but also the Commission on Forensic Psychiatry completely disregarded the public debate on possible or probable political motivation which had taken place. The psychiatrists' stripping NN of his political and ideological thinking, and their conclusion of insanity as a consequence, is grounded on a strict medical way of thinking. The road to prison is the main road, and that road has many thorns. But we also know now, if we didn't know before, that to confine someone in a mental hospital, possibly for life, is not an invitation to a rose garden.

The Second Committee
The second committee did make a difference. It was made official on 10 April 2012, a week before the trial started. The committee's report was over 300 pages long, its content was secret until the end of the trial, but its main conclusion was made clear that day. It contradicted completely the first report, which had concluded that the perpetrator suffered from *paranoid schizophrenia* and would, consequently, be exempt from punishment and sentenced to

---

33. Source: *Aftenposten*, 28 January 2012. Altogether, 772 Jews were arrested and deported in Norway during World War II. Only 34 of them survived. Same source.
34. Odd-Bjørn Fure, director of Norway's Centre for Studies of Holocaust and Life View Minorities.

compulsory psychiatric care. The second committee came down, in complete contrast to this, on the opposite side. The perpetrator was certainly deviant in important ways. He suffered from serious personality disorders. He fulfilled the criteria of the diagnosis "dyssocial behaviour" from before he was 15. The report said, *verbatim*: "In the observant's case there are not reported clues indicating distinct dyssocial behaviour during childhood and early years, though certain traits have been observed, so that he fulfils the criteria before 15." He was also narcissistic. But this did not make him unaccountable. He was accountable and not subject to impunity.

Why? Because the report brought to the fore a contextual political perspective which led to a radically different interpretation of the perpetrator's actions and beliefs. *Aftenposten* explained it on 11 April 2012 in the following words:

> In the new experts' report, which *Aftenposten* is partly familiar with, the picture of [the defendant] as paranoid schizophrenic and psychotic, is completely rejected…NN's statements about DNA-testing of all Norwegians, reservations for Norwegian "aborigines" and mass factories for births are interpreted by [the new psychiatrists] in a wider political and cultural context.

The following day *Aftenposten* went into further detail:

> *Aftenposten* knows the content of the new secret legal psychiatric report which was given to the Oslo Court on Tuesday. According to *Aftenposten*, the report goes much further in establishing that NN has greater support for his acts than we have known earlier…'[T]he experts base themselves on his [the perpetrator] having sympathisers in Norway and other countries…It is well known from the news and from home pages which the experts have visited that political subcultures exist which support the extreme political ideas which the observed individual has maintained…During remand he receives a steady stream of declarations of support from persons of the same opinion. The experts therefore do not find a basis for understanding the observed person's extreme and unrealistic political views and goals as expressions of psychotic thought processes'.[35]

---

35. Towards the end of the trial, in June 2012, many other psychiatrists (and health personnel from an observation period) appeared as witnesses. Not one of the psychiatric witnesses

Aftenposten's commentator followed up as follows, when reporting during the trial, on one of the witnesses for the defence (5 June 2012):

'[NN] is no mystery. He is a product of a political environment with a long tradition which he in his time [was inspired by]', the Court was told by Professor Mattias Gardell [Swedish history professor of religion]. Professor Gardell had looked—and he had found the Norwegian terrorist's source of inspiration.... The only thing the learned historian of religion had not found was something unique. Without doubting at all, he point blank ascertained that what two psychiatrists think is a symptom of illness, are rather ordinary reality conceptions in the environments where NN had found inspiration.[36]

Many other witnesses voiced similar views. Exactly as we argued above.

The Trial

Hundreds of journalists and numerous national and international television channels followed the trial. All the major newspapers and TV channels in Norway, and certainly a number of media channels with regional (European) and world coverage, were there. The international media noted how polite and dignified the Norwegian handling of the perpetrator was. The various actors in court even opened by shaking hands with him (while he greeted the audience with a Nazi-inspired salute for several days, until he was asked to stop that). The court was of five judges—two professional judges and three lay judges. The prosecution had two State attorneys—and the Attorney-General in the audience. The defence had three attorneys. The perpetrator was there, and was allowed to speak, but at times his voice was faded out.

---

agreed with the insanity conclusion of the first committee. The perpetrator, and consequently the defence, now also pleaded accountability. Most probably, the reason was the perpetrator's wish for political legitimacy. One experienced psychiatric witness forcefully maintained that neither of the two committees had come to a correct psychiatric diagnosis (paranoid schizophrenia, and consequently unaccountability; versus dyssocial personality disorder, which is not a psychosis and consequently leads to accountability). According to the psychiatrist in question, the perpetrator suffered from Asberger's syndrome and Tourette's illness, which do not constitute a psychosis. The differences altogether show the uncertainty attached to the psychiatric diagnoses.

36. But the commentator added that there was one "missing link" in this: The perpetrator had killed 77 people. Few if anybody in his environment had done anything similar.

So were the voices of other actors when they spoke of matters regarded as privileged information—the perpetrator's mother, who refused to [be a?] witness, as she had a right to.

The first week was filled by the perpetrator's own description of events. His main concern now was that of *being found sane and accountable, not insane and subject to impunity.* Sanity and accountability would make it possible for him to legitimise his acts as political. The deliberations in a Norwegian court are mainly oral, but he was allowed to read a prepared written statement out loud—a fairly lengthy description of events—before being questioned. He defended himself vociferously, but in a calm and rational way. His detailed coldness and lack of empathy were noticeable. The content of his descriptions of what happened on the island was cool but horrific. The only thing he regretted was that he did not manage to kill everyone on the island (over 500), but just 69 people. After most of the second week had passed, which was also filled with questions to him and to some of the many witnesses, several observers thought he was actually the leading actor on the stage.

Impeccably dressed in a white shirt and with a nice broad tie, pictured in the newspapers or in court as if discussing on equal grounds the intricacies of a complicated case, he symbolically appeared as if he was almost a winner.

However, finally, the Norwegian people answered. On Thursday 26 April 2012—ten days into the ten week long trial—some 40,000 people rallied at the main city square in Oslo and outside the courthouse—in the rain, bringing heaps of fresh roses, overwhelming the courthouse and singing a popular song—"Children from the Rainbow", a Norwegian version of a song by Pete Seeger. "We are the ones who win", said the singer who led the singing at the city square.[37] Even members of Parliament sang in a meeting hall in Parliament that day. One of the defendant's attorneys said that the perpetrator had understood that 40,000 had met up singing in the rain, but she did not want to convey how he had reacted. To rely once more on roses, which had been used right after 22 July 2011, was wise: It symbolised again that we, surrounding the court house, were on the winning side, and we were winning despite the perpetrator's actions and phrases inside the courthouse.

---

37. Source: *Aftenposten,* 27 April 2012. Thousands of people gathered in similar rallies throughout the country.

This rally was more than just important. It was a critical juncture. We, the masses of people, were back to the critical days on and after 22 July 2011. We were back to "more openness, more democracy".

You could have expected a demonstration with serious confrontations in front of the courthouse. With banners and loud cries indicating that the perpetrator should hang from the nearest telephone pole, or at least be shot. You saw and heard nothing of the sort. You saw tens of thousands of people, not as many as on 25 July 2011 but certainly very, very many, singing a children's song in the rain. Was it organized? Of course it was. Is that wrong? Of course it isn't. The organizing of it could have had an entirely different slant. Again, people were probably activated on Facebook. But they were receptive to this. If they hadn't been, there would have been far fewer people. Again we won.

. . . .

What happened in court during the rest of the trial appeared to be minor things. At one point a shoe was thrown at the perpetrator. Many applauded. The perpetrator remained cool. The court proceedings remained dignified. Towards the end, the two teams of psychiatrists, who had been present during the whole trial *inter alia* observing the perpetrator, were questioned for several days — without changing their positions. At the end the perpetrator was given the floor, and there were statements from victims' relatives, reminding everyone of the dire consequences of the terrorist's actions. Some wept, even the judges. We should be proud of the dignified atmosphere which remained throughout the trial.

In their summary statement, *the prosecution* went for insanity and the hospital conclusion — but with grave doubts. *The defence* went for sanity — and a punishment outcome. As I have said, the opposite of popular wisdom.

And the court? It landed unanimously on sanity and punishment. The reading of the sentence by the two professional judges took seven-and-a-half hours. The conclusion was unequivocal. The first psychiatric team, which had gone for insanity and placement in a closed hospital ward, as well as the legal-psychiatric Commission which had had no important comments on the first report (but unclear comments concerning the second report), were severely criticised by the judge who read the verdict. The importance of political context was a significant fact of the case. The perpetrator was punished by indeterminate preventive detention for 21 years (the maximum sentence) with ten years as a minimum, and the possibility of an extension for five years at a time by court orders. Extensions of this kind would be possible if the perpetrator was found to be still dangerous.

Everyone, possibly except the Attorney-General, who had gone against the very establishment of the second psychiatric committee, seemed happy. The others — the victims with their assistance lawyers, and the perpetrator with his lawyers — had argued for the second committee and concluded with sanity and punishment. The perpetrator had at first seemed indifferent and his lawyers had argued for insanity, but they had in the end swung around. There were no appeals from any of the parties, and the verdict became legally binding.

As I have said before, an unusual agreement between victims and perpetrator had occurred — with different motivations: just responsibility for his crimes on the part of victims, and, despite right-wing extremism, legitimacy of political views on the part of the perpetrator.

Will he ever be released? Nobody knows.

Conclusions

Among the many possibilities, there seem to be two overarching major conclusions to be drawn from this long story. The first one is this: What is the future of forensic psychiatry, in Norway and other countries with a similar system?

In a sense, the whole question of hospital versus prison, which preoccupied all of Norway intensely towards the end of the terrorist case, is a major but important departure from the main critical question in this *Epilogue* and this book — Norway's and Europe's future in defence against terrorism. But the future of forensic psychiatry became so pressing during the Norwegian terrorist case that it deserves some concluding remarks.

The Future of Legal Psychiatry[38]

Long before the second committee made its conclusions public, retired Supreme Court Judge Ketil Lund, a long-time critic of criminal justice control, *in effect* advocated a complete abolition of the use of legal psychiatrists in court cases (Lund 2012).

Lund maintained that it systematically discriminated "the sick". It took away the last remnants of their independence and responsibility. It would be better to subject all criminals to a punishment meted out by the court, and to discuss afterwards what should be done to the few individuals who did not know the difference between right and wrong. They would have to be given special care and consideration.

Norwegian legal psychiatry lies with a broken back. We have known it all along. Numerous clinical but also statistical studies indicate that predictions made by psychiatrists and others contain a vast number of errors (Mathiesen, 2011). The present Norwegian case shows that psychiatry is certainly not an exact science. Usually it gives the impression of solidity and finalised certainty. The present case, with its clash between two entirely different opinions, clearly shows that it is certainly not.

As a consequence the Attorney-General has advocated an evaluation of the role of psychiatrists in the legal system.[39] The Minister of Justice said that once the trial was over, the Government would appoint a committee which will look at the rules concerning accountability and how today's system functions.[40] Several psychiatrists have argued that the psychiatrists have too much power. They are much more than mere advisers to the court. In actuality they decide the future of the defendant. Yet they may, as we have seen now, be in total disagreement with each other. One of them argued as follows when the sentence had been passed, as Ketil Lund does:

---

38. The above statements on the questions of abolishing *forensic psychiatry*, or abolishing *the medical principle* in forensic psychiatry in order to open-up for contextual considerations (I here use the terms "forensic" and "legal" psychiatry interchangeably) — also address the future of legal/forensic psychiatry. In 2012, right before the trial came to its end, I published an article on these themes — in Italian — in *Studi Sulla Questione Criminale*.

39. Source: *Aftenposten*, 11 April 2012.

40. Source: *Aftenposten*, 13 April 2012.

> Perhaps psychiatry should be toned down a bit in the legal system. There will be more equality before the law by people receiving a punishment for what they have done, and then afterwards one can find out how punishment should be carried out.

In short, is not the moral of this that legal psychiatry should be abolished?

I sympathise with this view. To a considerable extent, my own professional work during the past 50 years has witnessed a deep uncertainty and moral unclarity attached to the role of forensic psychiatrists. Forensic psychiatrists have for years on end been severely criticised by prison inmates and others for lack of solid work, unpredictability in terms of conclusions, unclarity in terms of roles and illegitimate power.[41] The crux of their power lies in their role as advisers, in effect seen as decision-makers, in relation to the judges in court. Criticism has followed regardless of changes in the system of legal psychiatry.

But there is a difficulty: The *criminal asylum* looms in the background. The few who earlier were found insane and unaccountable, need help. A criminal asylum, perhaps within the prison system, may be established for them. Is that an improvement?

Improvement or not, Ketil Lund's approach at least opens-up the way for fresh thinking in an area which desperately needs just that.

· · · · · · · · · · · · · · · · · ·

Another approach for thinking is to leave behind, in Norway, what is called "the medical principle" in these matters. After the sentence in the terrorist case was passed, several psychiatrists wished to have the relevant section in the penal code (§44), giving impunity to the psychotic and the unconscious, changed. As far as a psychosis goes, the perpetrator is tied to an objective diagnosis regardless of its consequences for the criminal act in question.[42]

---

41. The first time I ran across these views was during my research among inmates at Ile preventive detention institution in Norway some 50 years ago. See Mathiesen 1965/2012, especially Chapter 5 ("Staff Distribution as seen by Inmates") and Chapter 6 ("Elements of a Patriarchal Régime").

42. Section 44 of the Norwegian Penal Code reads like this (translated by this author): "The person who at the time of the act was psychotic or unconscious, is not punished. The same holds for the person who at the time of the act is severely mentally retarded". One problem is

This is called "the medical principle" in Norwegian forensic psychiatry. The opposite is a "psychological principle", where a cause-effect relationship between the mental state and the deviant act may be found. The medical principle has been the core principle for years, at least since the penal code of 1842. But there are good reasons for saying that the medical profession is not the best equipped for the tasks involved.

History, and the current case, show that this is a fact. By leaving the medical principle, professions and types of perspectives and knowledge—in short, contexts—from elsewhere could be brought to the fore. Depending on the case, history, political science, social anthropology and so on may be relevant. In the present terrorist case, a view from political science in which the existence of right-wing extremism in the environment would be relevant, would be a case in point. If such extremism in the environment could be empirically ascertained, and if the perpetrator could be ascertained as influenced by this political stand (as in the present case), it would be a sign of "sanity" in the perpetrator. If it could not be ascertained, it would be a sign of the opposite. Other types of knowledge would be relevant in other types of cases.

The principle governing the forensic discipline should be psychological rather than medical, tying the mental state of the perpetrator to the deviant act rather than being a system of diagnoses independent of the act. The psychologist would be responsible for calling in other professionals when the context is relevant.

But the psychologist would be responsible for just one question—*accountability* or *unaccountability*. As it is now, the medical men and women in this area have responsibilities, and power—far beyond that. They are, for example, frequently called in to examine accountable persons suffering from dyssocial disturbances, persons who should not be subject to impunity but sentenced to preventive detention. This we should abolish.

But this is hardly enough. Even if based on a psychological principle, and therefore with a wider professional setting relevant for them, the professional experts will in reality be decision-makers rather than mere advisers

---

that the criteria of "psychosis" varies in time. Another is that there is a difference between the concept seen legally and psychiatrically. We do not go into these issues. The main point is that no cause-effect relationship is presupposed between the state of psychosis and the deviant act. Regardless of the relationship the person is not punished.

to the court. Responsibility will be pulverised, the judge will say that he has to listen to the expert and the expert will say that he is only an adviser. I would therefore prefer to have the roles of the professional split—one for the prosecution and one for the defence.

We know the disadvantages of this. As witnesses for the parties involved, the experts will easily be lured into extreme positions. But it also has an advantage—the judge will, at least probably, be in a freer position to decide. The expert will not be an adviser to the court which presents the judge with an opinion he *must* follow if the defendant is to be regarded as sane. The judge may be presented with agreement between the two, but not as an advisory truth-sayer, and often he will be presented with differences of opinion—even less of an advisory truth-sayer. Nils Christie has pointed to this possibility in an important article.[43] The judge will be freer to make a choice.

There is a desperate need for fresh thinking in what is now called "forensic psychiatry".

New Rules? Indications Both Ways

This story began with ideals of more openness, more democracy, compassion and love as our defence against terrorism. This is still with us, but in a more tempered form. The words are more rarely heard now. Even the relatively soft-minded Minister of Justice had to go, a new minister came instead. Is it beginning to go the wrong way? Towards harsher times, with more emphasis on punishment, even longer sentences and more surveillance—the core issue of this book?

The People's Voice

There are indications going both ways. On the one hand, an opinion poll,[44] made public in July 2012, shows that the positive attitudes which were present right after 22 July 2011 have in fact been kept up. The journalist Gudleiv Forr formulates it this way (Forr, 2012):

> Pluralism is in fact to a larger extent than before seen as something positive,
> immigrants are to a larger extent than before seen as contributors to the Norwegian

---

43. Nila Christie: "*Fem hjelpsomme feil*" (Five helpful errors), *Aftenposten*, 5 September 2012.
44. Ipsos MMI's "*Norsk Monitor*" (Norwegian Monitor).

economy. There are fewer who see immigrants as parasites on the Norwegian welfare system. Even the proportion who like rather than dislike the fact that Muslim religious communities establish themselves in this country, has increased.

A professor of political science (Ottar Hellevik), responsible for the study, tones down the effect of the terrorist case on 22 July: There is a continual trend in this direction from way back, since 1993. The Norwegian scepticism to immigrants has gradually become weaker. Ethnic Norwegians are more positive to immigrants. The greater the number of immigrants who arrive in Norway, the more positive Norwegians become towards immigrants and the cultural and economic consequences. "Knowledge begets friends" ("*kjennskap avler vennskap*") he says. Similar trends are present in Sweden (Gardell Norw. ed. 2011, pp. 206-211). Again, the higher the number of Muslims becomes, the more positive opinions turn out to be (pp. 109-111).

A further study if public opinion a year after 22 July 2011, showed somewhat less of a positive view of opinion, but still a positive view compared to all of the criticisms coming from the media and the political world. In their report "One Year After 22 July" Dag Wollebæk and associates (Wollebæk *et al,* 2012) followed up their initial report on opinion just before and just after 22 July 2011. Right after 22 July 2011 opinions had been very positive, showing a high degree of confidence and togetherness in relation to other people and to institutions, symbolised by the large masses of people participating in rose gatherings. Opinions a year afterwards were different. Opinions surveys and panel studies were carried out for four different periods, called April 2011, August 2011, May 2012 and August 2012 (right after the publication of the critical 22 July Commission). The data showed that a development back to the time before 22 July 2011 had occurred. *The terror event had neither become a societal collapse nor something like a permanent rose gathering.* In August 2012 the social engagement, confidence in people and confidence in institutions were back to *just about normal.* This corroborates findings in the US after the events of 9/11.

Fear and insecurity, as well as a belief in surveillance measures were also greater, but this may be due to the publication and widespread public debate on the 22 July Commission's Report, which also occurred in August 2012.

We do not know whether the support of surveillance measures were a short-term opinion sentiment or a more permanent change in opinion.

With regard to surveillance on the net there is a clear tendency of opinion towards more surveillance of communication during the past year. The terrorist's communications and his ideologically supportive web-sites are most likely behind this (p. 70). But there is an important difference between grown-ups and young people. Grown-ups to a larger extent accept surveillance of individuals and groups on the Internet. Young people to a larger extent have attitudes which do not exclusively demand more control and surveillance (p. 70). The question is why a culture of fear is not more clearly established among the young. The explanation may be tied to the fact that they live in a "high trust society" (p. 72):

> The terror has not led to a weakening among youths of trust generally in relation to other people. On the contrary. Trust in systems is also high among young people…

There was even trust in the police, but this was lower, probably due to the harsh public criticism of the police, perhaps especially criticism following the news of the report from the 22 July Commission in August 2012 (Wollebæk *et al*, 2012 b). In short, with some exceptions, public opinion one year after the terrorist event was back to normal. Possibly, the lowering of confidence in the police may turn out to be temporary, due to the particular public criticism of the police at the time (*op.cit.*, p. 45). In fact, according to a major public opinion study, confidence concerning the preparedness of the police was again on the rise in the late autumn of 2012, from 51 to 62 per cent between August and December 2012. Norway has a deep-rooted "confidence culture". The State is largely viewed as a "friend".[45]

To be sure, there were some signs which may turn out to the contrary, and they must be addressed. Strong reactions, outside the realm of the 22 July affair, came to the fore during the summer of 2012, due to an "invasion" of Romani people from Romania and Bulgaria. The Romani people came to Norway on the basis of free travel for three months at a time.[46] During earlier

---

45. Source: *Aftenposten*, 21 December 2012.
46. Romania and Bulgaria are not yet full Member States of Schengen, but are members of the European Economic Area (EEA).

summers there had been few Romani travellers to Norway, this year there were many. They lived by begging in the streets, they lived outside in the open or in tents, they were seen as filthy, leaving their excrements and other waste in public places, and had to escape from place-to-place when trying to camp. Very strong statements about them were cited in the newspapers, there were proposals to make begging forbidden, and even proposals for closing the borders to Romani people — the latter plainly an illegal measure.

A regulation which is relatively mild compared to these statements is an obligation to report the collection of money in public places (including begging) which has now been proposed by the Ministry of Justice. But a movement for their support was also raised. Toilet facilities, etc. were proposed, camping equipment was suggested, and a newspaper in their defence was published. Quite a few people protested against the negative statements quoted in the press, also by some higher ranking politicians. The proposal to forbid begging was met by statements stressing the immorality of denying people the elementary right to ask for help. In short, a real debate took place. The event may lead to more negative norms and attitudes, but in view of the movement established for them, which was a reality, it may also be viewed as another example of deeply rooted Norwegian humanitarianism. In other countries Romani people have been expelled.

In general, 13.3% of the population of Norway are foreigners from 219 different countries and self-governed regions (655,170 individuals). A total of 546,732 individuals are first generation immigrants. As of 2008 the largest group was from Poland, followed by people from Sweden, Pakistan, Somalia, Germany, Iraq and Denmark. Integration and adjustment to a Norwegian way of life increases with length of stay in the country, and second generation people are more adjusted than their parents.[47] During the past 20 years there have been 23 political action plans and, altogether, 673 measures taken for better integration. Nonetheless, unemployment is still threefold the size of the rest of the population.[48] However, the survey on attitudes towards immigrants and immigration conducted by Statistics Norway in July/August 2012 shows that the proportion agreeing strongly or on the whole that "Most immigrants make an important contribution to the Norwegian working life"

---

47. http://no.wikipedia.org/wiki/Innvandrere_i_Norge
48. Source: *Aftenposten*, 27 December 2012.

increased by five percentage points from 2011. The proportion disagreeing or being indifferent ("either-or" question) was reduced by two percentage points. The change is statistically significant. Eighty per cent agreed with the statement, which is the highest percentage measured so far. A little less than three out of four hold that most immigrants enrich the cultural life of Norway, 86 per cent think that immigrants should have the same job opportunities as Norwegians, seven out of ten think that labour immigration from non-Nordic countries to Norway makes a positive contribution to the Norwegian economy. One out of three thinks that immigrants abuse the welfare system of Norway, one out of three thinks that immigrants represent a source of insecurity in society; the population is split in two regarding the question of receiving refugees (43 per cent think there should be stricter rules; 44 percent think that access should remain as it is today; only seven per cent think access should be made easier; none of these differences conflict significantly with what was found a year earlier, in 2011).[49]

Negative attitudes towards foreigners from outside Western Europe and North American are of course present, but they are weak. There is reason seriously to doubt that negative attitudes to immigrants plays an important role in changing people's attitudes to criminal policy in a more negative direction.

The Politicians' Voice
In short, as far as the 22 July event is concerned, confidence among *the people* went back to normal, which was high, after a time. On the other hand, there was an opposite tendency among several high-ranking politicians and influential policy makers.

The Consultation Paper
Immediately following some rather sensational news about a Norwegian citizen who had converted to Islam and been trained to become a terrorist in one of al Qaeda's terror training camps in Yemen. *Aftenposten,* 12 July 2012 carried the news that the Government had dispatched a Consultation Paper on wide-ranging proposals for changes in the Norwegian terrorist legislation.[50] *Thinking about or the mere planning* of terrorist acts was not illegal in

---

49. Source: Blom 2012, p. 5.
50. "Consultation Paper: Consultation on Criminalising Preparation of Terror Acts, Expanded

Norway prior to the Consultation Paper. The proposal was to make it illegal.[51] Solo terrorists were a part of the thinking. *Receiving terror training*, which, as opposed to giving terror training, was not illegal prior to the Consultation Paper, was to be made illegal.[52] *The mere presence at a site* where terror training is going on (even if not taking part in the training) was to be made illegal.[53] *Possession of equipment* such as rubber gloves, so-called "finland hoods" (balaclavas) and communication equipment, which may be used for the purposes of terror, were to be criminalised.[54] There were also proposals for criminalising possession of information or obtaining information with a view to future terrorist acts. The Consultation Paper likewise considered an expansion of coercive methods — under certain circumstances room bugging to ward off threats to or attacks on people in authority, or expansion

---

Access to the Use of Coercive Methods, and Changes in the Penal Code of 1902 §60 a". The Ministry of Justice and Preparedness 12 July 2012.

51. On p. 7 in the Consultation Paper, the Norwegian Secret Service said: "There is a need for a general stipulation on criminalisation of the planning of terror acts. Such a stipulation will also hit solo terrorists in the planning phase." The Ministry commented on this as follows: "The Secret Service's proposal contains no further precise details of what is going to denote punishable planning. An unspecified stipulation would receive a very broad impact area, and may in view of that be very fit for use [*anvendelig*]. On the other hand it may be maintained that it becomes so vague that it would impair predictability". In 2002 a similar proposal was advanced, and turned down.

52. On pp. 14-15 the consultation paper said: "According to the Penal Code…it is a criminal offence to teach methods or techniques which are particularly suitable to contribute to the performance of certain terror - or terror-related acts, as mentioned in the stipulation. The stipulation does *not* apply to the reception of training…The Secret Service proposes that the reception of training or instruction useful for terror should be criminalised as an aggravating circumstance in relation to the proposal to criminalise presence at a place where terror training is taking place".

53. On p. 12 the Consultation Paper stated: "The Secret Service maintains the need for a stipulation which applies to the mere presence at a place where terror training is taking place. It is not a condition that the person in question himself/herself receives training." In the Consultation Paper p. 13-14, the Norwegian Secret Service wrote: "A stipulation which criminalises participation at a place where terror training takes place, could for example be formulated…[as follows] and read as follows: 'With prison up to six years a person is punished who is present at a place where teaching is carried out…Complicity is similarly punished'".

54. In the Consultation Paper p. 30 the Secret Service wrote: "A stipulation in the Criminal Code of 1902 could read like this: 'With prison up to six years a person is punished if he has the purpose of committing a criminal act producing or keeping objects or material which alone or together are especially suited to serve as an aid in implementing such an act. Under exceptionally aggravating circumstances prison up to ten years may be passed as a sentence'". Complicity was similarly punished.

of the possibility to hide the identity of service people acting as witnesses. The Secret Service also wanted to widen its *emergency* competence. There were also other proposals. The Government was not necessarily supportive of all of the proposals, which originated in the Secret Service and according to several submissions (reactions from outsiders) on the whole the presentation was poorly argued and vague. But it was, after all, the Government's consultation paper on coming changes.[55] This was exactly a month before the 22 July Commission on 13 August 2012 had made its critical report on the terror events public.

---

55. This is just a brief sketch of the many detailed reforms. The Norwegian *Data Protection Authority* has summarised the proposals after 22 July 2011 from the Norwegian Secret Service in the following points (23 May 2012, translated from the Norwegian by this author; proposals 1-8 were communicated to the Ministry of Justice and Preparedness, 1 November 2011, proposals 9-12 were communicated as the Norwegian Secret Service's reply to a Consultation Paper on the Regulation of data retention (10 April 2012).

Criminalisation of the *thought* as such about committing a future terror act, so-called "solo-terrorism".

Criminalisation of *presence* in places where training in activities takes place which may be used with a terror aim (for example training to fly an air carrier).

Criminalisation *of receiving training or instruction* in activities which the person has the intent to use in a terror act, but without the presence of a specified terror goal at the time when the training is received.

Criminalisation *of possession or acquisition of legal objects* where one thinks there are due grounds for suspicion of a terror goal (for example a pair of cutting nippers, rubber gloves or so-called "finland hoods" (balaclavas). It is not necessary for the prosecution to prove an exact terror goal.

Criminalisation of *possession or acquisition of information* where the goal of the information, not the holder's, is terror acts (for example military manuals).

Opens the way for *data reading*, which means to install a spy programme in computers in order to survey all information which is being sent or is stored encrypted.

Opens the way for *camera surveillance of private rooms*, such as staircases or basements.

Secure that the Secret Service in the future *may abstain from informing* the use of hidden coercive measures in cases which never become the objects of investigation, in full contrast to the recommendations of the Methods Report (NOU, 2009: 15).

Extend the duty also to store in the Data Retention Directive to *Internet cafés*.

Extend the duty to store in the Data Retention Directive *Norwegian web-sites* on the Internet (for example *Aftenposten, Vårt Land* og *Dagsavisen*).

Extend the duty to store in the Data Retention Directive also suppliers of *telecommunications services*.

Extend the Data Retention Directive, when net suppliers start using Network Address Translation (NAT), to cover *also information concerning which URL/IP-address* is visited on the net.

Public debates on punishment levels

And more came, a little later. Later in August 2012, a short while after the 22 July Commission had made its report known, it became clear, in the newspapers and on TV, that there had been meetings in the Labour Party and other political parties on raising the punishment level. Twenty-one years as a maximum was too limited, it was argued. Some politicians said it would really have to be for life for acts similar to what happened in 2012, others said more vaguely that a real life sentence would have to be introduced. In any case, chances are that the introduction of a real life sentence would stimulate longer sentences also for smaller crimes, and that Norway's reputation as a moderate and humane society, with relatively little violence also on the criminal side, would be weakened if not lost. At the beginning of 2013 the Government proposed that the maximum sentence of preventive detention be raised from 21 to 30 years. Extensions for five years at a time, if the person was still considered dangerous, existed already.

At the same time, a debate among politicians on the basis of the criticism of the 22 July Commission broke out. Some said that the Prime Minister, who had had the formal responsibility, had to leave office. Others said that the former Minister of Justice would have faced impeachment if he had not lost office earlier.[56] In Parliament towards the end of 2012, several members of the opposition turned out very critical towards the social democrats in power.

---

56. We also saw debates on the 22 July Commission report as such. While everyone during the first days or weeks was happy with and favoured the critique, criticisms countering some of the report's conclusions could be heard as time went on. Also, as these lines are written (September 2012), the *Chief Inspector of the Directorate for Cultural Heritage* has barred as confidential the information brought forward as working documents from high ranking politicians and civil servants by the 22 July Commission. The inspector's thinking has been that openness here might influence in a negative way the future of investigative commissions. The result has been scathing criticism from politicians, including Ministers, for protective and secretive activity at a time when full openness is the order of the day, and indeed emphasised from day one by the Prime Minister himself. Openness has become more controversial and more of an issue than in the beginning of this string of events. I inject these notes on debates to indicate the terrorist case had wide spread tentacles to and effects on Norwegian society, raising many questions beyond the case as such.

Parliament's Control and Constitutional Committee

Parliament's Control and Constitutional Committee had a five day hearing of high-ranking civil servants and Government politicians. Severe criticism followed. The committee's report arrived on 19 February 2013. Again, severe criticism, according to some almost to the point of a vote of no confidence, was launched against the Government.[57] The parties in Government were also critical, but tried to ward off devastating criticism of the Prime Minister. An excerpt from the report (p. 24) summarises much of the criticism as follows.

The committee is of the opinion that it is blameworthy that:

— Grubbegata [the street passing the main Government Building] was not closed faster
— Temporary measures for closing Grubbegata were not implemented
— The manning of the operative sections of the police had been too poor
— The police helicopter had not been held in readiness
— The national system of preparatory command did not function
— Important planning was not implemented, and utilised incompletely
— A request concerning assistance from the military came too late
— Securing central buildings such as the Parliament Building came too late
— The Police Directorate was not to a sufficient degree graded in terms of its work with societal security and preparedness
— The acknowledgement of risk seems not to have been high enough on the agenda neither with the police authorities nor the police
— The ability to take learning from exercises has been too small.

The Committee wishes to emphasise that these are serious circumstances which are blameworthy.

On the background of the critical 22 July Commission, the question of *responsibility* for things that went wrong was raised. Earlier there had been much talk of "system failures" (whatever that means), in contrast to "personal

---

57. *Innstilling fra kontroll- og konstitusjonskomiteen I Stortinget etter å ha behasndlet 22. Juli-kommisjonens rapport* (Recommendation from the Control and Constitutional Committee in Parliament after having discussed the Report from the 22 July Commission, 19 February 2013).

failures. Now, system failures faded into the background, whereas personal failures" remained an issue. The coming national elections in the autumn of 2013 may have been behind this.

White Paper from the Government

Finally the Government struck back. Its reaction to the critical reports from the 22 July Commission (13 August 2012) and from Parliament's Control and Constitutional Committee (19 February 2013) took the form of a voluminous White Paper to Parliament from the Government on terror preparedness issued on 20 March 2013 (White Paper No. 21 (2012-1013. 20 March 2013)). The Government proposed an evaluation of the district-wise structure of the police, in keeping with a strengthening of Norway's traditionally decentralised system close to the public.

A string of new measures against terror were to be evaluated and to some extent implemented. Altogether there were ten major measures involved. The four most important ones were the establishing of a national operative agency in order to strengthen police ability to coordinate responses in crises; a strengthening and further upgrading of the ability to muster police units in the various districts; increased training of police personnel earmarked for handling "shooting takes place" situations; and the establishing of a minimum manning of all operational police agencies and demanding special training of everyone working in the agencies. A seventh measure was, interestingly, the strengthening of the work of the Secret Service to establish a counter-terrorist centre and a proposal for opening-up access of the Secret Service "to administrative registers and to improve conditions for the exchange of information with other public agencies". From the point of view of this book, the latter measures may certainly contain dangers.

The Government seemed to go for cautious, well-planned and step-by-step procedures, not rushed and sensational measures. The opposition in Parliament was in considerable measure positive. According to the press, the Prime Minister was back in his usual optimistic and front line role. Beforehand (6 March 2013) Parliament had, on the basis of the Control and Constitutional Committee Report, unanimously criticised him, but also unanimously gone against his leaving office.

Interestingly, among the measures mentioned was not an increased emphasis on surveillance of planning and thoughts like those referred to at the beginning of this section on the Politicians' Voice. The Government appeared to be of the opinion that democracy and personal integrity demand careful evaluations before the Secret Service is given a legal basis for access to information about individuals. This also holds for access to information based on what is known as hidden measures. This may be good sign for Norway, though such an emphasis may still come, and though it may also mean that Norway is already in the process of adopting or implementing several of the EU systems, such as the Schengen Information System (already implemented) the Data Retention Directive and Prüm (the two latter systems under implementation). In fact the Government said that before the summer of 2013 a Bill was to be presented where rules opening-up the way for greater discretion on behalf of the police in taking action against the planning of criminalised acts, before the limit to criminalised attempts is reached, will be presented. The reference to the Consultation Paper mentioned at the beginning of this section is clear. Such discretion dangerously widens the scope of police action, brings in criminalisation of thoughts, and runs counter to a long legal tradition in Norway.[58]

As this book goes to press, in May 2013, the Government is presenting a Bill on the basis of the above mentioned Consultation Paper, which is expected to go through Parliament before Summer. The Bill is slightly more moderate than the Consultation Paper, due to the criticisms in many of the submissions, but contains many of the same proposals. The first paragraph of the summary runs like this:

> The Ministry of Justice and Preparedness stipulates in this Bill a number of proposals aimed at preventing terror acts. It proposes to criminalise the planning and preparation of a terror act shown by outward signs pointing towards implementation. It is proposed to widen the liability to prosecution for dealing with weapons and explosives with the aim of committing a crime. Reception of terror training [not just teaching it, TM] is also proposed to be criminalised. Finally, the

---

58. From the daily *Klassekampen*, 21 March 2013.

Ministry proposes to criminalise qualified participation in a terror organization by various forms of active support.

A number of other proposals are added. The maximum sentence is raised to 30 years in the Penal Act of 2005. The possibility of prosecution according to this stipulation is not to be statute-barred. The liability to prosecute organized crime is proposed to be widened. The definition of an organized criminal group is proposed to be widened so that it covers a flatter and looser structure. The modification "to criminalize the planning and preparation of a terror act shown by outward signs pointing towards implementation", shows somewhat greater emphasis on "objective" criteria and not just "thinking" inside people's heads, not just "criminalizing thoughts", but stipulations are vague and certainly subject to interpretation

Two Additional Incidents

It should be added that two important incidents did occur as the year 2013 was inaugurated.

Firstly, in January 2013, a major terrorist attack took place on a gas plant located in Algeria and owned by BP, the Norwegian energy company Statoil and the Algerian state-owned Sonatrach. Hostages were taken, and 37 foreign hostages, including five Norwegians, were murdered in a shoot-out between the terrorists and Algerian forces. Norwegian and international mass media covered the incident closely, and Norwegian political authorities used strong negative words about the terrorist case. The many sensible words from Norwegian politicians which could be heard and read right after 22 July 2011, were as if washed away. The evaluations of the mass media were dark and sinister.

Secondly, in February 2013 there was a great deal of media commotion around a drunk armed person who threatened to blow up the Parliament Building in the capital city of Oslo. The police took the incident seriously, invaded several apartment blocks while moving the inhabitants out, and blocked a wide area round the Parliament Building. The man was released from custody after a few days, hardly remembering anything from the incident. He was viewed as completely harmless. But it is worth noting that the latter incident received almost as many Norwegian headlines as the former one, and, indeed, that it was followed up by a threat image, provided by the Secret Police, showing that the serious and the harmless were integrated or blended in a media outlet which was close to a moral panic. It was as if Norway had not decided which way the country should go—towards a hard line or a cautious attitude, towards a tough new type of policing or towards a "cautious" (but not unprepared) line in keeping with old Norwegian values and traditions. "Are we on the road to a closed Norway?" was a main headline in the major daily *Dagsavisen* of the 18 February 2013. Several independent commentators argued against State measures which would be in conflict with human rights.[59]

We Have to Hark Back

If, then, the "tough" line, and legal reforms concerning surveillance based on thoughts and plans rather than concrete material proofs, such as those mentioned at the beginning of this section, are followed up or become realities, they cannot very well be traced back to the opinions of people living in our culture. They would above all follow on the political level and from debate or debates which have taken place for over a year, with a large number of rather wild arguments and conclusions reaching the front pages of many newspapers, and an equally large number of TV-debates and even talk shows. Excluded from this are several of the newspaper commentators.[60] In short, much seems to be *media-driven*. The media drive finds a receptive audience on the political level. The people have remained dignified and relatively calm, but the media has been aggressively active, and the politicians likewise. One-hundred-and-fifty-thousand articles may be found on this case in Norwegian newspapers between the events of 22 July 2011 and the end of the year. This is, for a small country, an enormous number, and it has even been carried further to the international world, by probably well over 80,000 articles in foreign media.[61]

---

59. *Dagsavisen* 18 and 19 February 2013.
60. A concrete exception is the role of the (Norwegian) journalists when covering the trial. I have no content analysis to rely on, but several of the journalists in the national newspapers were during the trial largely bringing thought-provoking and reflexive write ups. There had been meetings and discussions in various newspapers.
61. Source: *Aftenposten,* 5 January 2012. No other occurrence ever has been carried by so many articles in Norway, not the tsunami in Thailand, not the German occupation of Norway in

We must, therefore, hark back to a past which, after all, is not too distant, and which reminds us of Norwegian politicians' initial decisive quest for more openness and more democracy as a basic defence ideology not only against terrorists, but also and most importantly against the surveillant society. We must give this quest top priority. We must not forget how it all began.

Above all, we must *avoid introducing new legislation now.* Maybe a long time has to pass. We must wait patiently. We will then find that with the exception of a few points where efficiency could be strengthened (they are among those mentioned in the critical 22 July Commission report: a renewed police helicopter service, an improved and operable digital emergency network to make it possible for the police to react more quickly during hours of crisis, improved organizational networks also to make the police react more quickly, see above), we have legislation enough. Our defence should not be more dinosaur-like information and surveillance systems which will trample on the cherished values of openness and democracy, the very values which terrorists try to tear down — more openness, more democracy.

A Final Challenge

A final issue, a challenge: We have learnt that if the terrorist takes his precautions, he is extremely difficult to find — beforehand. He is especially difficult to find if he gains knowledge of the weaknesses and intricacies of the various surveillance systems. After the fact, after the terrorist has performed his deed, it is a different matter. Then the blood track can be seen and followed. But before the fact there is, provided the terrorist takes precautions, little or no evidence to be found. Internationally you find cases which counteract this, indicating that the terrorist has been found before the act. But they are rare, for reasons given in this book. They are also frequently warded off by civilians, neither by the information and surveillance systems nor by the Secret Service. A case in point is the action of passengers to prevent the hijacking of Kato Air in 2004, another is the equally resolute action of the passengers

---

1940 (note that we then had a more limited number of media, for example no TV, and after a short while German censorship came in). Figures are provided by *Retriever*, provider of *inter alia* media surveillance, editorial research and media analysis. District news on TV and direct transmissions on TV are not counted because counting is difficult. Neither is morning news on the radio covered. The figures given are therefore minimum figures.

who overpowered the hijackers on the fourth plane on 11 September 2001, making the plane crash rather than hit its target. The target was probably the White House of the USA.

This is also the case when the terrorist is not a lone wolf, but operating with others. Of course, it is easier then. But it is far from simple. Also groups can hide their tracks, not use their mobile phones, not leave other traces. Remember the stories about Indians that we read when we were children. They were completely silent, tip-toeing forward in the grass until they suddenly came, razing over the hilltop on their rapid ponies with loud and scary war cries, colours, feathers and bows and arrows. This was very noticeable as a fact during the American Indian War in 1862-63, when the Indians were on the verge of gaining total control (at least for a little while) of all or most of Minnesota State. The only reason why they didn't win was the American Civil War, which took place simultaneously, and disagreements among themselves.[62]

As I have said several times, this is a core message of this book, corroborated by the Norwegian story of the Norwegian terrorist 22 July 2011. This is a sledge hammer argument *against* supporting the development of vast surveillance systems such as those we have seen elsewhere in Europe and in the USA. We have to fight staunchly, basing ourselves on our values and using words — argumentation — as our main weapon. A staunch insistence on these values, and constant debates defending them against every attack on or corruption of them — in the family, in the neighbourhood, certainly in schools and universities, on the Internet, in the newspapers — should be our defence. The best arguments win. We have the best arguments.

Let us *not* look to the EU and the USA.

We leave the Norwegian reactions to the terrorist acts here, except for saying that a full scale study should be made of them in the future, when this story has finally come to an end.

---

62. See Karl Jakob Skarstein's important historical account of Norwegians against Indians during the Indian War 1862-1863 (Skarstein, 2005).

BIBLIOGRAPHY

Albanese, Jay (1989) *Organized Crime in America*, 2. edn. Anderson.

Altheide, David L (2006) "Terrorism and the Politics of Fear". *Cultural Studies, Critical Methodologies,* Vol 6 No. 4.

Anderson, Chris (2012) *Makers: The New Industrial Revolution*. Random House Business.

Andresen, Trond (1998) "Forbrukermakt via Internett" (Consumers' Power via the Internet). *Dagbladet* (Norwegian daily) 4 October 1998.

Atchison, Chris (1997) "Critical Criminological Applications of Computer Technology". *Critical Criminology*.

Aubert, Vilhelm (1958) "Legal Justice and Mental Health", *Psychiatry*, Vol. 21 No. 2, pp. 101-113.

Bakken, Børge (2005 edn.) *Crime, Punishment, and Policing in China,* Bowman& Littlefield Publishers.

   (2012) "The Chinese Surveillance State: The Rationalities of 'Social Management' in China", (paper presented at the Conference on Stability and Law, Australian National University, Canberra, 8-9 November 2012).

Bamford, James (2012) "The NSA Is Building the Country's Biggest Spy Center (Watch What You Say)". *Wired* 15 March.

Banakar, Reza (1994) *Rättens dilemma. Om konflikthantering i ett mångkulurellt samhälle* (The Dilemma of Law. Conflict Management in a Multi-Cultural Society). Bokbox Förlag.

Bell, Daniel (1973/1976) *The Coming of Post-Industrial Society: A Venture in Social Forecasting.* Basic Books 1973, 2 edn. with a new preface 1976.

Bill No. 56 (1998-99, Norway).

Bjørgo, Tore (2011) "Med monopol på vrangforestillinger" (With A Monopoly on Delusions), *Aftenposten* 7 December.

Blom, *Holdninger til innvandrere og innvandring i 2012* (Attitudes to Immigrants and Immigration 2012) Statistics Norway 2012.

Borch, Anita (1998) *Reklame rettet mot barn på internett — en forstudie* (Advertising oriented to Children on the Internet — A Preliminary Study), *Statens institutt for forbruksforskning, arbeidsrapport nr. 2.*

Brown, Felicity (2006) "Rethinking the Role of Surveillance Studies in the Critical Political Economy of Communication". IAMCR Prize in Memory of Dallas W Smythe.

Bruckert, Christine and Colette Parent (2002) "Trafficking in Human Beings and Organized Crime: A Literature Review", www.rcmp-grc.gc.ca

Bundesinnenministerium (2008) "Deutchland und die Niederlande schliessen Testphase beim Abgleich von DNA-Analysedateien erfloreich ab", press release; see also same date: "Dutch Ministry of Justice: Successful Exchange of German and Dutch DNA data".

Bunyan, Tony (2005) *Crossing the Rubicon: The Emerging Counter-Terrorism Regime.* Statewatch Report. London: Statewatch.

Bunyan, Tony (2006a) "The 'Principle of Availability'". Statewatch Analysis. London: Statewatch.

Bunyan, Tony (ed., 2006b) *The War on Freedom and Democracy.* London: Spokesman Books.

Bush, Heiner (2008) "Freier Binnenmarkt für Polizeidaten. EU ermöglicht gemeinschaftweiten Zugriffauf DNA-Informationen". *Grundtrechte-Report.*

Carlsen, Terje (2008) "Når kildene byr opp til DNA-dans" (When the Sources Invite to a DNA-dance). *Trønder-Avisa* (*The Trønder* Newspaper), 24 October.

Christie, Nils (1962) "Noen kriminalpolitiske særforholdsreglers sosiologi" (The Sociology of Some Specialised Legal Reactions), *Tidsskrift for samfunnsforskning*, Vol. 3 No. 1, pp. 28-48.

(2012) "Fem hjelpsomme feil" (Five helpful errors), *Aftenposten* 5 September.

Cohen, Stanley (1972) *Folk Devils and Moral Panics: The Creation of the Mods and Rockers.* London: Mac Gibbon & Kee.

Consultation Paper (2012) Høring—*kriminalisering av forberedelse til terrorhandling. Utvidet adgang til tvangsmiddelbruk og endringer i straffeloven 1902* § 60 a (Consultation on Criminalising Preparation of Terror Acts, Expanded Access to the Use of Coercive Methods, and Changes in the Penal Code of 1902 § 60 a. Ministry of Justice and Preparedness), July.

Dahl, Brungot *et al.* (including among others the present author; 2001) *Göteborg 14. til 17. juni 2001—15 norske beretninger fra EU toppmøtet* (Gothenburgh 14 to 17 June 2001. 15 Norwegian Stories from the EU Summit) ISBN

82-996149-0-2 (available at the Department of Criminology and Sociology of Law at the University of Oslo).

Dahl, Johanne Yttri and Lomell, Heidi Mork (2008): "Urealistiske forventninger til et utvidet DNA-register" (Unrealistic Expectations to a Widened DNA-register). *Adresseavisen* 25 August.

Davidow, William H and Michael S Malone (1992): *The Virtual Corporation. Structuring and Revitalizing the Corporation for the 21st Century.* Harper Business (Division of Harper Collins Publishers).

Diesen, Christian *et al.* (2005) *Likhet inför lagen* (Equality before the Law). Stockholm: Natur och Kultur Publishers.

Document No. 15 from Parliament 1995-96 ("The Lund-Report").

European Data Protection Supervisor: "The 'Moment of Truth' for the Data Retention Directive: EDPS Demands Clear Evidence of Necessity", 3 December 2010.

Europol (2011) General Report on Europol's Activities 2010, 20 May ENFOPOL 149.

(2011) TE-SAT EU Terrorism Situation and Trend Report.

(2012) TE-SAT EU Terrorism Situation and Trend Report.

Foucault, Michel (Eng. edn. 1979) *Discipline and Punish. The Birth of the Prison.* New York: Vintage.

Forr, Gudleiv (2012) Kjennskap gir vennskap (Knowledge gives friendship), *Dagbladet* 11 July 2012.

Fuchs, Christian (2012) "Critique of the Political Economy of Web 2.0 Surveillance", in Christian Fuchs *et al.* (eds.) *Internet and Surveillance. The Challenges of Web 2.0* and Social Media, Routledge pp. 31-70.

Gardell, Mattias (2010) *Islamofobi* (Islamophobia); Norw. edn. Spartacus Publishers 2011.

Gerth, Hans H. and C. Wright Mills (first published in English in1948). *From Max Weber: Essays in Sociology.* Oxford University Press.

Gjerding, Sebastian (2012) "Nye industrirevolusjon" (A New Industrial Revolution), *Klassekampen* 13 November.

Goldsworthy, Adrian (Norwegian edn. 2007) *Julius Cæsar.* Oslo: N. Gyldendal.

Guild, Elsbeth and Florian Geyer (undated) "Getting Local: Schengen, Prüm and the Dancing Procession of Echternach — Three Paces Forward and Two

Back for EU Police and Judicial Cooperation in Criminal Matters. http://
aei.pitt.edu/11629/1/1411.pdf

Hammerlin, Joakim (2009) *Terrorindustrien* (The Terror Industry). Oslo: Manifest Publishers.

Hayes, Ben (2004) *From the Schengen Information System to SIS II and the Visa
Infirmation (VIS): The proposals explained.* Statewatch Report. London,
Statewatch.

(2009) *Arming the Big Brother — the EU's Security Research Programme*,
Amsterdam: Transnational Institute.

Hayes, Ben and Mathias Vermeulen (2012) *Borderline. The EU's New Border Surveillance Initiatives.* Heinrich-Böll-Stiftung.

Hellum, Anne, Shaheen Sardar Ali, Anne Griffiths (2011.eds.) *From Transnational
Relations to Transnational Laws: Northern European Laws at the Crossroads.*
Ashgate.

House of Lords, European Union Committee (2007a) *Schengen Information
System II (SIS II).Report with Evidence.* London: The Stationery Office
Limited.

(2007b) *Prüm: An Effective Weapon against Terrorism and Crime?* London: The
Stationery Office Limited.

Hydén, Håkan (1997) "Hva är rättssociologi? Om rättssociologins forskningsup-
pgifter nu och i fremtiden". (What is Sociology of Law? On the Tasks of
Research in Sociology of Law now and in the future). In Håkan Hydén
ed. *Rättssociologi — då och nu* (Sociology Then and Now) Lund Studies in
Sociology of Law.

*Innstilling fra kontroll- og konstitusjonskomiteen i Stortinget etter å ha behandlet 22.
Juli-kommisjonens rapport* (Recommendation from the Control- and Constitutional Committee in Parliament after having discussed the Report
from the 22 July Commission, 19 February 2013).

Jewkes, Yvonne (2010) *Media and Crime.* 2 edn. London: Sage Publications.

Jones, Chris (2011) "UK: Mandatory data retention of communications data:
Update and developments". *Statewatch Bulletin*, Vol. 21 No. 2, pp. 19-21.

Jones, Chris (2012) "Complex, technologically fraught and expensive — the problematic implementation of the Prüm Decision". *Statewatch Bulletin*, Vol.
22 No. 1, pp.15-17.

Jones, Chris (2012) "Secretive Frontex Working Group seeks to increase surveillance of travellers", *Statewatch Bulletin*, Vol. 22 No. 2/3, pp. 23-27.

Karanja, Stephen K. (2005) *SIS II Legislative Proposals 2005: Gains and Losses* (pp. 81-103). Oslo: Norwegian Research Centre for Computers and Law, Yulex.

    (2006) Schengen Information System and Border Control Cooperation: *A Transparency and Proportionality Evaluation*. Unpublished PhD dissertation, University of Oslo.

Lampe von, Klaus (2009) "The Study of Organised Crime: An Assessment of the State of Affairs", in Karsten Ingvaldsen and Vanja Lundgren Sørli (eds.): *Organised Crime—Norms, Markets, Regulation and Research*, Oslo: Unipub pp. 165-211.

Larsen. Lena (2011) *Islamsk rettstenkning i møte med dagliglivets utfordringer* (Islamic Legal Thinking Meeting the Challenges of Everday Life), Ph:D. dissertation, University of Oslo.

Larsen, Torgeir (2012) "Hatets Europa" (Hatred in Europe). *Dagbladet* 25 November.

Lund, Ketil (2012) "Strafferettslig diskriminering" (Discrimination in penal law) *Klassekampen* 4 January.

Lyon, David: (2006) "9/11, Synopticon, and Scopophilia. Watching and being Watched". In Kevin D. Haggerty and Richard V. Ericson (eds): *The New Politics of Surveillance and Visibility,* University of Toronto Press.

Marx, Karl (n. edn. 1970) *Verker i utvalg 5, Kapitalen 1.* (Selected Works, Capital vol. 1).

Mathiesen, Thomas (1965) *The Defences of the Weak*, London: Tavistock Publications.

    (1997a) *Schengen: Politisamarbeid, overvåking og rettssikkerhet i Europa* (Schengen: Police Cooperation, Surveillance and Legal Protection in Europe). Oslo: Spartacus Publishers.

    (1997b) "The Viewer Society—Michel Foucault's Panopticon Revisited", *Theoretical Criminology.*

    (1999a) *Industrisamfunn eller informasjonssamfunn? Innspill til belysning av den høymoderne tid* (Industrial Society or Information Society? Ideas to the Illumination of Late Modernity). Oslo: Pax Publishers.

    (1999b) *On globalisation of control: Towards an integrated surveillance system in Europe.* London: Statewatch.

(2000a) On the globalization of control: Towards an integrated surveillance system in Europe. In Penny Green & Andrew Rutherford (eds), *Criminal Policy in Transition* (pp. 167-192). Portland: Hart Publishing.

(2000b) *Siste order ikke sagt: Schengen og globaliseringen av kontroll* (Last Word not Said: On Schengen and Globalization of Control). Oslo: Pax Publishers.

(2001) Die globalisierung der iiberwachung. In: C. Schulzki-Haddouti (ed.). *Vont Ende der Anonymitedt* (pp. 11-24). Hannover: Verlag Heinz Heisse 2000.

(2002) Expanding the concept of terrorism? In Phil Scraton (ed.), *Beyond September 11. An anthology of dissent* (pp. 84-93). London: Pluto Press.

(2004a) The Rise of the Surveillant State in Times of Globalization. In Colin Sumner (ed.), *The Blackwell Companion to Criminology* (pp. 437-451). Oxford: Blackwell Publishing.

(2004b) *Silently Silenced. Essays on the Creation of Acquiescence in Modern Society.* Winchester: Waterside Press.

(3rd edn. 2002, 5th edn. 2010) *Makt og medier. En innføring i mediesosiologi* (Power and the Media. An Introduction to Media Sociology.) Oslo: Pax Publishers.

(2011) *Kritisk sosiologi — en invitasjon* (Critical Sociology — An Invitation). Oslo: Novus Publishers.

(2012) "Malato di mente o assassino politico", *Studi sulla questione criminale.* ISSN 1828-4973. 5, pp. 83-91.

Michael, George (2012) *Lone Wolf Terror and the Rise of Leaderless Resistance.* Nashville: Vanderbilt University Press.

NOU (2009: 15) Skjult informasjon — Åpen kontroll (Norges offisielle utedninger/Norway's Official Reports -2009 No. 15, Hidden information — Open Control.

NOU (2012: 14) Rapport fra 22. Juli-kommisjonen (Norges offisielle utredninger/Norway's Official Reports — 2012 No. 14 Report from the 22 July Commission.

Official Journal L 344 28 December 2001.

Official Journal 2002/475/JHA.

Oscarsson, Mikael (2005) Lag eller ordning? — polisens hantering avEU-topp-
    mötet i *Göteborg* (Law or Order? — the police handling of the EU-summit
    in Gothenburgh). Stockholm: Jure Publishers (PhD Dissertation).

Peers, Steve (2011) "The Frontex Regulation — Consolidated Text after 2011
    Amendments". As Amended in 2007 and 2011. *Statewatch Analysis.*

Price, Simon and Peter Thonemann (2011) *The Birth of Classical Europe. A History
    from Troy to Augustine.* Penguin (first published by Allen Lane 2010).

Prodnik, Jernej (2012) "Toward a Critique of Surveillance in the Age of the Inter-
    net: A Reflection on the 'Internet and Surveillance'." Review of Christian
    Fuchs *et al. Internet and* Surveillance: The Challenges of Web 2 and Social
    Media. Routledge.

Rapport til Stortinget fra kommisjonen som ble nedsatt av Stortinget for å granske
påstander om ulovlig overvåking av norske borgere (Lund-rapporten) avgitt til
    Stortingets presidentskap 28. mars 1996 (Report to Parliament from the
    Commission appointed by Parliament to inquire into Allegations con-
    cerning Illegal Surveillance of Norwegian Citizens (the Lund Report),
    delivered to the Presidency of Parliament 28 March 1996.

Sabau, Isabelle and Jim Thomas (1997) "Theory and Praxis on the Internet: A
    Critical Exploration of the Electronic Frontier". *Critical Criminology.*

Simmel, Georg (1919/1950) "The Stranger". Free Press.

Simon, Jeffrey D (2013) *Lone Wolf Terrorism. Understanding the Growing Threat.*
    Amherst, New York: Prometheus Books

Simonsen, Gunnar (1976) *Pressen og virkeligheten* (The Press and the Facts),
    Department of Sociology of Law, University of Oslo, mimeographed
    report no 14.

SOU (2002: 122) *Betänkande av Göteborgskommittén: Göteborg 2001* (Report from
    the Gothenburgh Committee: Gothenburgh 2001.

Skarstein, Karl Jakob (2005) *Krigen mot siouxene. Nordmenn mot indianere 1862-
    1863* (TheWar against the Siouxs. Norwegians against Indians 1862-1863),
    Spartacus Publishers.

Statewatch analysis (2007; with H. Busch). *The Dream of Total Control — Status
    quo and Future Plans for EU Information Systems.* London: Statewatch.
  (2007a) London: Statewatch.
  (2007b) *Mandatory, Retention of Telecommunications Traffic to be 'nodded
    through' in UK.* London: Statewatch.

(1998) *Statewatch Bulletin.* September-October.

(2010) *Statewatch Bulletin.* Vol. 19 No 4.

(2011) *Statewatch Bulletin.* Vol. 21 No. 3.

Sundby, Nils Kristian (1974) *Om normer* (On Norms). Oslo: Norwegian Universities Press.

Teubner, Gunther (ed. 1997) *Global Law Without a State.* Aldershot: Dartmouth Publishing.

Teubner, Gunther (1997) "Global Bukowina: Legal Pluralism in the World Society". In Gunther Teubner, (ed. 1997) *Global Law Without a State.* Aldershot: Dartmouth Publishing pp.3-28.

Touraine, Alain (1969) *La Société post-industrielle.* Paris; Denoel.

Töpfer, Eric (2008) "Lubricating the flow of information in the EU". http://www.statewatch.org/analyses/no-134-dna-databases.pdf

(2009) "Network with Error". http://www.statewatch.org/analyses/no-139-eu-ims.pdf

Van Duyne, Petrus (2009) "Searching the Organised Crime Knowledge Grail: Disorganised EU threat methology", in Karsten Ingvaldsen and Vanja Lundgren Sørli (eds.): *Organised Crime—Norms, Markets, Regulation and Research, Oslo: Unipub pp. 119-163.*

Villasenor, John (14 December 2011) "Recording Everything: Digital Storage as an Enabler of Authoritarian Governments"; http://www.brookings.edu/research/papers/2011/12/14-digital-storage-villasenor.

Webber, Frances (1995) Crimes of Arrival: Immigrants and Asylum-seekers in the New Europe. Paper at the 23rd Conference of the European Group for The study of Deviance and Social control. Crossmaglen, Northern Ireland, 1-4 September 1995. Published by Statewatch.

White Paper NOU (2009:15) Skjult informasjon—åpen kontroll (Hidden Information—Open Control).

White Paper NOU (2013: 21) Tiltak mot terror—for et tryggere Norge (Measures Against Terror—for a safer Norway).

Wiig, Simen (2007) *Flyt og tilgjengelighet. En studie av det europeiske informasjons-samarbeidet innen politi, sikkerhets- og grensekontroll og dets konsekvenser for individers rettssikkerhet og rettigheter.* (Flow and Accessibility. A Study of the European Cooperation regarding Information within the Police, Security and Border Control and its Consequences for the Legal Protection and Rights of Individuals). Unpublished Masters thesis, Department of Criminology and Sociology of Law, University of Oslo.

Woon, Long Litt (17 June 2008) "Ta fremmedfrykt på alvor" (Take fear of foreigners seriously), *Politiken* (Danish daily).

Wijk, Erik (2002) *Orätt — Rättsrötan efter Göteborgshändelserna* (Injustice — the Legal Situation after the Gothenburgh Events). Stockholm: Ordfront Publishers.

   (2003) *Göteborgskravallerna og processerna* (The Gothenburgh Struggles and the Legal Processes). Stockholm: Karneval Publishers.

FWollebæk, Dag *et al.* (2011) *Hva gjør terroren med oss som* civilsamfunn? (What does the Terror do to us as a Civil Society?). Senter for forskning på sivilsamfunn og frivillig sektor, Oslo/Bergen.

   (2012) *Ett år etter 22. juli* (One Year after 22 July). Senter for forskning på sivilsamfunn og frivillig sektor, Oslo/Bergen.

   (2012b) "Tillit i Norge etter 22 juli" (Confidence in Norway after 22 July). In Helge Skirbekk and Harald Grimen (eds.): *Tillit i Norge* (Confidence in Norway), Res Publica.

Wright, Steve (1998) *An Appraisal of Technologies of Political Control.* Luxemburg: European Parliament, Directorate General for Research, PE 166.499.

Wright, Steve (1998) An Appraisal of Technologies of Political Control. (Working Document Consultation Version) European Parliament, Scientific and Technological Options Assessment (STOA) 6 January.

Zedner, Lucia (2007) "Fixing the Future? The Precautionary Principle as Security Technology", Keynote Speech at the conference *Technologies of (In)security,* University of Oslo 19 April.

   (2009) "Fixing the Future? The Pre-emptive Turn in Criminal Justice". In Bernadette McSherry *et al.* (eds): *Regulating Deviance. The Redirection of Criminalisation and the Futures of Criminal Law.* (Oñati International Series in Law and Society. Hart Publishing.

INDEX

F

J

K

L

suspicion

    low degrees of *125*

    mass suspicion *126, 133*

Sweden *30, 42, 48, 109, 143*

    Swedish Framework Decision *167*

Switzerland *102, 134, 136, 167*

symbolism *79, 214, 238*

synergy *164, 180*

Syria *44, 72, 80*

systems *61, 159*

    compatibility *130, 160*

    integration of systems *22, 159*

    interlocking systems *187*

    mother system *101*

    spy system *98*

    system failures *253*

T

tapping *156*

targets *155*

    legitimate targets *58*

Tarif, Wissam *44*

taxation *23*

technical procedures *17*

technology *26, 51, 96, 100, 155*

    political control, of *56*

TECS *112, 124*

Telecomix *44*

telegraph *25*

telephone *138*

    mobile telephones *97*

    satellite telephones *44*

    telephone directory *18*

    telephone tapping *58*

television *66*

Telia *30*

terrorism *xiii, 22, 61, 65, 124, 165, 171, 188*

    acquittals *200*

    Common Position *88*

    Framework Decision

        latent functions *93*

    increasing concern *92*

    meaning of *78*

    planning *248*

    preparation for *74, 106, 191*

    prosecution of *151*

    provocation to *90*

    purposes of *83*

    recruitment *74, 90*

    solo terrorists *249*

    terrorist financing *157*

    terror preparedness *253*

    third countries

        third-country nationals *165*

    training *90, 248*

    understandings of *80*

TE-SAT *201*

Teubner, Gunther *185*

theft *170*

thinking

    criminalisation of thoughts *254*

third

    third bodies *160*

    third countries *119*

    third parties *112*

    third States *160*

    Third World *34, 76, 78, 115*

threats *24, 109, 153*

    hidden threats *64*

Silently Silenced: Essays on the Creation of Acquiescence in Modern Society

by Thomas Mathiesen

Describing how people can be silenced almost without their realising it, Mathiesen outlines the many subtle and barely detectable methods that exist for absorbing political or unwelcome opposition. They are the 'methods and processes of everyday life' brought into and applied to the workings of power. As he shows in this brilliantly argued work, it is 'disturbingly clear' how easily and without our knowing it we are transformed into 'acquiescent human beings'.

'A highly original and provocative book …[Mathiesen is] a lone wolf in present day sociology - that makes his books worth reading': *Journal of Law and Society.*

Paperback ISBN 978-1-904380-15-3 | 118 pages | 2005

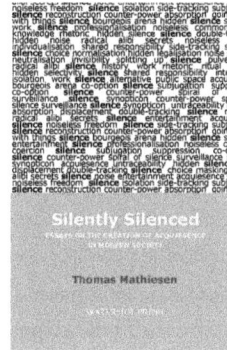

WatersidePress.co.uk/Silent

Dissenters, Radicals, Heretics and Blasphemers: The Flame of Revolt that Shines Through English History

by John Hostettler

A certain level of dissent, protest and open debate is a central part of UK history and democratic processes. Taking key events from both the past and modern times John Hostettler demonstrates how when legitimate avenues of challenge to the actions of the state or other powerful groups become closed to people then they are bound to assert their grievances in other sometimes less acceptable ways.

'This book is a glorious Molotov cocktail to be placed in the hands of every citizen and lobbed at the status quo': Helena Kennedy QC.

Paperback ISBN 978-1-872870-82-5 | 272 pages | 2012

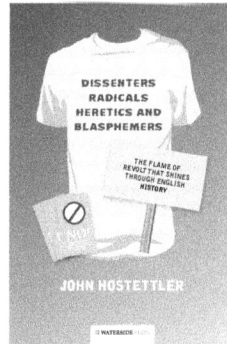

WatersidePress.co.uk/DRHB

Civilising Criminal Justice:
An International Restorative
Agenda for Penal Reform

Edited by David Cornwell, John Blad and
Martin Wright

Foreword by John Braithwaite

Probably the best collection there is, *Civilis-ing Criminal Justice* is an inescapable resource
containing a major re-appraisal of the state of
crime and punishment. The book combines
history, theory, developments and practical
advice in specially commissioned contribu-tions by widely respected commentators from
various countries making it a break-through
in bringing together some of the best argu-ments for long-overdue penal reform. The
book argues that there is an evermore urgent need to change outmoded ways of dealing
with crime: for a renewed restorative agenda. For full contents and contributors see:

Paperback ISBN 978-1-904380-04-7 | 568 pages | 2013

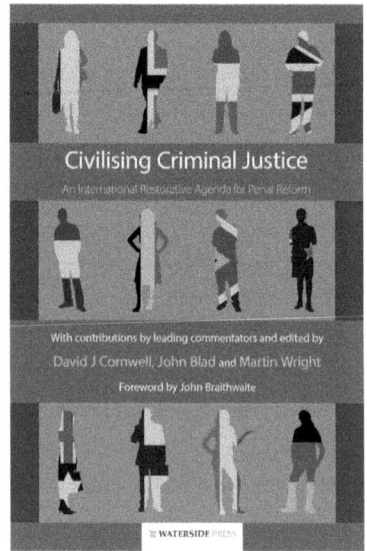

WatersidePress.co.uk/CCJ

Milton Keynes UK
Ingram Content Group UK Ltd.
UKHW020829280723
425958UK00008B/347